The Fu

This book was made possible by grants from the John D. and Catherine T. MacArthur Foundation in connection with its grant making initiative on Digital Media and Learning. For more information on the initiative visit www.macfound.org.

The John D. and Catherine T. MacArthur Foundation Reports on Digital Media and Learning

The Future of Learning Institutions in a Digital Age by Cathy N. Davidson and David Theo Goldberg with the assistance of Zoë Marie Jones

The Future of Thinking: Learning Institutions in a Digital Age by Cathy N. Davidson and David Theo Goldberg with the assistance of Zoë Marie Jones

Living and Learning with New Media: Summary of Findings from the Digital Youth Project by Mizuko Ito, Heather Horst, Matteo Bittanti, danah boyd, Becky Herr-Stephenson, Patricia G. Lange, C. J. Pascoe, and Laura Robinson with Sonja Baumer, Rachel Cody, Dilan Mahendran, Katynka Z. Martínez, Dan Perkel, Christo Sims, and Lisa Tripp

Young People, Ethics, and the New Digital Media: A Synthesis from the GoodPlayProject by Carrie James with Katie Davis, Andrea Flores, John M. Francis, Lindsay Pettingill, Margaret Rundle, and Howard Gardner

Confronting the Challenges of Participatory Culture: Media Education for the 21st Century by Henry Jenkins (P.I.) with Ravi Purushotma, Margaret Weigel, Katie Clinton, and Alice J. Robison

The Civic Potential of Video Games by Joseph Kahne, Ellen Middaugh, and Chris Evans

The Future of Thinking

Learning Institutions in a Digital Age

Cathy N. Davidson and David Theo Goldberg
With the assistance of Zoë Marie Jones

The MIT Press
Cambridge, Massachusetts
London, England

For information about special quantity discounts, please email special_sales@mitpress.mit.edu

This book was set in Stone Sans and Stone Serif by Westchester Book Group. Printed and bound in the United States of America.

Library of Congress Cataloging-in-Publication Data

Davidson, Cathy N., 1949–
The future of thinking : learning institutions in a digital age / Cathy N. Davidson and David Theo Goldberg ; with the assistance of Zoë Marie Jones.
    p.   cm.
Includes bibliographical references.
ISBN 978-0-262-51374-6 (pbk. : alk. paper)
1. Educational technology. 2. Internet in education. 3. Education—Effect of technological innovations on. 4. Educational change.
5. Organizational change. I. Goldberg, David Theo. II. Title.
LB1028.3.D275   2010   371.33'44678—dc22   2009024638

10   9   8   7   6   5   4   3

To John Seely Brown, who got us (all) going

Contents

Series Foreword

The John D. and Catherine T. MacArthur Foundation Reports on Digital Media and Learning, published by the MIT Press, present findings from current research on how young people learn, play, socialize, and participate in civic life. The Reports result from research projects funded by the MacArthur Foundation as part of its $50 million initiative in digital media and learning. They are published openly online (as well as in print) in order to support broad dissemination and to stimulate further research in the field.

Preface

The Future of Thinking: Learning Institutions in a Digital Age is a book about innovative, virtual institutions. It is at the same time an experiment that uses a *virtual institution* as part of its subject matter and as part of its process. Like such recent books as Chris Anderson's *The Long Tail: Why the Future of Business is Selling Less of More*[1] and McKenzie Wark's *Gamer Theory*,[2] this book had, as its beginning, a first draft hosted on a collaborative feedback and writing site. Where this book differs in some respects from others is that it uses this experiment in participatory writing as a test case for virtual institutions, learning institutions, and a new form of virtual collaborative authorship. The coalescence of meaning and method are a hallmark of participatory learning—and this book uses this participatory method to help support that meaning.

This has been a collective project from the beginning, and so the first acknowledgment goes to all those who supported it and contributed to it. Funded by a grant from the John D. and Catherine T. MacArthur Foundation, as part of its initiative on Digital Media and Learning, *The Future of Thinking: Learning Institutions in a Digital Age* began as a draft that was written together and then posted on a collaborative Web site developed

by the Institute for the Future of the Book (http://www.future
ofthebook.org) in January 2007. The draft remained on the Institute's site for over a year (and still remains there), inviting
comments from anyone registered to the site. A new digital tool,
called CommentPress, allowed readers to open a comment box
for any paragraph of the text and to type in a response, and
then allowed subsequent readers to add additional comments.
Hundreds of viewers read the draft, and dozens offered insights
and engaged in discussion with the authors or with other
commentators.

Three public forums were held on the draft, including one at
the first international conference convened by the Humanities,
Arts, Science, and Technology Advanced Collaboratory (HAS-
TAC, pronounced "haystack").[3] HASTAC is a network of academics and other interested educators who are committed to
creative use and development of new technologies for learning
and to critical understanding of the role of new media in life,
learning, and society. HASTAC is both the organizing collective
body around which this book developed and the subject of one
of its chapters. Without the energetic participation of those who
contributed to the Institute for the Future of the Book collaborative site, to the HASTAC network and conference, and to the
various forums on digital institutions, this book would look
different and certainly be less visionary. The names of project
participants are included in the contributors list. Where appropriate, specific contributions are also noted throughout the text.

In the print version of this book, text boxes offer examples of
learning institutions that have begun to chart visionary paths
for other institutions to follow.[4] In the online version, URLs
point to sites where one can find out more about innovative
digital learning experiments and institutions. Although the
scope of the main discussion is on university education and

digital communities among adults, Bibliography II includes an annotated listing of K–12 and youth-oriented institutions that are taking the lead in exploring what virtual learning institutions might accomplish and how.

Zoë Marie Jones, a doctoral candidate in the Department of Art, Art History, and Visual Studies at Duke University, joined this project in the fall of 2007. Collaboration (especially with so many participants) is an enormous amount of work, and Ms. Jones took charge of the complicated process of integrating the responses and feedback from the virtual contributors into the final draft in a way that allowed conscientious acknowledgement of those contributions, both individually (where appropriate) and collectively. She helped organize this input in a coherent fashion. She found models, resources, and bibliographic information that added practical wisdom and examples to the theoretical discussion of virtual institutions. We cannot thank her enough for her brilliance and dedication throughout this project.

As authors, scholars, teachers, and administrators, we are part of many institutions. One conclusion offered in this book is that most virtual institutions are, in fact, supported by a host of real institutions and real individuals. This is an important point because it is part of the mythology of technology that technology is "free." This book seeks to deflate that myth by underscoring how the most inventive virtual and collaborative networks are supported by substantial amounts of organization, leadership, and funding. Like an iceberg, sometimes the "free" and "open" tip of virtual institutions is what is visible, but it is the unseen portion below the virtual waterline that provides the foundation.

For example, HASTAC could not exist without the work of many individuals who contribute their time and energy, many of whom are located at the two institutions that provide the infrastructure support for HASTAC: Duke University and the University of California. We thank both of these institutions and their administrators for having faith in HASTAC back in 2002, when many were skeptical that a virtual organization could have any impact or staying power.

At Duke University, infrastructure as well as a community of energetic and commited colleagues comes from the John Hope Franklin Center for Interdisciplinary and International Studies and the John Hope Franklin Humanities Institute. For their early and continuing support, we thank: President Richard Brodhead; Provost Peter Lange; Vice-Provosts Gilbert Merkx and Susan Roth; Deans George McLendon, Gregson Davis, and Sarah Deutsch; and past John Hope Franklin Humanities Institute Director Srinivas Aravamudan (now Dean of the Humanities and Arts) and the current FHI Director, Ian Baucom. We also thank, for their tireless contributions to HASTAC and to this project, Mandy Dailey, Jason Doty, Erin Ennis, Sheryl Grant, Erin Gentry Lamb, Mark Olson, Fred Stutzman, Jonathan E. Tarr, and Brett Walters, and the three newest members of our Duke HASTAC team: Fiona Barnett, Nancy Kimberly, and Ruby Sinreich.

At the University of California, infrastructure comes from the University of California's Humanities Research Institute (UCHRI), the humanities institute serving the 10 universities making up the University of California system. We thank the following administrators for their support: University of California Irvine's Executive Vice-Chancellor and Provost Michael Gottfredson, University of California Irvine Vice-Chancellor for Research Susan Bryant; and former University of California Vice-Provost for Research Lawrence Coleman. As the founding Director of the California Digital Library, Dan Greenstein was enormously supportive in getting HASTAC off the ground. We also thank the staff members, present and former, at UCHRI for their engaged and sustained efforts on behalf of HASTAC: Dante Noto (formerly at the Office of the President and now the head of Development and External Relations at the Institute), Kevin Franklin (now Executive Director of the University of Illinois Institute for Computing in the Humanities, Arts, and Social Sciences at Urbana-Champaign), Suzy Beemer (now working in Advancement at Stanford University), Irena Richter (now the Associate Director of the Institute for Humanities Research at University of California, Santa Cruz), Shane Depner, Khai Tang, Justin Tang, Arielle Read, Jennifer Wilkins, Jessica Pham, and Stefka Hristova.

We are enormously grateful to Constance M. Yowell, Director of Education in the MacArthur Foundation's Program on Human and Community Development, and the visionary behind the Digital Media and Learning Initiative. This book would not be possible without her sustained and sustaining support. We also thank MacArthur Foundation President Jonathan F. Fanton, Vice President Julia Stasch, and our Program Officers for the MacArthur Foundation's Digital Media and Learning Initiative, Ben Stokes and Craig Wacker. Likewise, all those at the Institute for the Future of the Book have been terrifically helpful in hosting the collaborative project, notably Bob Stein and Ben Vershbow.

Finally, there are two people who have been interlocutors (perhaps more than they would have wished) in all things digital and all matters HASTAC: Ken Wissoker, Editorial Director of Duke University Press, and Philomena Essed, Professor of Critical Race, Gender, and Leadership Studies in the Antioch PhD Program on Leadership and Change. There is nothing virtual about their critical acumen and loving support—and we learn more from them every day.

Notes

All links are accurate as of July 1, 2009.

1. Chris Anderson, *The Long Tail: Why the Future of Business Is Selling Less of More* (New York: Hyperion, 2006).

2. McKenzie Wark, *Gamer Theory* (Cambridge, MA: Harvard University Press, 2007).

3. The forums took place on February 8, 2007, in Chicago, Illinois; April 21, 2007, at Duke University in Durham, North Carolina, at "Electronic Techtonics: Thinking at the Interface," the first international HASTAC conference; and on May 11, 2007, at the University of California's Humanities Research Institute in Irvine, California.

4. Although many conventional learning institutions have made great strides in recent years (see, for example, Jason Szep, "Technology Reshapes America's Classrooms," *New York Times*, July 7, 2008; and Bibliography II in this book), there is still significant progress to be made. Conventional learning institutions must reexamine their entire structure and approach to learning before they can truly enter the digital age.

Contributors

Principal Authors

Cathy N. Davidson   Duke University, Ruth F. DeVarney Professor of English and John Hope Franklin Humanities Institute Professor of Interdisciplinary Studies, Cofounder of HASTAC

David Theo Goldberg   University of California, Irvine; Professor of Comparative Literature and Criminology, Law, and Society; Director of the University of California Humanities Research Institute; Cofounder of HASTAC

Editorial and Research Consultant

Zoë Marie Jones   Duke University, Department of Art, Art History, and Visual Studies

February 8, 2007, Forum in Chicago, Illinois

James Chandler   University of Chicago, Barbara E. and Richard J. Franke Distinguished Service Professor, Department of English; Director of the Franke Institute for the Humanities

John Cheng   Northwestern University, Lecturer and Acting Director, Asian-American Studies Program

Allison Clark   University of Illinois at Urbana-Champaign, Associate Director, Seedbed Initiative for Transdomain Creativity

S. Hollis Clayson   Northwestern University, Professor of Art History, Bergen Evans Professor in the Humanities, Director of the Alice Kaplan Institute for the Humanities

Noshir Contractor   University of Illinois at Urbana-Champaign, Professor, Department of Speech Communication, Department of Psychology, Coordinated Science Laboratory, Research Affiliate of the Beckman Institute for Advanced Science and Technology, Director of the Science of Networks in Communities Group at the National Center for Supercomputing Applications, Codirector of the Age of Networks Initiative at the Center for Advanced Study

Dilip P. Goankar   Northwestern University, Professor of Communication Studies, Codirector of the Center for Transcultural Studies

Steve Jones   University of Illinois at Chicago, Professor, Department of Communication, Associate Dean of Liberal Arts and Sciences

Julie Thompson Klein   Wayne State University, Professor of Humanities, Interdisciplinary Studies Program, Faculty Fellow in the Office of Teaching and Learning, Codirector of the University Library Digital Media Project

Martin Manalansan   University of Illinois at Urbana-Champaign, Associate Professor of Anthropology

Lisa Nakamura   University of Illinois at Urbana-Champaign, Associate Professor, Asian-American Studies, Institute of Communications Research

Mary Beth Rose   University of Illinois at Chicago, Professor of English and Gender Studies, Director of the Institute for the Humanities

Craig Wacker   John D. and Catherine T. MacArthur Foundation, Program Officer in Digital Media and Learning

April 21, 2007, Forum in Durham, North Carolina

Ruzena Bajcsy University of California, Berkeley, Professor of Electrical Engineering and Computer Science, Director Emerita of the Center for Information Technology Research in the Interest of Society

Anne Balsamo University of Southern California, Professor of Interactive Media and Gender Studies in the School of Cinematic Arts and of Communications in the Annenberg School of Communications

Allison Clark University of Illinois at Urbana-Champaign, Seedbed Initiative for Transdomain Creativity

Kevin Franklin Executive Director, University of Illinois Institute for Computing in the Humanities, Arts, and Social Sciences, Senior Research Scientist for the National Center for Supercomputing Applications

Daniel Herwitz University of Michigan, Mary Fair Croushore Professor of Humanities, Director of the Institute for the Humanities

Julie Thompson Klein Wayne State University, Professor of Humanities, Interdisciplinary Studies Program, Faculty Fellow in the Office of Teaching and Learning, Codirector of the University Library Digital Media Project

Henry Lowood Stanford University Libraries, Curator for History of Science, Technology, and Germanic Collections

Thomas MacCalla National University, Vice President, Executive Director of the National University Community Research Institute in San Diego

Stephenie McLean Renaissance Computing Institute, Director of Education and Outreach

Tara McPherson University of Southern California, Associate Professor, Gender and Critical Studies, School of Cinematic Arts, Founding Editor of *Vectors: Journal of Culture and Technology in a Dynamic Vernacular*

Mark Olson Duke University, Visiting Professor, Department of Art, Art History, and Visual Studies; Director, New Media and Information Technologies, John Hope Franklin Center for Interdisciplinary and International Studies

Douglas Thomas University of Southern California, Associate Professor, Annenberg School for Communication, Director of the Thinking Through Technology Project, Coinvestigator on the Metamorphosis Project

Kathleen Woodward University of Washington, Professor of English, Director of the Walter Chapin Simpson Center for the Humanities

May 11, 2007, Forum in Irvine, California

Anne Balsamo University of Southern California, Professor of Interactive Media and Gender Studies in the School of Cinematic Arts and of Communications in the Annenberg School of Communications

Jean-Francois Blanchette University of California, Los Angeles, Assistant Professor, Department of Information Studies, Graduate School of Education and Information Studies

Tom Boellstorff University of California, Irvine, Associate Professor of Anthropology, Editor-in-Chief of *American Anthropologist*

Allison Clark University of Illinois at Urbana-Champaign, Seedbed Initiative for Transdomain Creativity

Edward Fowler University of California, Irvine, Professor and Chair of East Asian Languages and Literature, Professor of Film and Media Studies

Deniz Göktörk University of California, Berkeley, Associate Professor of Department of German, Cofounder of *TRANSIT*, the first electronic journal in German studies

Diane Harley University of California, Berkeley, Senior Researcher at Center for Studies in Higher Education, Director of the Higher Education in the Digital Age Project

Adriene Jenik University of California, San Diego, Associate Professor, Computer and Media Arts, Visual Arts Department

Rosalie Lack University of California, Office of the President, California Digital Library, Digital Special Collections Director

Toby Miller University of California, Riverside, Professor and Chair of Media and Cultural Studies

Christopher Newfield University of California, Santa Barbara, Professor, English Department, Innovation Working Group, Center for Nanotechnology in Society

Vorris Nunley University of California, Riverside, Assistant Professor of English

Mark Poster University of California, Irvine, Professor of History

Todd Presner University of California, Los Angeles, Associate Professor of German Studies, Chair of Center for Humanities Computing and Director, Hypermedia Berlin

Ramesh Srinivasan University of California, Los Angeles, Assistant Professor of Information Studies and the Graduate School of Education and Information Studies

William Tomlinson University of California, Irvine, Assistant Professor, Informatics Department, Bren School of Information and Computer Sciences

K. Wayne Yang University of California, San Diego, Assistant Professor of Ethnic Studies

Institute for the Future of the Book[1]

Christine Alfano Stanford University, Lecturer, Program in Writing and Rhetoric and the Department of English

Craig Avery

Anne Balsamo University of Southern California, Professor of Interactive Media and Gender Studies in the School of Cinematic Arts and of Communications in the Annenberg School of Communications

Mechelle Marie De Craene Florida State University, Department of Art Education and K-12 Teacher (Special Education/Gifted Education), Founder HASTAC on Ning

Kevin Guidry Sewanee: The University of the South, MacArthur Information Technology Fellow

Steve Jones University of Illinois at Chicago, Professor, Department of Communication, Associate Dean of Liberal Arts and Sciences

Becky Kinney University of Delaware, Instructional Programmer, User Services

LAC

Edward Lamoureux Bradley University, Associate Professor, Multimedia Program and Department of Communication, Codirector of the New Media Center

Eileen McMahon University of Massachusetts, Boston, Senior Instructional Designer, Communication Studies

Jason Mittell Middlebury College, Associate Professor, American Studies and Film and Media Culture

rcsha

Alex Reid

Michael Roy Wesleyan University, Director of Academic Computing Services and Digital Library Projects, Founding Editor of *Academic Commons*

K. G. Schneider, Blogger Free Range Librarian

Patricia Seed University of California, Irvine, Professor, History of Science and Technology

Trevor Shaw   *MultiMedia & Internet@Schools* magazine

David Silver   University of San Francisco, Assistant Professor, Department of Media Studies

Bruce Simon   State University of New York, Fredonia, Associate Professor of English

Tpabeles

wheat

Ben Vershbow   Editorial Director, Institute for the Future of the Book

Sarita Yardi   Georgia Institute of Technology, PhD Student, Human-Centered Computing Program

Additional Scholarly Contributions

Anne Allison   Duke University, Chair of Department of Cultural Anthropology

Richard Cherwitz   University of Texas at Austin, Professor, Department of Communication Studies and Department of Rhetoric and Writing, Founder and Director of Intellectual Entrepreneurship Consortium

Jonathan Cummings   Duke University, Associate Professor of Management, Fuqua School of Business

Diane Favro   University of California, Los Angeles, Professor, Department of Architectural History, Director of the Center for Experimental Technologies

Alice Kaplan   Duke University, Professor, Department of Romance Studies, Literature, and History

Robin Kirk   Duke University, Director of the Duke Human Rights Center

Timothy Lenoir Duke University, Kimberly Jenkins Professor of New Technologies and Society, Director of Information Sciences+Information Studies Program

Richard Lucic Duke University, Associate Department Chair and Associate Professor of the Practice of Computer Science, Director of External Relations, Information Sciences+Information Studies Program, Curriculum Director of the Department of Computer Science

Robert Nideffer University of California, Irvine, Professor of Art, Codirector of the Arts, Computation, and Engineering (ACE) Program, Director of Center for Gaming and Game Culture

Simon Penny University of California, Irvine, Professor of Art and Engineering, Codirector of the ACE Program

Ken Rogerson Duke University, Lecturer, Sanford Institute of Public Policy

Carol Hughes University of California, Irvine, Associate University Librarian for Public Services

Kavita Philip University of California, Irvine, Associate Professor of Women's Studies, Anthropology, and the ACE Program

Todd Presner University of California, Los Angeles, Associate Professor of German Studies, Chair of the Center for Humanities Computing, Director of Hypermedia Berlin

John Taormino Duke University, Director of the Visual Resources Center

Contributors to Bibliography II: Resources and Models

Mechelle Marie De Craene Florida State University, Department of Art Education and K-12 Teacher (Special Education/Gifted Education), Founder of HASTAC on Ning

David Harris University of São Paulo, PhD Student, Director of the Global Lives Project

Kenneth R. Jolls Iowa State University, Professor of Chemical and Biological Engineering

Julie Thompson Klein Wayne State University, Professor of Humanities, Interdisciplinary Studies Program, Faculty Fellow in the Office of Teaching and Learning, Codirector of the University Library Digital Media Project

Michael Roy Wesleyan University, Director of Academic Computing Services and Digital Library Projects, Founding Editor of *Academic Commons*

Notes

1. These contributors cited here made comments on the Institute of the Future of the Book Web site between January 2007 and January 2008. Many of the contributors to the site used (often cryptic) usernames in order to register and thus could not be identified in terms of their institutional connections. This does not make their comments any less valuable and is instead a natural product of digital collaboration. Users were contacted and asked permission to use their real names and institutional affiliations. If no response was received, the name or pseudonym used on the site is reflected here. Comments contibuted after January 2008 have not been incorporated into this book.

The Future of Thinking

age centers challenge collaborative community complex cultural definition digital distributed education emergence field formation forms future hastac humanities important individual information institutions interactive internet knowledge learning media mobilizing models networks offer open organization peer-to-peer people possibilities productive public resources scholars sites social tail technologies thinking traditional university virtual web year

1 Introduction and Overview: The Future of Learning Institutions in a Digital Age

A university classroom. The instructor is reading aloud from a passage in the assigned work for the week. He looks up to find his students all deeply engrossed. Their rapture, alas, is not with him but with their laptop screens, their attention worlds away.

Later that day, the professor fires off an email to his colleagues suggesting that laptops be banned from the classroom because of incidents like this.

Response one: This is an outrage, more and more familiar. Students are distracted by what their laptops make available to them, their attention too readily drawn away from the class activities and lesson.

Response two: Perhaps a professor shouldn't be sitting at the desk reading out loud from a book.

There may well be merit in each of these responses. At the very least, each response deserves consideration. The latter response raises questions about the book itself as a technology. It did not always exist, after all. But the history and form of teaching methods warrant renewed consideration, too. Why is a professor at the front of the classroom at all? Why is he reading out loud? What are the forms of learning implicit in such an act, and how do those forms edify our concept of learning, education, and the whole process of communicating ideas? How do laptops change the way we learn? And how *should* they change the way we teach?

These are the kinds of questions that every educator should be thinking about today. Modes of learning have changed dramatically over the past two decades—our sources of information, the ways we exchange and interact with information, how information informs and shapes us. But our schools—how we teach, where we teach, whom we teach, who teaches, who administers, and who services—have changed mostly around the edges. The fundamental aspects of learning institutions remain remarkably familiar and have been for around two hundred years or more. Ichabod Crane, that parody of bad teaching in Washington Irving's classic short story "The Legend of Sleepy Hollow",[1] could walk into most college classrooms today and know exactly where to stand and how to address his class.

There are other questions, too. If we are going to imagine new learning institutions that are not based on the contiguity of time and place—*virtual* institutions—what are those institutions and what work do they perform? What does a virtual learning institution look like, who supports it, what does it do? We know that informal learning happens—constantly and in many new ways—because of the collaborative opportunities offered by social networking sites, wikis, blogs, and many other interactive digital sources. But beneath these sites are networks and, sometimes, organizations dedicated to their efficiency and sustainability. What is the institutional basis for their persistence? If a virtual site spans many individuals and institutions, who or what supports (in practical terms) the virtual site and by what mechanisms?

Conventional institutions of learning have changed far more slowly than the modes of inventive, collaborative, participatory learning offered by the Internet and an array of contemporary mobile technologies. This slow pace of change makes us think we know what a learning institution is—or we think we do. But what happens when, rivaling formal educational systems, there are also many virtual sites where learning is happening? From young kids customizing Pokémon (and learning to read, code, and use digital editing tools), to college kids contributing to Wikipedia, to adults exchanging information about travel or restaurants or housing via collaborative sites, learning is happening online, all the time. Are these Internet sites *learning institutions*? And, if so, what do these institutions tell us about the more traditional learning institutions such as schools, universities, graduate schools?

One of the best examples of a virtual learning institution in our era is Wikipedia, the largest encyclopedia compiled in human history and one "written collaboratively by volunteers from all around the world."[2] Sustaining Wikipedia is the Wikimedia Foundation, Inc., with its staid organizational charts and well-defined legal structures. What is the relationship between the quite traditional nonprofit corporation headquartered in San Francisco and the free, open, multilingual, online, global community of volunteers? Is the *institution* the sustaining organization, the astonishing virtual community, or the online encyclopedia itself?

When considering the future of learning institutions in a digital age, it is important to look at the ways that digitality works to cross the boundaries within and across traditional learning institutions. How do collaborative, interdisciplinary, multi-institutional learning spaces help transform traditional learning institutions and, specifically, universities? For example, how are the hierarchies of expertise—the ranks of the professoriate and also the divide of undergraduates, graduate students, and faculty (including adjunct faculty, tenure-track junior faculty, and tenured and distinguished faculty)—supported and also undermined by new digital possibilities? Are there collaborative modes of digital learning that help us to rethink traditional pedagogical methods? And what might learning institutions look like—what *should* they look like—given the digital potentialities and pitfalls at hand today?

This book addresses these intertwined questions and the myriad implications they provoke; the book is neither utopian in its prognostications of the future, nor bleak in its assessment of the present, nor nostalgic in its construction of the past. Rather, the book assumes that the future will be as complicated and contradictory as is the present (and as the past has always been). Similarly, its focus is not on the intrinsic value of new technologies but, rather, on how we can most creatively explore new technologies to better understand what it means to learn. As technologies change, potentials and problems also shift, even as some cultural, psychological, educational, social, and political values remain consistent, though not necessarily constant.

This book investigates the character of learning institutions and how they change, how they change those who belong to them, and how we can work together to change them. The primary focus is on higher education. It is daunting to think that universities have existed in the West since medieval times and in forms remarkably similar to the universities that exist today. Will they endure for hundreds of years more, even as learning increasingly happens virtually, globally, and collaboratively? Will thinking about the potential of new ways of knowing inspire us to revitalize those institutions of advanced formal learning?

Digital Learning

A key term in this project is *digital learning* or, as it is sometimes called, *participatory learning*. In this form of learning, many contribute to a final product. The Institute for the Future of the Book's collaborative site, for example, on which the first draft of this project was posted and to which many responded and engaged in dialogue, would be an example of digital, participatory learning.

Digital, participatory learning has been promoted both by the Humanities, Arts, Science, and Technology Advanced Collaboratory (HASTAC) and by the John D. and Catherine T. MacArthur Foundation's Digital Media and Learning Initiative. Digital learning begins from the premise that new technologies are changing how people of all ages learn, play, socialize, exercise judgment, and engage in civic life. Learning environments—peers, family, and social institutions (e.g., schools, community centers, libraries, museums)—are changing as well. The concept of digital learning is different from instructional technology (IT), which is usually a toolkit application that is predetermined and even institutionalized with little, if any, user discretion, choice, or leverage. It also tends to be top down, designer determined, administratively driven. In digital learning, outcomes typically are customizable by the participants. When the draft essay was placed on CommentPress, the Web-based tool developed by the Institute for the Future of the Book, authorship became a shared and interactive experience in which the essayists engaged in online conversation with those reading and responding to the work (figure 1.1).[3] That is a version of digital learning.

Box 1

The Institute for the Future of the Book

Figure 1.1

Screenshot of the first draft of the *Future of Thinking* project (http://www.futureofthebook.org, accessed on August 13, 2008).

Our tools of learning are shifting increasingly from the printed page to digital media. The Institute for the Future of the Book (http://www.futureofthebook.org) takes as its mission the chronicling of this shift and the development of digital resources to promote innovative reimaginings of the book. In 2007, the Institute released free, open-ended software called CommentPress (a variation of the blogging software, WordPress) that allows an online text to be "marked up" in a manner reminiscent of margin notes.

Digital learning is not simply about interaction (we all have plenty of that in our lives) but of interaction that, because of issues of access, involves cocreation with myriad strangers who have the anonymity to respond as they wish, candidly. From such a process, we learn and continue to learn from people met only virtually (if at all) and whose institutional status and credentials may be unknown.

With digital learning, the play between technology, composer, and audience is no longer passive. Indeed, digital learning begins to blur these traditional lines. This does not happen often in a scholar's life, where almost everything is based on peer review and institutionally ordained authority, all within certain professional norms. In conventional learning institutions, the lines of authorship and authority are clearly delineated, and the place of teacher, student, and technology are well known. With digital learning, these conventional modes of authority break down. As a model, though, the pressing question is that of the sustainability of conventional modes of learning. It challenges us accordingly to think of new and more compelling modes of learning practice and process that can be pressed into productive play in productive ways.

Remix Authorship

As has often happened in the history of technology, a significant breakthrough in hardware or software has an impact on social and political conditions. These impacts may be large or small, general or local. On the local end of the spectrum, in the case of the CommentPress tool, the concept of publishing changed, as did the concept of authorship. Is the first or the final version of the text the "published" version of the essay? Are both? The concept of authorship (a subject to which we return in chapter 3) must be reassessed because of the interactive publishing process.[4] As any historian of the book knows, one cannot change a part of the publishing circuit without changing all others, from the materiality of its production (books or Web sites) to its distribution and its readership (which brings into question issues ranging from access to literacy).[5]

The implications of the CommentPress interaction are fascinating for thinking about the future of learning institutions. Anyone could join the CommentPress Web site and make notes on the essay, without the benefit of any specific institutional membership. Anyone who heard about the project from some source—*networking* is another crucial component of digital learning that we return to in chapter 3—could register and comment. Given that someone could log on from an Internet café in Thailand or from a graduate research program in Boston, this process raised important issues of access, authority, and anonymity. It also offered the retreat, if not the vanishing altogether, of traditional institutional structures and implicit notions of institutional membership and hierarchy marking most forms of feedback to scholarly work—such as shared membership in a classroom, an academic department, or a professional association. Participation in CommentPress required only access to a computer and enough literacy to be able to read, comprehend, and respond to the essay. In many ways, the Institute for the Future of the Book is an extension of the first subscription libraries. Benjamin Franklin established the Library Company of Philadelphia in 1731 to give readers broader access to knowledge. The Internet, surely, has redefined access (and its limits) for the twenty-first century.

The process of interactive authorship and readership seems different from previous forms, such as coauthored books and book clubs, especially in its institutional implications. Hybrid forms of authorship and production resemble other hybridized forms of cultural expressions emerging at this particular historical moment. Sampling and remixing are now part of almost every aspect of expressive culture, from music and art to fashion and architecture. Here, too, authorship is remixed in the sense of transforming working comments, insights, and critical remarks from CommentPress interlocutors into revisions of this book. Remix authorship (like all collaborative forms) comes with its attendant issues of intellectual property and credit, which are explored in chapter 2. Intriguingly, the more collaborative the project, the more we must think about individual credit, even in cases such as this where profit is not an issue.

One purpose of this book is to document these forms of production and the features that seem unique to them, for they both fashion and reflect emergent institutional learning practices. New technologies make possible instantaneous revision, repositioning, reformulation. There are clearly benefits to this, though there may be drawbacks, too. If we do not hesitate to reword, we likewise may not take the time to reflect. Analyzing the transformations that new technologies have made to modes of learning requires looking honestly at the pros and cons. The moment is fresh enough that it is still visible to us, and we can influence these developments before they settle in to become routine, the assumed, the given.

This book's form of remix authorship has many traditional elements instructive about the nature of learning as well. Someone, individually or collectively, must take responsibility for the product, for the learning environment, the technologies, the content. In this book, two authors have made the final "call" about what to include and what to exclude from the feedback and the process of soliciting feedback itself. Like teachers, the authors assumed responsibility for organizing the forums and choosing the participants who offered insights. Those choices are not made in a vacuum, absent a charge or parameters of writing or learning, of subject matter and audience, of funding mandates and institutional review. This interactive form of research is different from the carefully hidden series of revisions that emerge in the public eye as a fully finished book, with the labor of its various readers, copy editors, and others acknowledged in a sentence, but, in a sense, banished from the final product. In other ways,the traditional sense of authorship was retained, since the authors sorted through the commentary and selected elements to include in the final book. Teachers and learners make similar selections about materials from input by others, with expertise and experience as guides.

Was this interactive writing process worth the effort? It has certainly been more work—not less—than a single-author production or a traditional coauthored work. Hidden behind the enterprise, for example, are the people at the Institute for the Future of the Book who wrote the software for the collaborative system and who maintained its efficient Web presence for the duration of the project. Not so hidden are the comments (for all the world to see) that range from castigations for misspellings (e.g., the first draft used "UTube" instead of "YouTube") to pointing out issues simply overlooked (e.g., libraries were omitted from the first draft) (figures 1.2 and 1.3). For most senior academics, warts are not noted quite so publicly. Yet, given the new worlds of discourse in the snarky blogosphere or on the irreverent Facebook "wall," perhaps we all must accept that we are in the midst of a change (yet again) in the status of the author, the teacher, and, indeed, the learner. The author may not be dead, as Roland Barthes first pronounced in 1978 in *Image-Music-Text*, but the author is now digital.[6] From the process, one learns not only content but form and voice, and

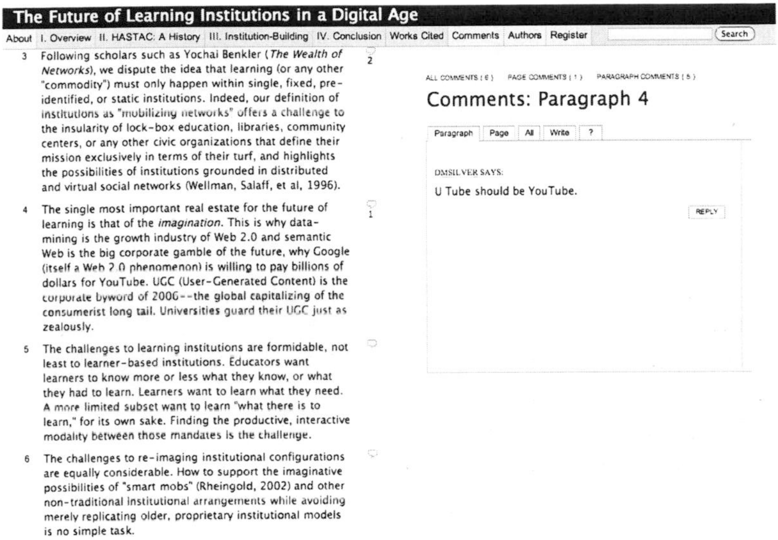

The Future of Learning Institutions in a Digital Age

About I. Overview II. HASTAC: A History III. Institution-Building IV. Conclusion Works Cited Comments Authors Register   [Search]

3   Following scholars such as Yochai Benkler (*The Wealth of Networks*), we dispute the idea that learning (or any other "commodity") must only happen within single, fixed, pre-identified, or static institutions. Indeed, our definition of institutions as "mobilizing networks" offers a challenge to the insularity of lock-box education, libraries, community centers, or any other civic organizations that define their mission exclusively in terms of their turf, and highlights the possibilities of institutions grounded in distributed and virtual social networks (Wellman, Salaff, et al, 1996).

4   The single most important real estate for the future of learning is that of the *imagination*. This is why data-mining is the growth industry of Web 2.0 and semantic Web is the big corporate gamble of the future, why Google (itself a Web 2.0 phenomenon) is willing to pay billions of dollars for YouTube. UGC (User-Generated Content) is the corporate byword of 2006--the global capitalizing on the consumerist long tail. Universities guard their UGC just as zealously.

5   The challenges to learning institutions are formidable, not least to learner-based institutions. Educators want learners to know more or less what they know, or what they had to learn. Learners want to learn what they need. A more limited subset want to learn "what there is to learn," for its own sake. Finding the productive, interactive modality between those mandates is the challenge.

6   The challenges to re-imaging institutional configurations are equally considerable. How to support the imaginative possibilities of "smart mobs" (Rheingold, 2002) and other non-traditional institutional arrangements while avoiding merely replicating older, proprietary institutional models is no simple task.

ALL COMMENTS (6)   PAGE COMMENTS (1)   PARAGRAPH COMMENTS (5)

Comments: Paragraph 4

| Paragraph | Page | All | Write | ? |

DMSILVER SAYS:

U Tube should be YouTube.

REPLY

Figure 1.2
Screenshot of the Institute for the Future of the Book Web site (http://www.futureofthebook.org, accessed on August 13, 2008).

maybe even some dissociative distance from one's own still-in-process products. All of this is intrinsically *interesting*. And because it is, the process has been worth it. In many ways, the process has revealed the crucial features of the concept of digital learning that this book considers and promotes.

Likewise, this printed version is not final. As a product of Web 2.0 knowledge formation, it is open-ended and revisable. An electronic version of the book will remain on the HASTAC Web site, and comments will continue to be accepted. As with the previous comments, this is part of the enterprise of thinking collaboratively about the future of learning and its institutions.

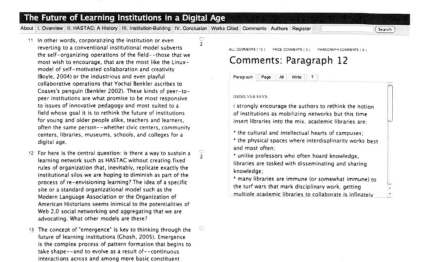

Figure 1.3
Screenshot of the Institute for the Future of the Book Web site, (http://
www.futureofthebook.org, accessed on August 13, 2008).

Youth Access

This book addresses both formal and informal learning and
educational environments. Although the chief focus is on college students and higher education, younger learners are also
considered. For those who are still minors, there are many special issues of security and privacy that are relevant to digital
production, networked circulation, and remix authorship. Digitality offers new possibilities for youth; there are also areas
where guardianship and supervision are clearly necessary. There
are issues of "protecting" digital youth where media hysteria
creates, as much as it documents, a social problem.

Once there is open access (with no gatekeeper ensuring the participant is over 18 or accompanied by a parent or guardian), myriad new issues arise. Once kids can participate freely with adults in an atmosphere of anonymity, issues of credibility and vulnerability arise. We might not know whether a particularly salient remark was offered by a distinguished professor or a twelve-year-old (and does it matter?). We only know that the interaction helped us think through a thorny problem. And yet that anonymity might equally hide other vulnerabilities—of manipulation, enticement, attraction, indeed addiction—that young folk have not yet developed the judgment to recognize or resist.

For minors, all of the important and sensitive issues concerning access, privacy, and security for youth in a digital age take on special weight and force. Readers who are especially concerned with kids are referred to Bibliography II, an extensive collection of sources that might help guide teachers, parents, administrators, policymakers, researchers, teachers, and students (of any age). Bibliography II provides models and examples of innovative digital learning projects already underway for youth (some more successful than others). What is the complex relationship between access and protection when it comes to kids? Different digital learning environments and virtual worlds have addressed this issue, and some insights from those experiments are provided.

Mobilizing Networks

In thinking through new versions of digital learning, authorship, and participation in this book, new ideas of institutions are also explored. It is typical for social scientists to define an institution in terms of the structures and mechanisms of control, social order, rules of regulation, and cooperation that govern the behavior of its members and that, sometimes, by extension, exert control or definition over those excluded from the institution's official membership. This book proposes a deliberately provocative alternative definition of *institution*: An institution as a *mobilizing network*.

This counterintuitive (and even cantankerous) definition is a way to rethink the limits of an institution and its potential. Given that the aim is to consider learning institutions for a digital age, what might follow from a definition of *institution* that emphasized its flexibility, the permeability of its boundaries, its interactive productivity, and its potential as a catalyst for change rather than its mechanisms of cooperation, order, control, and regulation? Is it possible to see institutions as mobilizing rather than restraining? Or even mobilizing *and* restraining?

Much of social science thought has gone into parsing out the guardian functions of institutions. What might follow from thinking about what flows into and out of institutions from other sources and the ways existing institutions themselves (sometimes unwittingly) produce or at least mobilize change? How can the digital connections that transcend the walls (literally and figuratively) of institutions enable us to transform some of the most bounded and frustrating aspects (the "silos") of institutions of higher learning? For example, we are all too familiar with the difficulties of teaching courses as intellectually complex as our digital era (the subject of chapter 4). It is not easy to circumvent departments, disciplines, schools, and the special prejudices held by each. In this grant-driven era in higher education, we also acknowledge the problem of writing a grant that transcends schools and departments. Who will receive the income (the so-called indirect cost recoveries) from the grants when many contribute?

Chapter 5 offers an extended definition of institutions as *mobilizing networks* that is designed to help us move away from the frustrations of attempting to revolutionize institutions and, instead, to invigorate the concept of institutions by highlighting the fluid networks that operate within, through, around, across, and outside traditional boundaries of even the most solid and seemingly unchangeable institutions. This definition is a thought experiment. How can beginning with a counterintuitive definition help us rethink the institutions we belong to and envision the kinds of institutions we desire? If, at present, too many learning institutions pose obstacles to the free flow of thinking, to collaborative knowledge formation, and to interactive learning almost as formidable as the obstacles imposed by corporations and by governments, then how do we create free-flowing institutions?

This line of thought leads, once again, to a series of interconnected questions. How can the networked social relationships characteristic of digital worlds and peer-to-peer learning be supported by equally distributed institutional structures, by peer-to-peer institutions as innovative, flexible, robust, and collaborative as the best social networking sites? Is it possible for a successful peer-to-peer institution such as HASTAC to help lead a generation of scholars in the conception and creation of flexible institutions for youth (e.g., libraries, civic centers, community centers, schools) that take advantage of new digital forms of learning and self-organization that characterize everyday life and learning for many young people today?

In order to create a new field of digital learning, we must bring together research, knowledge, methodologies, and expertise from radically distributed existing fields—from the media and design arts to history, sociology, communications, psychology, philosophy, education, policy studies, political science, the computational sciences, engineering, and all points in between. A field cannot exist without institutional grounding. But at what point do loose affiliations between and among those in different fields (what Harvard sociologist Mark Granovetter calls "the strength of weak ties"[7]) constitute the critical mass necessary for a new field with all of its apparatus—conferences, journals, networks of authorities, debates, theories, practices, pedagogies, and (meaningfully contentious) subfields? If we are moving toward distributed institutions—with peer-to-peer training, review, and certification—what can we do to support and sustain those institutions in creative new ways?

This book draws its strength from the richness of its sources. Feedback was gathered from the general public and from numerous leaders who have been instrumental in the development of new interdisciplinary fields. In the sciences, these fields include cognitive neuroscience, biomedical engineering, genomics, and bioinformatics. In the social sciences and the humanities, the fields include cultural studies, visual studies, African and African-American studies, film and media studies, postcolonial studies, queer theory, comparative literature, and gender and women's studies. Leaders were consulted individually and in groups in order to learn their histories and profit from their insights.

Second, the successes and shortcomings of the Humanities, Arts, Science, and Technology Advanced Collaboratory, the innovative peer-to-peer learning institution that was conceived of in 2002 and launched in early 2003, provided a wealth of data. A case study and a potential next-generation model, HASTAC is an entirely voluntary consortium, a network of networks, with no dues, no written rules of association, no headquarters, and no formal organizational structure. Yet, its accomplishments to date include collaborative tool building, successful negotiation efforts (to ensure that the complex data needs of human and social sciences are included in national funding efforts of various kinds), research and development with leading scientific agencies, and collaborations with leading national supercomputing centers, as well as consulting with national and international agencies, and field-building educational efforts in collaboration with foundations, learning institutions, and corporations.

Although HASTAC is *voluntary*, it is not *without cost*. It receives significant support for core infrastructure from two established institutions, Duke University and the University of California. Without their investment in the digital future of learning, HASTAC would not have developed, let alone flourished and played the leadership role it has over the last several years. Additionally, support for various activities comes from the other member institutions—collaborations, conferences, workshops, and scholarships to undergraduate and graduate students. During 2006–2007, 80 institutions collaborated on an In|Formation Year, offering courses, seminars, lecture series, conferences, and public events, as well as rolling out new software and hardware, all supported in a distributed fashion by the individual institutions and then publicized centrally by HASTAC. These efforts also received significant foundation support—from Digital Promise, the National Science Foundation, and, most significant, the John D. and Catherine T. MacArthur Foundation.

As we consider the most visionary interdisciplinary and institutional projects, we also must reflect on the traditional funding institutions (i.e., state and federal granting agencies,

private foundations, and corporations) that help them to flourish. The relationship between virtual and traditional institutions can take many forms. For example, the John D. and
Catherine T. MacArthur Foundation, one of the most respected
private foundations in existence, had the boldness to invite
HASTAC, a virtual institution, to administer its first open
competition in Digital Media and Learning. In this instance,
HASTAC's extensive virtual network of networks helped the
MacArthur Foundation to extend its reach into new communities, and the support of the MacArthur Foundation helped
HASTAC to flourish.

The collaboration between a virtual institution and a major
private foundation resulted in the HASTAC/MacArthur Foundation Digital Media and Learning Competition (figure 1.4). The
first competition was announced on August 14, 2007, with an
application deadline of October 15, 2007. The extensive HAS-
TAC communication network, in tandem with a $2 million
prize and the impeccable reputation and reach of the MacArthur Foundation, turned out to be a winning combination. The
competition received 1,010 final submissions, more than three
times as many as the organizers expected, which suggested that
this first competition should not be the last.[8] Those submissions
tended to be radically cross-disciplinary and cross-institutional,
often with complex collaborations of institutions of various
sizes, kinds, and missions—collaborations of a kind that many
people would have thought impossible even a year before. It is
clear that something is happening. Maybe institutions *are* mobilizing networks.

Through the collaborative process of gathering responses to
the first draft of this book and then by synthesizing these comments into a coherent analysis and action plan, partly stimu-
lated by and symbolized by the HASTAC/MacArthur Foundation

Figure 1.4
Screenshot of the first Digital Media and Learning Competition (http://www.dmlcompetition.net, accessed August 13, 2008).

Digital Media and Learning Competition, peer-to-peer learning institutions and environments have been mobilized, encouraged, and celebrated in a way that addresses the future of lifelong learning and the institutions that will serve and sustain them in a digital age.

2 Customized and Participatory Learning

Customized Learning

"Common culture" is dead, claims *Wired* magazine editor Chris Anderson In *The Long Tail. Why the Future of Business is Selling Less of More*,[1] the smash bestseller of summer 2006.[2] Anderson argues that the effect of the Internet has been to expose consumers to limitless choices. Remote niche markets and a global range of products are available to anyone with a laptop and a credit card. Social networking sites that develop among consumers with shared interests also communicate the best Web sources providing these goods. The result is a new kind of market. In contrast to the *Pareto tails* of the standard statistical distribution in the common culture regime (where 20 percent of products account for 80 percent of revenue), on the Internet *98 percent* of products are chosen by someone, thus skewing the 80:20 ratio.[3] Anderson argues that the savvy cultural purveyor, like the smart businessperson, understands that it is now necessary to offer young consumers a plethora of possibilities, including personalized or self-designed products and projects.

This book focuses less on the consumer choices now available through the Internet and more on the customized learning opportunities offered by the Internet (although, as any parent knows, there is no hard-and-fast boundary between "consumer choices" and "learning opportunities" for kids today). So-called serious games are the most overt educational adaptations of online entertainment, but there is seemingly an endless array of choices, especially if learning is considered to include all forms of new knowledge acquisition and formation.

Consider Pokémon, for example. A five-year-old masters the equivalent of a third-grade reading vocabulary in order to play online and also customizes the game with digital graphic tools that, only a generation ago, would have been considered sophisticated for a professional designer. That five-year-old makes friends online through game play that requires memorizing hundreds (the number expands every day) of characters with different attributes and skills and learns how to fix, customize, program, or hack a computer in order to participate in this compelling online world of play. You do not have to force a child who is interested in Pokémon to practice at the computer. Technical skills, programming, literacy, social life, aesthetics and design, narrative-making, socializing, and fun are all woven together, and, for many preschoolers, the only brake is the parent who worries about the child spending too much time (or money) on Pokémon. Innovation has responded to one parental concern: SoftwareTime has developed a popular program to limit children's time at the computer.[4]

This multidisciplinary learning world, where play and learning are inseparable, is diametrically opposed to our federal education program and the No Child Left Behind Act of 2001 (NCLB).[5] With its lockstep national standards and standardized testing, where school districts are penalized with reduced funding if students do not perform to a certain level, NCLB rewards teachers for teaching to the tests. National standards and assessments have replaced other measures of learning, including those gauged by classroom teachers themselves. Indeed, public education has been privatized to a shocking degree by NCLB, since private testing businesses are now frequently hired, at taxpayer's expense, to construct the tests that purportedly measure outcomes but do not necessarily gauge real learning. It is an intrusive, forced model of education, and it is no surprise that we face a decline in teachers willing to stay in public education.

In an increasingly customized world, we have standardized public education that is far closer to an early nineteenth-century model than a twenty-first century one. If one purpose of formal education is to underscore what modes of learning are valued by our society, we are in an oddly mismatched time, where success and failure of a school district or a student are determined by standardized tests at a time of vast potential for customized, collaborative learning. To return to Anderson's point, public education in America is still in the common culture model; NCLB has a very stubby tail.

What, then, are the implications of the long tail for learning and for learning institutions in this new world where choice and customization seem to prevail? How might we expand learning possibilities within conventional learning institutions to keep pace with our consumer choices? And is such expansion desirable? If people are, in fact, self-educating via the Internet, how are we, as educators, using students' skills to help transform learning practices, both in the classroom and out? The Internet offers unprecedented access to an enormous range of information and the possibility of an extraordinary range of learning modalities, not all of which have been tested. Uninformed choice may be as much a waste of talent (overlooking compelling options) as it is talent-enhancing.

Equally important, what are the implications of not address-ing changes in the way young people learn and interact? The United States currently ranks *seventeenth* among industrialized nations in the educational attainment of its populace.[6] Although social and economic factors correlate strongly with educational dropout rates (with lower income contributing to higher attri-tion rates), the last decade has also witnessed dropout rates increasing across economic groups, across cities and rural areas, and across all areas of the country, with boys dropping out at notably greater rates than girls.[7] One reason, some argue, is boredom, and a mismatch between the lively online lives of youth today and the one-size-fits-all national educational agenda. Although more research remains to be done on this topic, many of the current conventional institutions of learning (both K–12 and higher education) do not fully, creatively, or completely address their students' needs and interests. We con-tinue to push old, uniform, and increasingly outdated educa-tional products on young learners at their—and, by implication, society's—peril.

Innovative and experimental ideas for schools are being fueled by a mix of existing knowledge and cultural institutions, as well as new digitally enabled possibilities (for more informa-tion, see the Portfolio of Virtual Learning Environments at the end of this chapter). A Museum School draws on five New York City museums to offer classrooms for the development of inter-disciplinary projects, sewing together science and culture, his-tory and natural history. Opening in Fall 2009, the Quest to Learn school in Manhattan will draw on game design and inter-active gaming methods and strategies as the basis for an innova-tive curriculum to teach traditional and nontraditional subjects, practices, and forms of wise decision-making. Computer gam-ing offers the possibility of developing important skills for the knowledge economy—computer and information literacy, database development and management, knowledge networks, data analysis—as well as more traditional skills associated with reading, writing, arithmetic, and social interactions.

Collaborative Learning

Anderson's point about the long tail can be customized into an important pedagogical principle for the twenty-first century. Because of the deep cultural shifts of our times to new modes of online learning available especially (but not only) to youth, there is a challenge to identify and comprehend the multiple preferences of dispersed and diverse learning populations. Learning is no longer one size fits all, and we need to learn to appreciate and foster learning in all its sizes and varieties. The hard part—and, arguably, the single most important skill for future educators—is finding ways that individual learners with individual skills and interests can share with others who possess different skill levels and interests.

This model of peer-to-peer information-sharing happens routinely, if casually, on social networking sites such as Facebook and YouTube and is being adopted and developed into a method by an increasing number of innovative educators, on all educational levels and in all institutional environments. The point is not to cannibalize or invade social networking sites that kids use to interact with one another. Many educators have objected to this invasion of privacy. A better model is to study, in a careful ethnographic way, the kinds of interactions that occur on these sites and then to apply that research to new ways of thinking about informal learning and formal education.

Successful social networking sites for youth provide models that educators might productively adopt for educational purposes.[8] In addition, social networking sites such as HASTAC on Ning (figure 2.1), Classroom 2.0, Shaping Youth, and many others offer educators their own social networking sites where they can use digital tools for collaborative thinking about pedagogical issues (e.g., privacy) that arise in new digital environments.[9]

Collaboration is another key issue of digital learning. If the first step toward envisioning a model of learning for the twenty-first century is appreciating and cultivating the various and sometimes eccentric skills and learning interests of individual students, the next step is creating learning environments where collaboration across diverse skill sets is rewarding for individuals and groups. Preliminary ethnographic research of social networking sites by a team led by Mizuko (Mimi) Ito suggests that kids socialize online much as they do offline, with the same close network of friends.[10] If this preliminary finding holds, then a challenge for educators is finding ways of extending and diversifying the reach of the individual students by using social networking tools, much as school-sponsored global pen-pal programs (often supported by international study abroad programs) did in an earlier era.

Box 2
HASTAC on Ning: A Synergistic Symposium for the Cybernetic Age

HASTAC on Ning (http://hastac.ning.com) is a social network created by secondary school teacher Mechelle De Craene. The network was started as a companion site to HASTAC and is a way for members of the HASTAC community to learn more about each other and share ideas and information. Members of HASTAC on Ning can post videos and links and participate in a group blog in order to promote new models for thinking, teaching, and research.

Box 2
(Continued)

Figure 2.1
Screenshot of HASTAC on Ning (http://hastac.ning.com, accessed on July 29, 2009).

Ning is a Palo Alto, California-based company that allows participants to create their own customizable social network (http://www.ning.com).

The best way to extend the reach of student networks is to involve youth in the learning process, encouraging them to explore their individual talents and guiding them as they work together to find ways that those talents can contribute to larger projects. This reshaping of learning as a continuing, customized, and collaborative project is as important for preschoolers as it is for retirees, for K–12 institutions as it is for research universities. Learning has as long a tail as commodity consumption, and we need institutions that recognize and support learning as a lifelong process.

Although this book uses *The Long Tail* as a jumping-off point for a discussion of customized, participatory learning, there are many points with which one could argue in *The Long Tail*, including its commodity emphasis. Educational preferences should not be marketed like new kinds of cola, and some of the corporate attempts to turn education into something "entrepreneurial" begin to resemble capitalist boot camp rather than a moment's respite from rampant commercialism (see discussion of the School of the Future in Philadelphia in the Portfolio of Virtual Learning Environments at the end of this chapter).

That said, Anderson makes some good assumptions about the effects of interactivity on intellectual choices and on the new kinds of affiliations (by self-defined choice) allowed by the Internet. His insights on the possibilities for learning, social action, and intellectual affiliation as a result of the virtual associations available on the Web are compelling.

Collaboration and Intellectual Property

The Long Tail began as an open-source research project on Anderson's blog (http://www.thelongtail.com). Open-source writing projects raise issues of intellectual property and authorship that exemplify a contradiction or even ambivalence about collaborative thinking that may be characteristic of the present moment.

Anderson began by offering ideas and draft text on the blog, and these ideas were improved and tested by numerous readers. That method is standard for our digital era. However, once that blog became a book, both traditional and peer-to-peer models of authorship were operating simultaneously. *The Long Tail* thus offers an interesting economic case study. It is, in part, a consumer- or user-designed product. However, it is Anderson and his publisher, in the traditional role of author and producer, who most directly benefited financially from the book's popularity, not the open-source researchers who added to or transformed Anderson's ideas.[11] Who owns ideas in a peer-to-peer environment? It is hard to say.

As a model of authorship, leadership, collaboration, originality, intellectual property, profit, and sustainability, *The Long Tail* is both a provocation to experiment with new forms of collective authorship but also a cautionary tale about the necessity of finding ways to give full credit to collaborative contributions. One lesson for learning institutions, then, is that they should be collaborative while also being respectful of individual efforts, and, accordingly, they need to develop reward systems suitable for collaborative efforts.

If collaborative learning challenges the traditional model of authorship, traditional authorship also challenges the assumptions of collaboration. On the Institute for the Future of the Book Web site, Alex Reid has raised some of these related and interrelated issues. "Authorship is fundar   the operation of the university from the grading of st   to the granting of tenure for faculty-   notes.[12] "How much time can I de   kind of writing when I know no   How can I convince my students   vince them of the validity of my   their individual work is so d   peers? In part I think the ar   with recognizing the differe marketplace function of the author-as-owner and a more material-technological understanding of the networked practices of composition."

Reid's point seems exactly right. *Authorship* is not one thing but various things. Anderson's model of authorship begins in the material-technological world of "networked practices of composition" and ends squarely in the "author-as-owner" model. There are countless examples of faculty taking students' ideas or products and making them their own. So the challenge, as much institutional as individual, is how to establish and reward interactive, collaborative outputs.

This book recapitulates aspects of this multiple construction of authorship, footnoting contributors where appropriate and listing the names of all participants in the contributors list. In addition, the authors are not profiting materially from this project.

But what if the authors of this book had not established this particular collaborative writing project—with its feedback from online drafts and public forums—as open-source, open-access, and nonprofit? Would that make a difference? What if, like Anderson's book, this book were to become a surprise bestseller? What are the open-source economics of the conversations and contributions leading to a publication? And are these online and face-to-face contributions different *in kind* than the kind of interchange that happens at conferences or even in the classroom as we make our way from a draft presentation to a final chapter, incorporating feedback and responses and insights along the way? Laws are themselves a form of institutional-ion. How do laws around intellectual property support or the future of digital learning and virtual institutions

The music industry, for example, is not monolithic. Some parts of the industry have moved toward a more open-source or pay-what-you-wish model. Currently both Radiohead and Nine Inch Nails are among the bands experimenting with different kinds of downloading options. Yet other parts of the industry are taking a hard line, arresting ten-year-old file-sharers and testing questions of influence, reference, sampling, remix, and citation in the courts.[13]

New digital and collaborative modes of learning, writing, communicating, and publishing inevitably disturb traditional definitions. In transitional moments such as the present one, assumptions become visible and also require serious rethinking. The issues are complex and intertwined. Juries rarely can unravel them, and monetary judgments are often capricious, inconsistent, and offer little in the way of guidelines for future decisions. One part of considering the future of learning institutions in a digital age is to try to understand the connections between and across the array of legal and social arrangements loosely grouped under such seemingly transparent terms as *copyright, patent law, intellectual property, publishing*, and *authorship*. As we see from the history of copyright law in the United States, transitional moments test the boundaries of accepted legal practice because new uses of media cannot be decided by past legal precedents. Seemingly familiar terms such as *author, artist*, or *owner* take on complicated and legally contested meanings when, for example, a poster artist is sued by the Associated Press because he downloaded a photograph of a presidential candidate from the Web and colorized it in a style that itself was subsequently imitated, parodied, or commercialized innumerable times by others.[14]

Fair Use

Fair use has multiple and often contradictory meanings. Legal organizations such as Creative Commons have tried to argue the importance of fair use, but upheavals in the recording and publishing industries make it difficult, sometimes, to be able to think clearly and productively about what constitutes use that is "fair" versus what constitutes use that exploits someone's labor without benefit of remuneration for that labor.[15]

The issue of fair use for educators can be almost as complex as it is for the music industry, where file-sharing can cut into profits. Since the currency of much of higher education is reputation, the issues of fair use must be configured partly in terms of peer review and citation.

Fair use in education is also in a transitional phase. If someone uses your ideas, does he or she have to pay you for them? What if that person is not making money from them? Is citation sufficient? Where does one draw the line between collaboration and plagiarism, between fair use (as it has long been defined) and theft of someone else's ideas? If one must pay Kinko's or another commercial copy center to make a coursepak of published chapters or articles, does one need to have the same respect for copyrighted material in an online resource? What about books and articles on reserve at the library? How about text cited or images used within a specialized scholarly publication?[16] What if the five lines of text in a chapbook is a poem versus the lyrics from a Dylan song? Why does one have to pay for the latter but not the former? What is the relationship between payment and authorship?

Clearly these are complex questions, made more complex by the fact that many universities now require faculty to put course syllabi and lectures up on the Web as a "public good" but will not support faculty when they wish to use movie clips or snippets of recorded music protected by copyright in their courses. For those in the humanities and media studies, this is a kind of double indemnity. If a faculty member is teaching a film course, his or her ideas (in the form of a syllabus) might be available to anyone, but he or she might be denied the right to include film clips or images in those texts. Henry Jenkins, one of the finest commentators on new media, has written eloquently on this inconsistency. He has testified in public hearings on the contradictions for educators around university policies on intellectual property, open access, and, ultimately, authorship in our digital age.[17]

To address these issues in one domain—the use of popular culture images and sounds in not-for-profit documentary filmmaking—the Center for the Public Domain has created a graphic novel designed to exemplify the choices one has, the laws that may apply, and the laws that do not apply (figure 2.2). *Tales from the Public Domain: Bound By Law?* is an activist document, encouraging documentary filmmakers not to censor themselves because of fear of copyright infringement where a case for fair use can be made.[18] The authors of *Bound By Law?* chose the comic format because the visuals illustrate (literally) issues of visual citation confronted by documentary filmmakers. In one segment, a television happens to be on in the background as a subject is being interviewed. Does the filmmaker need to pay for that use or edit it out? Or a kid walks by on a city street with a boom box playing a pop hit in the middle of a protest march. Documentary filmmakers cannot afford to pay for all of the incidental sights and sounds of a culture, sights and sounds that make up the texture of the culture they are documenting.

Probably the most famous case of fair use involves the powerful Public Broadcasting Service documentary of the U.S. civil

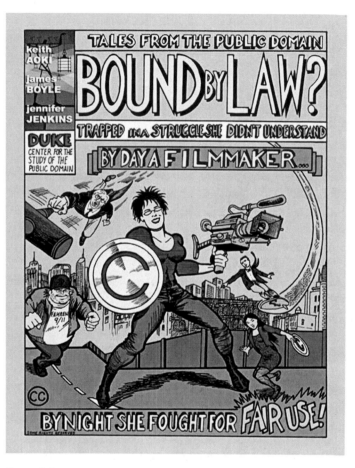

Figure 2.2
Reproduced by permission from Keith Aoki, James Boyle, and Jennifer Jenkins, *Tales from the Public Domain: Bound by Law?* (Durham, NC: Duke University Center for the Study of the Public Domain, 2006, page 1).

rights movement, *Eyes on the Prize: America's Civil Rights Years (1954–1965)*,[19] where expiration of the licenses of the copyright to archival footage prevented the documentary from being shown. Without the intervention of the Ford Foundation, which paid for the renewal of the rights, this documentary would not have been shown. *Bound By Law?* attempts to make these issues visible to all who are trying to figure out the rules of this era.

Digitality and Reputation

These examples of collaborative authorship, open access, and fair use underscore how the digital issues of this era are neither transparent nor trivial. They make good topics for the university classroom, especially for graduate students intending to go into the academy where authorship is a stepping stone to advancement. Academics typically have reputations, not royalties, at stake. But, as Reid's comment suggests, reputations are the currency in our academic realm and hiring, tenure, and promotion are all based on reputation. Single-author contributions are not the only ones, although in some fields, they continue to be the most important contributions to one's career.

As academics, we are a long way from facing the plight of the music business, yet we are clearly at a liminal moment, too. For example, many of the individual fields within the humanities, arts, social, natural, and biological sciences have been based on collaborative work (in labs, at archeological or ethnographic sites, and in published articles and books) and, despite multiple authorship, individual reputations are made and judgments of worth are still possible. Traditional single-author publishing fields can learn how to assess and reward individuals from the reward systems that have been developed in fields where multiply authored contributions are standard.

Learning from one another's expertise and experience is, after all, the theme of this text. Customized, collaborative digital learning cannot apply just to that which we educators deliver to our students. Indeed, we need to not only practice what we preach, but we must also learn to listen to what those more conversant with digital technologies have to tell us. In some cases, that means listening carefully to our students.

This reversal of who is teaching whom, who is learning from whom, and the constantly shifting hierarchies of expertise and the ability to appreciate those shifts when they happen and to value them are central to digital learning. The individuals' desire and need to learn from new collaborators and the shift in knowledge and ignorance can be unfamiliar and, at times, intimidating. And yet defamiliarizing our ways of knowing is also inspirational. It means rethinking not only what knowledge we possess but how we possess it, from what sources, and what that body of knowledge actually means, what it is worth. It means moving beyond our comfortable world of peers and all the tokens of esteem, value, respect, and reward that that world holds.

No one should take such risks on behalf of new ideas without a safety net. Institutions of learning provide the safety net for many of us. What happens if, instead of protecting us, these institutions are so set in older hierarchies of fields, departments, disciplines, divisions, and professional schools—the "silos" of the post-Humboldtian university—that they cannot adapt to the new modes of digital learning?[20] If that is the case, then it is important to work toward institutional change, not simply individual change. The cost is too high for individuals to bear alone, and value and esteem are conferred as part of institutions of credit and credentialing.

For those working within learning institutions, these are challenges. In fact, our institutions *are* changing. We see that all around us. Catalyzing and defining those changes are complex processes, but our digital era holds promise only if we are prepared to work toward transforming our learning institutions. Such transformation is not just part of this book's aspirations for digital learning but, at the same time, fulfills its aspirations for the future of learning institutions.[21]

Portfolio of Virtual Learning Environments

Innovative and experimental ideas for schools are being fueled by new digitally enabled possibilities (see figures 2.3–2.11).

Box 3
Gaming and Virtual Environments in Education

> Not only is educational gaming starting to be perceived as a viable alternative to formal education, other types of virtual environments and massively multiplayer online games are being recognized for their educational components. Some of the most popular examples of these educational alternatives are described below.
>
> **Virtual Worlds**
>
> An undergraduate course, "Field Research Methods in Second Life," conducted entirely in the virtual world of Second Life, was taught by Ed Lamoureux of Bradley College in January 2007. Due to the success of this class, Lamoreux, known as Professor Beliveau in Second Life, created two courses based on the same principles, "Introduction to Field Research in Virtual Worlds" and "Field Research in Virtual Worlds."

Box 3
(Continued)

Figure 2.3
Bradley College professor Ed Lamoureux with his avatar, Professor Beliveau. (http://www.bradley.edu/hilltopics/07spring/campusview, accessed May 2, 2009)

Figure 2.4
Ryan Cult with his avatar, Judge Canned. (http://www.bradley.edu/hilltopics/07spring/campusview, accessed May 2, 2009)

Box 3
(Continued)

Single Player Computer Games

Classic computer games such as *SimCity* and *Civilization* are being given a new life through their use in the classroom because of their ability to simulate complete environments. These games are often used to teach students about building and maintaining social and physical institutions.

Figures 2.5
Screenshot of *SimCity*.

Box 3
(Continued)

Figures 2.6
Screenshot of *Civilization*.

Massively Multiplayer Online Games

Massively multiplayer online games are attracting scholarly attention as an important social phenomenon. Games such as *World of Warcraft* offer alternative worlds where social functions, learning, and the development of social, tactical, and work skills can be practiced in a virtual environment. Researchers are also beginning to look at these games as a way to model societies and social interactions.

Box 3
(Continued)

Figure 2.7
Screenshot of *World of Warcraft*.

Serious (or Educational) Games

The Gamelab Institute of Play (http://www.instituteofplay.com) promotes gaming literacy (which it defines as "the play, analysis, and creation of games") as a foundation for learning, innovation, and change in a digital society. Although the Institute has been involved in several initiatives that target teenagers, such as the Quest to Learn school (see p. 24), it offers programs for all ages and technical abilities. In fact, one of its primary goals is to foster collaboration and an exchange of ideas between students, educators, and professionals. Through gaming, the Gamelab Institute of Play hopes to explore new ways to think, act, and create.

Box 3

(Continued)

Figure 2.8

Screenshot of Gamelab Institute of Play.

Box 4

Quest to Learn School: New York, New York

Scheduled to open in Fall 2009, the Gaming School is a joint venture between the Gamelab Institute of Play (http://www .instituteofplay.com) and the nonprofit organization New Visions for Public Schools (http://www.newvisions.org/index.asp). This innovative middle and high school, conceptualized by Katie Salen, director of graduate studies in the digital design depart-

Box 4
(Continued)

ment at Parsons School of Design, redefines the learning paradigm. The school actively seeks to blur the traditional line between learning and play. It aims to prepare students for a digitally mediated future through a curriculum structured around the creation and execution of alternate reality games. The project will also act as a demonstration and research site for alternative trends in education funded in part by the MacArthur Foundation Digital Media and Learning Initiative.

Figure 2.9
Students of the Institute of Play (http://www.flickr.com/photos/instituteofplay/2902732252/in/set-72157607611770213, accessed June 29, 2009).

Box 4
(Continued)

Figure 2.10
Students of the NYC Museum School, New York (http://www
.southstreetseaportmuseum.org/index1.aspx?BD=9079, accessed
June 29, 2009).

The 400 high-school students at the NYC Museum School (http://
schools.nyc.gov/SchoolPortals/02/M414/default.htm) spend up
to three days a week at a chosen museum (either the American
Museum of Natural History, the Metropolitan Museum of Art,
the Children's Museum of Manhattan, or the South Street Seaport Museum) studying with specialists and museum educators. Students work on different projects depending on which
museum they choose (i.e., geometry and computer animation
at the Children's Museum or navigation at the South Street
Seaport Museum). At the end of their senior year, students
share a thesis-like project on a chosen theme. The NYC Museum

Box 4
(Continued)

School was founded in 1994 by a former Brooklyn Museum assistant director in partnership with a former teacher with the Lab School in New York. It has been featured in the Bill and Melinda Gates Foundation "High Schools for the New Millennium" report.

Box 5
The School of the Future, Philadelphia

The School of the Future in Philadelphia is unique in that it is the first urban high school to be built in a working partnership with a leading software company, Microsoft Corporation. The school opened in September 2006 and serves approximately 750 students in a state-of-the-art, high-tech, and 'green' facility. Microsoft's Partners in Learning initiative played an integral part in the design and conceptualization of the school, not through a monetary donation (the School of the Future is funded by the School District of Philadelphia) but through the development of new technologies for both teaching and administrative purposes. Among the most innovative, and controversial, of these technologies is a smart card that allows access to digital lockers and that tracks calories consumed during school meals (breakfast and dinner are also served before and after school). Class schedules and locations change every day (the goal is to break down our culture's dependency on time and place), and all rooms are designed with flexible floor plans to foster teamwork and project-based learning. Instead of a library and textbooks, all students are given a laptop with wireless access to the Interactive Learning Center, the

Box 5
(Continued)

Figure 2.11
Screenshot of the School of the Future, Philadelphia, Pennsylvania (http://www.westparkcultural.org/?q=node/246, accessed June 29, 2009).

school's hub for interactive educational material. These laptops are linked to smartboards in every classroom and networked so that assignments and notes can be accessed even from home. The building itself is also unique in its holistic approach. Rainwater is caught and repurposed for use in toilets, the roof is covered with vegetation to shield it from ultraviolet rays, panels embedded within the windows capture light and transform it into energy, room settings auto-adjust based on natural lighting and atmo-

Box 5
(Continued)

spheric conditions, and sensors in the rooms turn lights on and off depending on whether the space is being used. In short, the School of the Future incorporates many innovations but also has high-tech interactivity that borders on extreme surveillance that makes it a questionable model for future digital learning initiatives. For more information, see http://www.microsoft.com/presspass/press/2006/sep06/09-06MSPhiladelphiaSOFPR.mspx and http://www.microsoft.com/education/SchoolofFuture.mspx.

3   Our Digital Age: Implications for Learning and Its (Online) Institutions

The Challenge

This book does not promote change for the sake of change. Implicit in its sincere plea for transformation is an awareness that the current situation needs improvement. In advocating change for learning institutions, this book makes assumptions about the deep structure of learning, about cognition, about the way youth today learn about their world in informal settings, and about a mismatch between the excitement generated by informal learning and the routinization of learning common to many of our institutions of formal education. This book advocates institutional change because our current formal educational institutions are not taking enough advantage of the modes of digital and participatory learning available to students today.

Chapter 2 focused on learning institutions that are being predicated on and fashioned around the engagement with digital technologies; this chapter considers the shifts in learning premises and practices prompted by an engagement with such technologies.

Youth who learn via peer-to-peer mediated forms may be less likely to be excited and motivated by the typical forms of learning than they were even a decade ago. Conventional modes of learning tend to be passive, lecture driven, hierarchical, and largely unidirectional from instructor to student. As Wheat (log-on name) notes on the Institute for the Future of the Book Web site, "open-ended assignments provide the opportunity for creative, research-based learning."[1] Yet, in the vast majority of formal educational settings, partly as a concomitant of cutbacks to education resulting in increased class size and partly a function of contemporary culture obsessed with testing, multiple-choice tests have replaced research papers or more robustly creative group-produced projects.

On the K–12 level (primary and secondary public schools), governmentally mandated programs, including those such as NCLB,[2] overwhelmingly reinforce a form of one-size-fits-all education based on standardized testing. Are *cloned learning*, *cloning knowledge*, or *clones* the desired products? Such learning models—or *cloning cultures*[3]—are often stultifying and counterproductive, leaving many children bored, frustrated, and unmotivated to learn.[4]

Close to 35% of those who begin public schools in the United States drop out before graduating.[5] Of special urgency is the surging gap between the wealthy and the poor, a gap that correlates in both directions with educational levels.[6] Youth from impoverished backgrounds are statistically most likely to drop out of school; high school dropouts earn less than those with a diploma, and significantly less again than those with a university degree. Incarceration rates, which have soared more than tenfold since 1970, also correlate closely with educational failure and impoverishment. Seventy-five percent of those imprisoned are illiterate, earning less than $10,000 per year at the time of arrest.[7] Currently, according to Human Rights Watch, America has the highest incarceration rate of any nation, with 762 of every 100,000 U. S. residents currently in jail (compared with incarceration rates in the United Kingdom of 152 per 100,000 residents, and, in Canada and France, 108 and 91, respectively).[8]

In the United States, incarceration correlates with poverty, and digital access correlates with educational opportunity and wealth. The *digital divide* is not just an old concept but a current reality. Access to computers remains unevenly distributed. Even the most basic resources (including computers) are lacking in the nation's most impoverished public schools, as well as in the nation's poorest homes.

Wealth, formal education, race, and gender are important interacting factors in the certification of what constitutes *merit* and *quality*. Nevertheless, despite the digital divide, there is a generational shift in learning happening by those both living above the poverty line and those more impoverished youth accessing such media in more limited form (often through community centers and libraries). An increasing number of people born after 1983 (the advent of the desktop computer) and 1991 (the advent of the Internet) learn through peer-to-peer knowledge networks, collaborative networks, and aggregated private and open-source social spaces (from MySpace and Facebook to delicious).

Given that the entering college class was born in 1989, this cultural change in learning touches every aspect of the educational system, as well as informal learning environments for all ages. The so-called Millenials are, in fact, not the only age group being transformed by digital technologies. The average age of a *World of Warcraft* game player is 28.[9] *Born again* has much more than religious resonance.

Because of the Internet, more and more choices are available
to the public, in everything from consumer products to software, social networks, modes of play, knowledge and data repositories, and cultural archives. Learning, too, has a "long tail,"
where more and more is available virtually, to potentially much
wider, more distributed, and diverse ranges of people. This book
does not solve these massively complex social issues, nor does it
explain the relationships between and among these various
developments. However, the opportunity exists to mobilize educators to more energetic and productive learning ends. Interactive technologies and collaborative learning have inspired
enormous excitement, and contemporary youth exhibit great
facility in negotiating the use of new media. Learning institutions can be developed to do a better job of enlisting the imagination of youth and to use the excited and specialized interests
of young people for the purposes of placing in practice wise and
rigorous forms of knowledge sharing.

To accomplish this, educators must rethink their most cher-
ished methodologies and assumptions. It is not easy to rethink
knowledge in the Net Age.[10] As open-source legal theorist and
activist James Boyle notes in "A Closed Mind about an Open
World," we have been conditioned by a confluence of factors,
economic and social, political and cultural, to acquire an "openness aversion."[11] The familiar is safe, easy, and reliable. Boyle
suggests that aversion to openness—to be disposed against the
challenge of the unforeseen—is an actual cognitive bias that
leads us to "undervalue the importance, viability and productive power of open systems, open networks and non-proprietary
production." To overcome this bias requires that knowledge
producers (those involved in the practices of teaching, in whatever current institutional configuration) rethink every aspect

(from economic theory to citation form) of what is thought of as "knowledge production."

Digital Presence and Digital Futures

Digital technologies increasingly enable and encourage social networking and interactive, collaborative engagements, including those implicating and impacting learning. Yet, traditional learning institutions, both K–12 and institutions of higher learning, continue to prioritize individualized performance in assessments and reward structures. After a century and a half of institutional shaping, maturing, and hardening, these assessment and reward structures have become fixed in place. They now serve to weigh down and impede new learning possibilities.

Digital technologies have dramatically encouraged self-learning. Web interfaces have made for less hierarchical and more horizontal modes of access. The Web has also facilitated the proliferation of information, from the inane and banal to the esoteric and profound, from the patently false, misleading, even (potentially) dangerous and destructive, to the compelling, important, and (potentially) life-enhancing and life-saving. But the relative horizontality of access to the Web has had another surprising effect: It has flattened out contributions to knowledge making, making them much less the function of a credentialed elite and increasingly collaboratively created.

What are the implications of this dual horizontality—of access and contribution—for learning, then?

First, self-learning has bloomed, from the earliest moments children figure out online possibilities through adulthood. In the digital era, informal learning is often nonhierarchical, more peer-to-peer and peer from (often anonymous) peer. There is increasing evidence, from numerous studies, that youth learn a range of complex skills—from protocols of interaction to those of etiquette, from negotiation to moral judgment, from time management to powers of concentration and self-discipline, and from strategic reasoning to collaborative facility—as a result of massively multiplayer online games.

Even online reading, according to Alan Liu, has become collaborative, interactive, nonlinear, and relational, engaging multiple voices.[12] We browse, scan, connect in mid-paragraph if not mid-sentence to related material, look up information relevant or related to what we are reading. Sometimes this mode of relational reading might draw us completely away from the original text, hypertextually streaming us into completely new threads and pathways across the information highways and byways. It is apt that the Internet is called the "web," sometimes resembling a maze, but more often than not serving as a productive, if complex and challenging, switchboard.

Networking Authority, Authoritative Networks

These emerging modes of learning entail a shift in trust. Where sources of knowledge making and authority become less visible, less face-to-face, more anonymous, and less concretely institutionalized, what or whose sources are we to trust as authoritative? And how do we discern the acceptable from the unacceptable, the trustworthy from the misleading or manipulative, the demonstrably compelling from the half-truth or the flatly false?

Second, this puts pressure on how learning institutions—schools, colleges, universities, and their surrounding support apparatuses—enable learning. Institutional education has traditionally been authoritative, top-down, standardized, and predicated on individuated achievement measured on standard tests.

Increasingly today, work regimes involve collaboration with colleagues in teams. Multitasking reinforces capacities to work around problems, work out solutions, and work together to complete projects. Given the range and volume of information available and the ubiquity of access to information sources and resources, learning strategy shifts from a focus on information as such to judgment concerning reliable information, from memorizing information to how to find reliable sources. In short, learning is shifting from learning *that* to learning *how*, from content to process.

Accordingly, learning is shifting from issues of authoritativeness to distinguishing good knowledge sources and substance from those that are questionable. Increasingly, learning is about how to make wise choices—epistemologically and methodologically, concerning productive collaborative partnerships to broach complex challenges and problems. Learning increasingly encompasses how to resolve issues regarding information architecture, interoperability and compatibility, scalability and sustainability, and how to address ethical dilemmas. It concerns issues of judgment in resolving tensions between different points of view in increasingly interdisciplinary environments, what knowledge authorities and claims to trust in complex learning environments.

We are being moved to interdisciplinary and collaborative knowledge creating and learning environments in order to address objects of analysis and research problems that are multidimensional and complex, and the resolution of which cannot be fashioned by any single discipline. Knowledge formation and learning today thus pose more acute challenges of trust. If older, more traditional learning environments were about trusting knowledge authorities or certified experts, that model can no longer address the complexities of relational constitution of knowledge domains. Today, we find ourselves challenged not just by trusting an individual in a domain but trusting teams, partnerships, when to cede authority to others and when to retain it, not just in determining outcomes but in the posing of the questions. Our sense of trust has shifted from authorities in substantive knowledge to questions of trust in formulating judgment itself.

Collaborative Knowledge Building Online

The Wikipedia experience provides a good illustration of collaborative knowledge creation and the emerging protocols and various challenges for learning surrounding it (figure 3.1). Initiated in 2001, Wikipedia was intended as an online, free, and openly fashioned and created encyclopedia. It would expand through contributions, edits and corrections, rephrasings, and replacements on most any subject of interest to its community of users. Wikipedia was both an early instigator and exemplary icon of the sort of collaborative, social networking production that quickly came to define Web 2.0. Currently the largest general reference source available—on the Web or in print—by the close of 2007, it boasted almost 10 million articles in more than 250 languages. The reference work of choice and often the source first consulted, Wikipedia consistently is in the top 10—and usually in the top five—of all visited Web sites.

Today, Wikipedia is the reference source most broadly consulted by students at all levels when working on an assigned project. Entries are crafted collectively and collaboratively, multiauthored and multiedited, sometimes leading to authorial investment, errors and inconsistencies, trivia, and irrelevance. These latter concerns, along with the ease of access and the irreverence for credentialed knowledge creation and authoriza-

WIKIPEDIA

English
The Free Encyclopedia
2 899 000+ articles

日本語
フリー百科事典
590 000+ 記事

Deutsch
Die freie Enzyklopädie
912 000+ Artikel

Español
La enciclopedia libre
478 000+ artículos

Français
L'encyclopédie libre
810 000+ articles

Polski
Wolna encyklopedia
608 000+ haseł

Italiano
L'enciclopedia libera
572 000+ voci

Português
A enciclopédia livre
482 000+ artigos

Русский
Свободная энциклопедия
304 000+ статей

Nederlands
De vrije encyclopedie
540 000+ artikelen

Figure 3.1
Screenshot of the Wikipedia home page (http://www.wikipedia.org, accessed July 29, 2009).

tion, have rendered some scholars and teachers skeptical about Wikimania. This skepticism, in turn, has generated analysis. Recent studies have shown Wikipedia to be in general no less reliable—and sometimes considerably more reliable—than the most credentialed traditional encyclopedias such as Britannica.[13] No matter; teachers in secondary and higher education have been moved either to limit or completely restrict use of Wikipedia for course assignments or to issue stringent guidelines for Wikipedia consultation and reference.

Alan Liu has circulated a useful and levelheaded set of guidelines he issues to students in his undergraduate college classes about consulting Wikipedia for formal coursework purposes (figure 3.2). Like any encyclopedia, Wikipedia provides a good entry point to knowledge on a wide range of subjects. But, Liu points out, its entries can be uneven, sometimes misleading, open in the unregulated world of Web 2.0 knowledge creation to manipulation, contestation, unsettlement, obfuscation, and, indeed, error. It should not, he concludes, be the sole source informing students' work. In addition, given that the central strength of socially networked knowledge formation is its ability to constantly and more or less instantaneously reform itself, Liu recommends that any citation to Wikipedia material include the date of consultation.

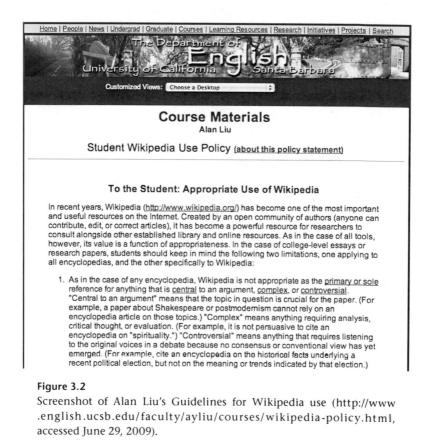

Figure 3.2
Screenshot of Alan Liu's Guidelines for Wikipedia use (http://www .english.ucsb.edu/faculty/ayliu/courses/wikipedia-policy.html, accessed June 29, 2009).

Liu's guidelines for Wikipedia use apply more generally to Web consultation for learning practices. Web information requires independent corroboration, either from other Web-based sources or from other media deemed at least as reliable. Web 2.0 learning is effective in generating an attitude of healthy epistemological skepticism, motivation to keep an open mind, a disposition to extend knowledge seeking, and the honing of the capacity to refine modes of judgment. On the production side, it is a call to collaborative knowledge making, to constant revision in the wake of new information and expertise, to updates in the wake of new insights and resources, and to seek others out as complements, domain experts, and checks on one's own knowledge and capacities.

Liu, however, goes further. He exhibits not just prudent protocols for developing, circulating, and drawing on Web 2.0 knowledge and learning capacities. His elaborated views demonstrate the limits of importing older modes of recourse to authoritative education deeply at odds with the newer Web 2.0 modalities. Thus, Liu argues that "we" should "police" and "control" entries made to Web 2.0 collaborative knowledge-creating sites (Liu, 2009).[14] By "we," he seems to mean domain experts, those credentialed authorities belonging to a community of experts licensed—by credentialing institutions, authoritative knowledge networks in a field, or standing associations—to determine what is reliable knowledge and what is not.

Liu's reinstatement of traditional knowledge authorities overstates the case for expertise and undervalues new collaborative modalities of knowledge creation.[15] For one, it assumes credentialed experts have a premium on authoritative knowledge and fails to acknowledge that "experts" also are open to error, bias, and the already given, whether individually or collectively. And it belies the productive strength of collaborative Web 2.0

knowledge formation. Liu fails to consider, in addition, that domain experts likewise are leaning increasingly on Web 2.0 strategies and technologies for creating collaboratively produced knowledge in or across their fields of expertise. They are drawn to the collaborative interaction, the ease of accessibility, the speed of interaction, and the dissemination possibilities. Thus, E. O. Wilson, the noted biologist, has been leading a major online undertaking in collaboration to provide a comprehensive, open-source, online catalog of knowledge about every known biological species. It is, as the home page announces, "an ecosystem of websites that makes all key information about all life on Earth accessible to anyone, anywhere in the world" (well, anyone with Web access). The project seeks contributions from the general public but nevertheless has stringent oversight of the quality of contribution, looking to domain experts as content editors.

Liu no doubt is right to call for greater transparency about the production of Web 2.0, to make technologically evident the debates, exchanges, differences, and controversies and the edits, deletions, revisions, and reformulations that occur in fashioning knowledge in online knowledge sites such as Wikipedia. Revealing these background conflicts for anyone to consult is itself a learning tool and also enables the possibility of people deciding for themselves what are the most compelling or insightful interventions, no matter the final or most polished version of the contribution posted to the site. This condition holds as much for domain expert contributions as it does for popularly created sites. Thus we urge the same condition of the comprehensive *Encyclopedia of Life* as we do of Wikipedia (figure 3.3).

Currently, technological interest in interactive digital modalities lies in expanding open access, in ensuring interoperability of systems and their applications, and in enabling as wide and

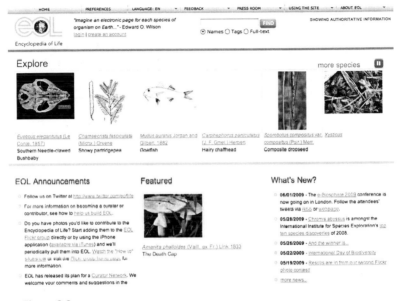

Figure 3.3
Screenshot of the Encyclopedia of Life (http://www.eol.org/index, accessed June 29, 2009).

robust a set of social networking tools as possible, whether for purposes of consumption, recreation, cultural production, revenue generation, research, or knowledge formation. The prevailing interest is in applications that connect one to others, peer to peer, many to many. Considerable interest prevails in development and application of virtual learning environments, in mapping and mash-ups, in simulation and animation, in textual analysis and language exploration tools, in distributed data collection, in archiving, and in analyzing applications. Internet 2, Lambda Rail, high-performance supercomputing, Grid networks, and other technologies allow for almost instantaneous sharing and manipulation of massive amounts of data. Work is also being devoted, though somewhat more remotely, in Web 3.0 strategies to semantic Web considerations, rendering it possible ultimately for machines to understand what is being written (and perhaps much further out what is being said, drawn, in general represented and expressed in multiple formats).

Learning Futures, Futures of Learning

Given these expansive directions in technological prowess, how might learning opportunities and modalities, applications, and tools be thought about, designed, or put to work in socially networked and mobile learning? If virtues, technological as much as social, are vested in dispositions of adaptability, flexibility, and transformability, in improvisation and in translation capacities, how might these virtues be embedded in learning practices to position learners most effectively to take advantage of these emerging technologies? How is trust to be reinstated in the shifts from knowledge authorities to knowledge sources, from institutional arrangements and authorities to process and collaboration?

First, if education has increasingly become about "learning that"—learning of and for facts, unproblematically presumed—the digital and increasingly mobile movements dispose learners to figuring out process. The latter concerns how to do things and why some ways work and some do not, indeed, more deeply, why things have come to be as they are and how they could be different and improved. So, the first shift in regimes of learning is from fact to question, from the static of "knowing that" to learning to ask the right, most revealing questions. In questioning, a good part of the lesson is not just in figuring out the nature of things but in the realization that *how* the question is asked—the frame, the tone, the addressee—can be as important as the question posed.

Second, collaborative learning is more often than not more productive than the sort of individualized learning that has become the central force of contemporary educational systems. Collaborative learning is peer-to-peer learning, laterally rather than hierarchically fueled. Digital technology is conducive to collaborative learning by condensing the space and time across which learning can usefully take place. It is all learning, all the time, across distributed distances and location, and through the extended social networks that Web 2.0 technologies have made conceivable and realizable.

Socially networked collaborative learning is predicated on expected practices, at best imposed as a form of discipline by individualized learning. There are a set of virtues, dispositional habits, which are constitutive of expected practices, including taking turns in speaking, posing questions, and listening to and hearing others out. By extension, they also imply correcting others and being open to being corrected oneself and working together to fashion workarounds when straightforward solutions to problems are not forthcoming. It is not that individualized learning can not end up encouraging such habits and practices. But they are not natural to individual learning, which tends to be a social framework that stresses the competitive, winner-takes-all, and domination of the successful rather than cooperation, partnering, and mediation. If individualized learning is chained to a social vision prompted by "prisoner dilemma" rationality, in which one cooperates only if it maximizes narrow self-interest, networked learning is committed to a vision of the social—stressing cooperation, interactivity, mutuality, and social engagement for their own sakes and for the powerful productivity to which it more often than not leads. The power of 10 working interactively will almost invariably outstrip the power of one looking to beat out the other nine.

Networked learning is central to the fabric of open-source culture.[16] Open-source culture seeks to share openly and freely in the creation of culture, in its production processes, in its product, and its content. It looks to have its processes and its products improved through the contributions of others by being freely available to all. If individualized learning is largely tethered to a social regime of copyright-protected intellectual property and privatized ownership, networked learning is committed to an open-source and open-content social regime. Individualized learning is hierarchical: One learns from the teacher or expert, on the basis of copyright-protected publications bearing the current status of knowledge; networked learning is peer-to-peer and more robustly many-to-many, or *many-to-multitudes*. Many-to-multitudes interactivity fuels digitally-driven social networking, as much in learning as in economic practices. It provides the circuits and nodes, the combustion energy and driving force for engaged and sustained innovative activity, sparking creativity, extending the circulation of ideas and practices, providing the test sites for innovative developments, and providing even the laboratory for the valuable, if sometimes painful, lessons to be learned from failure.

The connectivities and interactivities made possible by digitally enabled social networking in its best outcomes produce learning ensembles in which the members both support and sustain, elicit from, and expand upon each other's learning inputs, contributions, and products. Challenges are not simply individually faced frustrations, Promethean mountains to climb alone, but mutually shared, to be redefined, solved, resolved, or worked around—together.

An application such as Live Mesh allows one to unite and synchronize one's entire range of devices and applications into a seamless web of interactivity. It enables instantaneous file-and data-sharing with other users with whom the user is remotely connected, thus allowing for seamless and more or less instant communication across work and recreational environments. Our technological architecture thus is fast making net-*working*, in contrast with isolated, individualized working, the default. Slower to adapt, the organizational architecture of our educational institutions and pedagogical delivery are just starting to catch on and catch up.

Reading and writing practices in higher education, for example, have been traditionally individualized. We traditionally have marked up papers or books by underlining our own copies and writing in the margins. We might look up a reference, usually in serial and linear form, proceeding from one publication to another. Even reading groups operate by bringing together our individual perspectives into an occasional meeting, the collective experience ultimately feeding our individualized understanding and production, and leading to our own usually discrete outputs (at least outside of the sciences). Merit reviews of work have reinforced these individualizing ritual practices.[17]

Contemporary reading and writing practices are transforming before our eyes. Interactive reading and writing now increasingly engage us. One can read together with others remotely, commenting between the virtual lines and in the margins, reading each others' comments instantaneously, composing documents together in real time by adding words or sentences to those just composed by one's collaborators. The lines between one's own words and those of another's—let alone between whole sentences—become quickly blurred. (The authors of *this* text would be hard-pressed to identify exactly which one, in the end, wrote which word!) Hyperlinking has encouraged reading not just *within* and then *between* discrete texts but much more robustly *across* texts, inter-referencing and interweaving insights and lines of referencing. How texts relate, as a consequence, has become dramatically magnified, making visible what hitherto has been hidden largely from view.

Hyperlinking and inter-referencing have become so robust, so constitutive of online compositional and reading practices, that they have dramatically affected the design of published materials, as much in hard as in virtual copy. The first impact could be seen in magazine publishing. Traditional magazine layout consisted of complete pages of linearly produced written text in continuous and uninterrupted narrative. You got lines of words on the page, interrupted (if at all) by an illustration or photograph. In the wake of Internet influence, this layout has given way to pages cut up into segments, boxes, with multiple sources of information interweaving but also discontinuous and disconnected. The effects on textbook, academic, and trade book monograph production have become more recently palpable. It remains an open question whether this design change will have an equally telling transformative epistemological impact, leading to changes both in how and what we know as well as to the sorts of philosophical changes hinted at the outset of this chapter in *how* we know how we know.[18]

Principles and Protocols of Digital Learning

The consequences of these shifts can be summed up in a series of pointers. First, the sort of peer-to-peer redistribution to which we have been drawing attention is predicated, at least in principle, upon *sharing among equals*. There has been a rising call for equality of collaboration and communication with those who could not possibly share resources because of social disparities and unequal distribution of wealth, access, and technology. Sometimes age (lack of resources among youth, lack of attention to what drives youth now) might constitute a barrier; sometimes class, nation, culture (or culture tied to gender) or other factors might be the barriers. At least some (or some of those in) richer organizations with a fuller array of resources are looking to work, as equals, with those who offer other kinds (and not seldom more compelling forms) of intellectual, cultural, or social capital but who do not have the economic or technological assets to collaborate as equals without some transference of technologies. The fluidity and creativity of technological sharing in order to facilitate shared learning can be breathtaking. *Top-down* and *bottom up* do not begin to capture the subtler dynamics of production, distribution, exchange, circulation, and consumption. Influences run in all directions; influence is never a one-way street.

For example, mobile phones have had far greater impact in poorer societies such as those throughout Africa than laptops have had. For one, they are cheaper to own, more mobile, and more easily shared within (extended) families or across segments of villages. Researchers are just beginning to recognize the possibility of designing learning programs for hand-held devices that are likely to revolutionize learning in such societies. The Mobile and Immersive Learning for Literacy in Emerging Economies (MILLEE) project designs robust story-based games to fit mobile phones in developing countries to facilitate interactive language learning. Partnering with Sesame Street India, for instance, MILLEE has created a mobile-phone game environment for young girls working in rural fields to learn English as a second language.[19] To be effective, design engineers must learn local culture and understand learning motivations, challenges, cultural practices, and protocols. These practices and protocols, in turn, alter the syntax and semantics of the (cultural) language learned. For these changes witness, for one, the transformations in any credible English dictionary over time.[20]

Second, this *mixed reality* is knotted with mixed media, with the drive to *mash up* culture and modes of production. So many projects now abundantly flow in and out of the screen, in and out of the streets. Virtuality and digitality are part of the face-to-face world, more so with cell phones and iPods but also with laptops (even ones minimizing costs, whether the admirable undertaking of "One Laptop Per Child" (figure 3.4), committed to widespread and worldwide distribution of $200 machines, or Intel's equally ambitious "Classmate" (figure 3.5), its $400 educational computer "for the developing world"). The hype of digitality cordoned it off from the real world. Projects are meshing, unmeshing, and remeshing virtual and real in all sorts of ways, across time and place, almost seamlessly, sometimes ubiquitously. Mash-up characterizes "the real," material life as much as the imagined creations. Witness here, too, the transformative impact on the designs of the machines themselves.

Third, the spread of mobile technologies and inexpensive laptops suggest that, increasingly, digital learning is *global* learning. Learning projects more and more have a global vision, global partners, and global reach. It is the World Wide Web, after all, and at no time in history has it been easier to learn in tandem with digital partners half a world away. Digitalities have gone global. The growing globalization of the everyday—politically, economically, culturally, or in terms of our daily living practices—requires that learning must have global scope, too. Learning's global scope (or maybe the plural *learnings*, to stress the multiplicity of dispositions, practices, impacts, and implications) has transformative effects on Internet culture,

Figure 3.4
One Laptop Per Child (OLPC) is an association founded by the MIT
Media Lab to develop a low-cost, low-power agile and rugged computer
with applications to provide every child in the poorest countries with
appealing and appropriate learning possibilities. "OLPC espouses five
core principles: (1) child ownership; (2) low ages; (3) saturation; (4) connection; and (5) free and open source" (http://laptop.org, accessed June
29, 2009).

too, ranging from aesthetic to translation programs, from game
design and social networking protocols to Internet protocol
considerations.

Fourth, the "bowling alone" pronouncements about the lonely
life of the Internet-obsessed youth are over, initially undone by
massively multiplayer online games and the popularity of social
networking sites. These digital learning projects show that
learning together has a much broader reach than might have
been expected. In all ways—imaginative, social, communicative,

Figure: 3.5
Intel's Classmate PC, a small, economical and mobile educational solution that Intel has developed specifically for students all over the globe (http://www.intel.com/pressroom/kits/events/idffall_2008/photos .htm, accessed June 29, 2009).

and educational—people, young and not-so-young, are learning how to be digital *together* and *digitally* together. Sociality is online, offline, and all points in between. Go into any coffee house in America, as elsewhere, and there are people deeply embedded in their laptops one moment, as they might be in a book, and laughing with one another the next. They are also working together over a shared interface, whether a common computer or communicating at a distance, even if that distance is simply the table between them. And, in any case, where youth look like they might be on their own, their instantaneous connectivity and multitasking facility—through mobile devices and text messaging—quickly belie the appearance. This is an incredibly social time, if these projects are any indication. The digital sociality of youth does not look like past forms of social interaction, but that is what being young is about!

And finally, it has become obvious that, from the point of view of learning, there is no finality. *Learning* is *lifelong*. It is lifelong not simply in the Socratic sense of it taking that long to realize that the more one knows, the more one realizes how little one knows. It is lifelong in the sense also, perhaps anti-Platonically, that the increasingly rapid changes in the world's makeup mean that we must necessarily learn anew, acquiring new knowledge to face the challenges of novel conditions as we bear with us the lessons of adaptability, of applying anew lessons known to unprecedented situations and challenges. It is not just that economic prospects demand it; increasingly sociality and culture now do, too.

Examples abound of the complex interplay of these conditions of possibility in the newly emergent culture of learning. Some, like Doug Thomas, have cited the unpredictably robust learning possibilities from massively multiplayer online games, such as *World of Warcraft*, from economic transactions and strategic thinking to principles of collective behavior and moral decision-making. There are abstract learning possibilities at play in such a game, but it also reinforces the thrill of warmongering and war-making, of resolving issues through prevalent force and the recourse to violence to get one's way. There are other gaming opportunities to prompt the affirming lessons without warring belligerence that deserve much greater pedagogical and market focus.

Examples include many "performative play" games profiled by Persuasive Games[21] and AgoraXChange, the political game about nationalism, inequality, and state-making.[22] There are extraordinary possibilities afforded by learning creatively— precisely through a *game* such as *GameStar Mechanic* (figure 3.6) or of the innovative reskinning of war-game engines, as in Virtual Peace, to promote hands-on learning about mediation and conflict resolution.[23] This affords players the opportunity to learn how to design games, most notably through modding existing (even commercial) platforms. These learning possibilities range from aesthetic and design practice, narrative construction, interactive storytelling, and storyboarding to systems analysis, the logics and rules of games, programming and computing skills, and intellectual property challenges. They extend

Figure 3.6
Screenshot of the home page for Gamestar Mechanic (http://www. gamestarmechanic.com, accessed June 29, 2009).

also across social and economic skills in working with others, being held to timelines, thinking about budgets, as well as the negotiation of multimedia.

Other exciting possibilities include the environmental studies game, Black Cloud,[24] drawing together into an interactive mix of high school students in Los Angeles and Cairo, Egypt. Using pollution sensors placed by the gamers in each city, teams divide into role-playing either real estate developers or environmentalists to determine compelling sites for additional development or conservation. Lessons here include the science of pollution production and testing, the politics of property development, and cross-cultural global communication. Microsoft's *Worldwide Telescope* (figure 3.7) offers visualization software that enables one's personal computer to become a high-powered telescope to explore the astronomical universe. It offers extraordinary possibilities to people of all ages, guided by scientific experts or on their own, to immerse themselves in astronomical knowledge, from the most basic to the most complex. Above all, because it is fun and enticing to engage, it can serve as a primary exploration tool for people at almost any level of expertise or a compelling supplement to classroom instruction at almost any level.

Taken together, the viral pull of many-to-multitude learning, the lure and challenges of sharing among equals, the attractions and necessary negotiations of globally interactive learning, the enormous benefits and challenges of robustly networked knowledge formation and acquisition, and the transformative realities of lifelong learning represent the range and varieties of digitally-driven modes of learning.

The larger questions remain pressing, even universal: What to believe and on what grounds?, On what rests the credibility of sources, on what basis are claims to be trusted, and what are

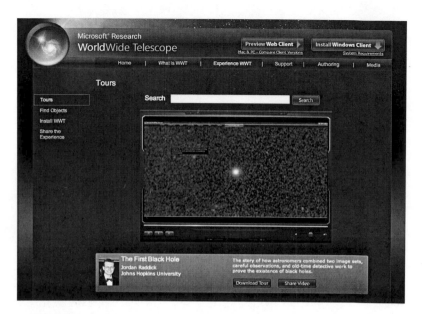

Figure 3.7
Screenshot of the interface for WorldWide Telescope (http://www
.worldwidetelescope.org, accessed June 29, 2009).

the most and least compelling uses of available knowledge? The
most convincing responses to these questions may themselves
be transforming, if less wholly or quickly, alongside the rampant transformation in mode and media of knowledge formation, circulation, acquisition, and authorization.

Challenges from Past Practice, Moving Fast Forward

This book stresses the range of opportunities and the transformative possibilities for learning at all levels as a result of readily
available and emergent digital technologies and acknowledges

the challenges, limitations, and misdirections—in short, the opportunity costs—resulting from these developments. Some of these costs are inevitable when unsettling long-established ways of doing things. When well-established modes of knowledge making and acquisition stagnate, they can become restrictive, if not unproductive. As new modes emerge, the old institutional structures can either dig in and refuse to respond other than to dismiss the new modes, or they can seek to work out renewed and renewing regimes to take advantage of possible productive elements.

The challenges by digital learning to institutional order in higher education (though these challenges count, too, in thinking about other institutional levels) range from the banal to the constitutive, from the disciplining of behavioral breaches of protocol and expectation to normative conceptions of what constitutes knowledge and how it is authorized.

A common complaint among educators today, most notably classroom instructors, concerns the divided attention during class time as a result of mobile device access and multitasking in the classroom. If students can "backchannel" or "google jockey" (or google jockey *and* backchannel) during a lecture, it not only can distract but can potentially undermine the authority of the instructor as views are questioned by access to alternative sources and circulated dissent. This may not be a bad thing—undercutting claims to authority in favor of truth claims. But students with Wi-Fi mobile access through laptops, personal digital assistants (PDAs), and cell phones are increasingly attention challenged as a result of multitasking and may be lured via connectivity to worlds away from boring lectures. Reports have students in lectures ordering consumer goods (one of the juicier reports involved purchase of a wig), playing online games, text messaging with friends, breaking up with boyfriends or girlfriends, making dates, or reading online news-papers (not so different from an earlier moment of the rustling newspaper at the back of the class).

Colleagues have called for a complete or partial ban of lap-tops and other mobile apparatuses from the classroom, with some reporting a dramatic increase in quality of classroom par-ticipation as a consequence.[25] This is one response, but it fails to address all the underlying factors pushing students to look elsewhere for sources of engagement. It addresses the symptom rather than the cause. Another response might be to seek, in novel and challenging ways, to incorporate creative technolo-gies into the classroom. The google jockey can rotate through the class roster; rotating laptop note-takers can be restricted to, say, two per session, who then must share their notes with other students in the class; all laptops can be hooked up to data pro-jectors so that what is on a screen can be projected for all to see without notice; and so on. The point is that one could be restric-tive or productive, curtailing or creative. No policy-driven one-size-fits-all solution is called for or will succeed.

Second, there is a proliferating array of creative invocations of technology to support learning activities. Students most often are broken up into collaborative groups to work together to produce conjoint course products related to the material dis-cussed in class. The outcomes can be terrifically productive, promoting all sorts of skill development from online research skills to collaborative sharing capacities to technological facil-ity. But as often as not they can also produce a disposition to romance the technological for its own sake, an aestheticism and formalism that at best ignores the development of knowl-edge content and at worst leaves completely unchallenged deep errors about a subject matter for which, as much as anybody, the instructor is ultimately responsible.

Third, the more or less openness and easy anonymity of Internet culture enable, if not license, the proliferated circulation of untruths and half-truths. This has been especially pernicious in political and commercial venues, where smears, innuendo, rumor, and misrepresentation have the potential to do enormous damage quickly. The less educated, lesser informed, judgment challenged, and insular nativists are prone to manipulation and exploitation. But the compelling response here is not to insist on authoritarian modes of learning, on top-down assertion by some small class of experts; rather, it is to shift focus from authority claims to assessment of authority claims and the stature of authority itself. The point is not to abandon or restrict contemporary technology—what could that possibly mean, in any case?—but to put it to good use, to acquire the tools for wise judgment about what it does, what it delivers, how and whom it benefits and harms, and what sort of sociality and polity it can and does enable.

There is the challenge of how to assess and accredit learning under these morphing models. In a posted response to a *Future of the Book* draft, C. Avery suggests that there are two assessment models at play: what has become institutionally dominant as "satisfy the gatekeeper" outcomes in which candidates must satisfy institutional review to be certified and open-ended discovery driven by individual interests and the development of tools instrumental to satisfying those interests. If the former is assessment driven, the latter is outcome oriented.[26]

We have been suggesting another form. This concerns productive learning by creating together and learning from that coproduction—about process, about content, about modes of production, about sociality, about ethics, about leadership, about temporal discipline, about multitasking, about distributed tasking, and so on. Call this "collaborative-interactive."

Issues of collaboration are crucial to the future of learning institutions. But so, too, are originality, reward, accountability, and sustainability (including public and private sponsorship and support).

The modes of institutional assessment that are just starting to be elaborated here would be particular to the elements of learning involved, and require the sort of creativity equal to that of the elements involved. Some of the traditional criteria of assessment would be incorporated regarding knowledge content in a field, for instance. Some criteria would need to be newly forged regarding the facility to multitask productively, to google jockey and not lose the broader thread of argument in a talk or class period, or to identify and successfully pursue novel funding sources for not easily fundable projects (a facility widely ignored in traditional undergraduate and graduate education).

Mark Bauerlein has chastised the age group under 30 today as "the dumbest generation." He skewers all members of the technological generation—of "digital natives"—as incapable of book reading, as lacking the capacity to spell, of being narrowly self-concerned with looks and fashion and the latest craze, as incapable of thinking and writing, as consumed with facile games and incapable of remembering, and of being unconcerned with the broader world around them.[27] Though there no doubt are young people who fit this stereotype, this far from exhausts an extraordinary array of young people who are more technically facile than previous generations ever were (or are), that speak multiple languages fluently, that are at ease across and in multiple worlds, that are deeply engaged in collaborative projects of various creative kinds, and, if the Obama presidential campaign is anything to go by, that are deeply involved not just in traditional political activities but care deeply about their own and other worlds. If there is cause for critique here, it is to be directed at key elements of the reductive, rote-based education system that has come to mark much of mass institutional education in the United States. No wonder students look elsewhere for their engagement. What narrow-minded and self-possessed world, we wonder, does Professor Bauerlein inhabit?

Futures of Our Pasts

We have been reexamining some of the key premises and the role they have played in shaping learning institutions in general and higher education more particularly, especially since the end of World War II. Access to education at all levels for larger and larger segments of the population was crucial to settling class conflict and the development of middle class aspiration in the wake of the Great Depression. Publicly funded schools, community colleges, technical training institutions, and universities drew rapidly expanding numbers, shaping what it meant to be an educated citizen, a productive employee, and a moral person. As a consequence, income and wealth expanded from the 1930s to the 1980s, though significantly more so for some groups than for others. Demand for labor outstripped its supply, creating an upward spiral for wages and subsequent wealth and quality of life, in particular from one generation to the next.

All this began to change at the onset of the 1980s. The neoliberal cuts in state services, including notably to educational resources at all levels, driven in the past three decades by the marriage of political economy and the culture wars, has meant a resurgence in inequality tied to educational access, the insistence on test-driven pedagogy, and class bifurcation, racially molded, in access to creative learning practices. The earlier emphasis on public education has given way to its privatizing erosion at all levels, whether through charter schools and vouchers, through distance-learning programs for the racial poor on reservations, the dramatic privatization of higher education, or through the introduction of user fees for libraries and museums and their transformation by the cultural industry model of urban branding into sites for tourist attraction.[28]

No institution of higher education in the country today has tested in a comprehensive way new methods of learning based on peer-to-peer distributed systems of collaborative work characteristic of the Internet age. At the school level, social psychologists such as Joshua Aronson and Claude M. Steele have established conclusively that collaborative learning is beneficial across class, culture, race, and religion. These new modes of distributed collaborative engagement are likely both to attract a broad range of motivated learning across conventional social divisions (think of the anonymous interactions across classes and races in online gaming) and to inspire new forms of knowledge and product creation. But can we really say, in 2008, that the *institutions* of learning—from preschool to the PhD programs—are suited to the new forms of learning made available by digital technologies? Is there an educational enterprise anywhere in the world redesigned with the deep assumptions of networked thinking core and central to its lesson planning? Has anyone yet put into institutional practice at the level of higher education what John Seely Brown is calling a "social life of learning for the 'Net age'"?[29]

If we face a future where every person has (easy access to) a laptop or networked mobile device, what will it mean? What will it mean for institutionally advocated, mediated, and activated learning? How will educators use these tools and this moment? How *can* we use them to inspire our most traditional institutions of learning to change? The next chapter focuses on what learning institutions currently offer and the obstacles they pose to innovative learning that takes advantage of the online learning practices and possibilities available. By assessing some of the institutional barriers and some of the institutional promise, institutions can be mobilized to change, with formal, higher education as part of a continuum with (rather than a resistance to) the collaborative, participatory, networked interactions that our students engage online today.

.

4 FLIDA 101: A Pedagogical Allegory

The University as Traditional and Transitional Learning Institution

It is often noted that, of all existing institutions in the West, higher education is one of the oldest, most enduring, and most stable. Oxford University, the longest continuously running university in the English-speaking world, was founded in the twelfth century (figure 4.1).[1] Only the Catholic Church has been around longer in the West and, like the Catholic Church, today's universities bear a striking structural resemblance to their medieval counterparts. The medieval university was a separate, designated, physical location where young adults (students) were taught by older and more experienced scholars, professors, and dons who imparted their special knowledge, chiefly by lecturing. Over the years, such features as dormitories, colleges, and, later, departments were added to this *universitas* (corporation). The tendency toward increasing specialization, isolation, departmentalization, and advanced training (i.e., graduate and professional schools) developed in the wake of the Enlightenment, gathering steam through the nineteenth century.

Figure 4.1
Main entrance of Balliol College, Oxford University (http://www.head
ington.org.uk/oxon/broad/buildings/north/balliol_college.htm).

Admission to the university indicated not just intellectual
ability but explicit or implicit class affiliation as well. A physical
space, a hierarchy of professor and student, limited access, and
the conferral of a degree are among the persistent structuring
forms of the traditional institutions of higher education in the
West that have endured for hundreds of years.

That is a sobering thought for anyone who seeks innovation.
In academe, the institutional obstacles to collective, collaborative, customized, participatory, and interdisciplinary teaching,
research, and learning range from arduous (at the most flexible
institutions) to insurmountable (at the most hidebound). It is not
easy to traverse departments, fields, disciplines, divisions, and
schools, the so-called silos of the modern research university.

And, yet, for all the solidity of the traditional university, there are also many features that have changed dramatically over the last several centuries. Were that not the case—were traditional learning institutions impervious to change from internal and external forces—there would be no point in thinking about the future of learning institutions and the ways that new modes of participatory, digital learning might be incorporated into existing structures, pushing those structures toward innovation (figure 4.2).

Figure 4.2
Entrance to Princeton's Second Life campus (http://ald03635.files .wordpress.com/2009/03/princeton-university_001.png?w=340&h= 238, accessed March 1, 2009).

There have been rapid transformations in learning environments in the past two decades prompted by emergent digital technologies. Increasingly, these developments have prompted people to participate in media and the learning possibilities they entail, rather than simply consuming them. Feedback regarding their participation has become far more immediate. Learning tools and content can be shared nationally and internationally. Learning environments and techniques can be customized. There is almost instantaneous and easy access to vast amounts of new information. And new media such as massively multiplayer online gaming environments and virtually enabled social networks pose not only new challenges to learning—new worlds require that we learn about them—but also new possibilities for learning media themselves.

Digital media accordingly have significant potential for learning when people use digital means for creative production or to communicate with one another and contribute their knowledge and expertise to solving a problem, to a body of collective knowledge, or to reporting on community activities in a responsible way. Technologies that promote participatory engagements across physical distance enable people who might not otherwise know one another to meet together online for a collective purpose, adding their knowledge to a common and public site. They offer the possibility of learning from each other (through digital dialogue and communication), as much from those who share the same interests as those who do not. Collaboration in learning, spanning geographic distance, has broad potential for significant impact.

These new possibilities come with significant challenges. To be precise about the kinds of difficulties and possibilities faced by academics interested in participatory learning within a traditional university environment at this historical moment, this chapter considers one case study. This example is fictitious, designed to highlight the different kinds of issues that academics negotiate on a regular basis.

Let us say that two professors want to coteach an introductory course on The Future of Learning Institutions in a Digital Age (aka FLIDA 101). For the sake of discussion, let us assume that those two professors are this book's authors, who teach at Duke University and the University of California at Irvine. Duke University is a private university of 6,000 undergraduates located in the Southeast; the University of California at Irvine is a public institution with more than 21,000 undergraduates (and growing) located in Orange County, California. Team-teaching such a course means traversing physical distances between the East and West Coasts, cultural differences between the student bodies of each university, and institutional disparities between private- and state-funded universities. It is hard enough to teach across the many campuses of the University of California system, let alone across the country and across divergent institutional structures.

The sort of virtual learning environments that Web technologies have enabled offer genuinely new learning spaces, with new possibilities, novel learning relationships—to texts, to educational authority, to other learners—and distinct challenges. They differ even as they draw on traditional structures of higher education institutions. But they are different, too, from earlier models of correspondence education, where one worked alone, isolated at home or at a residential institution (e.g., for incarcerated individuals who resolved to better themselves) with snail-mail written feedback from an instructor or supervisor with whom one had scant interaction. They differ again from more recent distance-learning programs that have tried to mimic the traditional classroom environment as much as possible, but with instruction beamed in remotely, and interaction with the instructor mediated by the distance and the limitations of the technology. Virtual environments have freed up learning in all sorts of ways—undercutting the demands of physical presence, opening up a range of possibilities for delivery of learning materials, for participatory and collaborative interaction even at a distance, and for instantaneous response.

Virtual environments proliferate the challenges faced in setting up a course such as FLIDA 101. For one, there are disciplinary differences to consider. Davidson is an English professor and historian of technology. She is also a professor of interdisciplinary studies, who publishes widely on gender and race in Americanist contexts. Goldberg is trained as a philosopher and is a professor of comparative literature and criminology, law, and society. He publishes widely on race and race theory. One is a former full-time university administrator; the other currently is an active administrator. Although both professors are cross-disciplinary in their intellectual interests and approaches and have worked extensively on other projects together, the disciplines they cross are different. This new course in "The Future of Learning Institutions in a Digital Age" has never been taught before, by either of us or by anyone at either of our institutions. It is a blank slate. What might such a course look like? What institutional obstacles might they face? What possibilities for digital learning might they explore?[2]

Steve Anderson and Anne Balsamo note in one of the best essays theorizing the implications of teaching in new digital environments, "A Pedagogy for Original Synners," that it is hard to "gain perspective on the contemporary scene of digital learning" precisely because we are in the midst of it.[3] They quote cyberpunk writer William Gibson's provocative comment on the problem of studying the contemporary or prognosticating "the future": "The future is already here, it's just distributed unevenly."[4] By focusing on a specific (if hypothetical) course, this book makes tangible some institutional problematics in an unevenly distributed future of participatory and digitally aided learning.

FLIDA 101: Course Design

Given the topic of the course and their commitments to exploring digital forms as learning platforms, the professors are determined to teach FLIDA 101 in a virtual environment that the class will build out together. Specifically, this involves multiplayer online games and other kinds of virtual environments as spaces for a new form of interactive, participatory, digital learning. They plan to meet, virtually, in such an environment for biweekly class sessions. Second Life (SL), a product of Linden Research, Inc., is the most obvious choice of an environment at this historical moment, although it is not without its problems (and there is no predicting what environments might appear and trump SL within the next decade).[5]

The challenges of virtual learning environments, in general, and of the problems posed by SL, in particular, will be the focus of some of the course discussion (figures 4.3 and 4.4). Indeed, almost every feature of the arrangements of the course will also be a topic for consideration and debate. The professors will want to consider what it means to use SL as a virtual substitute for the physical gathering place that has been the hallmark of the traditional university since medieval times. What features does SL share with the more typical campus (in any of its possible configurations), and what features are new? What is productive about SL in enabling traditional learning practices, in transforming those practices, and in prompting new learning practices and possibilities not otherwise available?

Figure 4.3
The New Media Consortium's campus in Second Life (http://www.nmc
.org/sl/about, accessed June 30, 2009)

Figure 4.4
Poster for a Second Life course led by Ed Lamoureux at Bradley
University.

SL would thus function in three interlocking ways in FLIDA 101. These functions are themselves a hallmark of the form of participatory digital learning the professors are advocating. First, SL will be their meeting space, a way of making a new collaborative bicoastal learning site, a virtual geography of proximity even when the participants may be living in different places. Second, SL will be their subject (one focus of their critical, historical, and theoretical analysis of the future of learning institutions). Finally, SL (or at least their particular island or piece of projected real estate) will be created by the students, a product of their individual and collective creative, computational, and customizing skills.[6]

The professors expect that typical FLIDA students will be used to customizing the social technologies with which they work. One demographic of students who will be drawn to such a course is exactly the do-it-yourself (DIY) student who already spends a lot of time customizing online. The professors also expect, however, that even the most dedicated DIY customizers will *not* be used to assessing the theoretical, historical, ethical, social, political, and technological implications of the social technologies with—or on—which they work. The professors assume that the discussion of these matters will take on added force because of the amount of time, dedication, and personal investment involved in creating a virtual environment or an avatar. The most theoretical discussion of identity, for example, gets quite personal when the focus is on a remix of the identity of the avatar someone has painstakingly created.

The theoretical issues the professors plan to discuss throughout the course as part of the future of learning institutions include such things as virtuality as a form, persistence, access, privacy, intellectual property, social contracts and social organization (in virtual as well as in real spaces), participation and collaboration, work credit, social privilege, digital divides, the nature of institutions, virtual "statehood" (and its geopolitical virtual boundaries), and the definition of learning. Race and gender will also be key issues, as will be all matters of disparity and prejudice that are developed and enacted in the design of a virtual culture. These issues will likely have an unusually visceral (if virtual) component.

For example, intellectual property, individual rights, and fair use discussions may turn up when the professors focus on the creations of the class. "Information wants to be free!" is a rallying cry of this creative generation. Peer-to-peer file-sharing of music, DIY videos of television shows posted on YouTube, and other activities that infringe on patent or copyright law occur daily as part of youth culture and the cry for open access. Remix culture is all about adapting someone else's initial creation and reusing it for one's own creative purpose. Most students today have no argument with a remix model. But how will they react when the professors suggest that others be allowed to take and remix the avatars and the real estate the class develops? Since our SL environment and the students' avatars are being generated in a nonprofit educational context and might be useful to other students and teachers, once class is over, the professors might decide to allow anyone anywhere in the world to take over the classroom and to use the student-created avatars and repurpose them however they wish. Information, after all, wants to be free. Or does it?

Putting together creative technology development with critical thinking forces certain issues in new ways. What, in fact, if the professors propose to be open source with the avatars while the course is in process and not just after the course is "finished"? Would that serve as a firsthand lesson in the limits of the anarchic? A discussion of authorship and publication might take on new energy if posed in this way. It will likewise raise interesting questions about avatar design appropriate to different environments, about thorny questions of race, class, and gender representation, and about wise decision-making on the Web.

Since the professors do not spend their leisure hours customizing their personal SL environments, this course also makes certain assumptions about differential expertise. Some students in the class no doubt will be far more expert at SL than other students or than the professors. This raises another interesting question about the traditional hierarchies of learning and the future of participatory learning. If the hierarchy of who teaches and who is taught is one of the persistent features of the traditional university, what happens in a course that, structurally, puts the professors in the position of learners? Hierarchical models of learning—the conceptions of pedagogical authority and respect they entail—give way to different learning dispositions. Flat (more horizontal) learning environments suggest the need for greater openness to multiple inputs, to more experimental trial and error, and to less authoritative classroom arrangements. Instructors end up being less like content-experts in every domain on which the course touches and more like effective learning coordinators, identifying who best might lead the learning trajectory at each moment. These issues of pedagogical collaboration, leadership, and hierarchy, too, would serve as topics for discussion in the class since the future of learning is tied to tacit hierarchies of who has what to learn and from whom and to a collaborative and participatory spirit of learning well from one another.[7]

Since we will be meeting in SL, every member of the class must customize an avatar to represent himself or herself online. The classroom itself will be in a space that the class develops and customizes together. Basic affordances such as classrooms are usually a given in the traditional university setting—yet that given is also full of ideological and hierarchical assumptions (the challenge more traditionally posed when an instructor proposes to hold a class outside on the lawn on a sunny summer day makes that stabilizing underpinning clear). In this virtual learning environment much, if not all, is a matter of choice, or at least of choice within SL's parameters (see figures 4.5 and 4.6). Even one's presentation of a pedagogical self—the quiet student, the contentious student, the studious student, the flake—is rarely so visible as when one actually must make a visible representation of oneself to be performed in a public, virtual space.

Figure 4.5
Schome Park, a classroom run by the pupils in Teen Second Life (http://www.schome.ac.uk/wiki/Schome_Publicity_Pictures, accessed July 5, 2009).

Figure 4.6
Lecture Hall at Kansas State University (http://www.ke5ter.com/tag/
education, accessed July 29, 2009).

There is also the question of time. Digital technology has certainly compressed space and time, famously speeding up activities such as instantaneous communication, the capacity to check
facts and sources, the possibility to produce work. The seduction
of speed often blinds one to just how time-consuming digital
production can be. It is not just that one receives so many more
communications, wanted and unwanted, than one did in digital
prehistory, nor that one has instantaneous access to so many
more sources of information. It is also that the setting up of the
infrastructure, the testing of new applications, the creation of
user spaces, the inhabitation of landscapes of identity, and the
experiment of working across varying institutional cyberinfra-
structures can all be enormously taxing. These considerations
(the hidden labor of instant communication) will create subject
matter for the course.

These issues of time and labor are theoretically urgent, but
they also have a practical component. One quarter (10 weeks) or

one semester (14 weeks) is likely too short to go from conception through construction to the full service of a virtual classroom—especially if one expects the virtual environment to be fully serviced and comfortably inhabited by students and instructors. A full additional term probably would be required: one for creating the space and one for actually deploying a course within it. We are looking at a year-long course—in short, a real commitment.

Since the goal of FLIDA is to understand the potentials and limits of virtual environments as collaborative learning spaces—learning institutions of the digital future—one of the course objectives is to prompt thought about the social and intellectual implications of the design choices made for the environment to be inhabited and for the avatars class participants make to represent themselves. It is important, for example, that the class not just assume it is going to set up a classroom in SL. The class must select SL as the site from among other available possibilities and carefully consider why it is making this particular selection. What if the class had decided that, in fact, learning is not about being in a shared space (virtual or physical) but is about the *agon* of ideas? The class might then have decided that the educational equivalent of *World of Warcraft* would be a better environment and a better way to embody the future of learning institutions in a digital age.

The point is that in traditional education much is already a given: the physical setting, the structure, the institutional rules, the admissions policies, the requirements for graduation, and the assumptions about what constitutes learning. If teachers and our students are selecting which kind of environment best represents learning needs and objectives, they are also thinking profoundly about what learning is and what constitutes a learning institution. One of the professors' jobs will be to remind students by reminding themselves that every conversation about the virtual and the future is also a tacit reflection on the actual and the present, and the historical conditions that shaped that past and may haunt the present.

There is a pedagogical method implicit in this participatory form of learning. At HASTAC, this method is *collaboration by difference*, and it is the method by which many of our interactions across disciplinary boundaries are structured. That is, when one is working with people who do not share one's basic assumptions and skill sets, who are (in whatever way) different from one, many keywords, assumptions, terms, and material conditions that once seemed obvious suddenly require explanation and redefinition before any significant collaboration can happen. It often turns out that what seemed obvious or the same is actually opaque and alien.[8]

Analyzing such embedded contradictions and unbraiding and unbundling terms—a methodology most commonly associated with Derridean deconstruction and probably as dated as Socrates—is one aspect of participatory learning that the professors of FLIDA intend to encourage. However, prodding likely will not be needed since one mode of youth discourse in the Internet age is snarky backchanneling (typically, instant messaging that provides a countercommentary to the teacher or other authority figure, a quietly twittering form of critique shared by those put in the position of normally passive listeners). Backchanneling is a tool of participatory learning.

SL is an exceptionally well-developed Metaverse, already inhabited in 2008 by over 13 million residents. The FLIDA class is not building a future learning institution from scratch but rather erecting an establishment within a well-populated virtual world. A first issue for the course will be the advantages and disadvantages of locating the class in a virtual world that is

already populated by millions of people, that offers the ameni-
ties of cities (including well-established learning institutions)
and many pastoral places and includes abundant goods and services (from operas and art exhibits to gambling and prostitu-
tion).[9] SL is a virtual world that now comes with an array of
established institutions (many of which mimic the physical
world). It operates on existing social rules (although these are not
autocratically or corporately enforced). And it has a relatively
stable economy (see http://secondlife.com/whatis/economy_stats
.php). Most anything can be purchased within SL with Linden
dollars, valued in April 2009 at L$270 to one U.S. dollar.[10]

The discussions leading to the selection of SL as the FLIDA
meeting place and digital learning institution are not limited
to one discipline. The authors' syllabus of secondary readings is
long. It is also evolving and expanding. It is hard to imagine
any social science discipline that would not contribute to an
informed choice about a virtual living space. Similarly, various
issues in the biological, environmental, and computational sciences must be considered. Nor are the issues purely virtual. In
the real world, SL takes up an extraordinary amount of server
space. Servers, like most computer hardware, are full of toxic
materials and consume excessive amounts of energy, both when
they are being produced and when they are operating. Here
again the knowledge hierarchy becomes an issue, since the
authority figure on a given topic shifts constantly. An undergraduate major in environmental studies may well know more
than the professors about the specific contribution of the Internet, desktops, mobile phones, and other technologies to global
warming, but that same student may know little about history,
science fiction, graphic design, ethics, critical race theory, intellectual property law, or programming.

Ideal students in FLIDA 101 are interested in virtual learning and would be willing to put their knowledge into practice and think critically about their practices. That is a lot to ask of students. Students must also risk feeling at sea some of the time. Since students do want to be certified to enhance job prospects as well as to learn, this poses a different kind of challenge. Not everyone will be equally good in FLIDA 101 all the time. The potential to receive a mediocre grade is high when one may fail to understand some of the core topics or possess all of the skills a course demands. The ideal FLIDA student also must be willing to translate since, in many instances, the student will have specialized knowledge not shared by other members of the class. Whether that specialized knowledge comes in the form of code, equations, or the specialized language of critical theory or social psychology, there will be terms, concepts, and assumptions that will need to be translated for other intelligent people whose knowledge, aptitudes, and interests are at a more basic level. As in any such translation, a FLIDA student is not just traversing virtual worlds but is exploring a range of disciplinary, hierarchical, and affective frontiers as well.

As noted earlier, professors sometimes forget the environmental impact of digital technologies, but, as a lesson in being cognizant of our environmental footprint, one collective class project might be recording daily the energy consumed by FLIDA 101 as well as the pollutants produced and putting that information in perspective with other forms of learning. Creating the design of the experiment, measuring it, analyzing and interpreting the data, putting the findings in institutional and historical perspective, and then presenting the findings to the world in a compelling multimedia format that would have maximum impact would require a range of skills and different forms of knowledge.

The professors also expect that the course will constantly surprise. For example, SL presents programmers with choices, and with limitations. Navigating virtual worlds to their fullest is not trivial, in a computational sense, especially as one sport among engineers is to see if they can outsmart the owners of Linden Labs as well as current residents by building ever-new and challenging applications, devices, tools, and weapons. One of HASTAC's summer interns, Evan Donahue, for example, working with Mark Olson, HASTAC's Director of New Media at the time, was able to develop a way of simulcasting real-time multisite video conferences in SL, a capacity that SL supposedly lacks.[11] Outside of his internship, Evan Donahue was also written up in his Brown University newspaper as a "virtual arms trader" for the SL weapons he created and sold (for real money) on eBay. This aspect of customizing would also be a class topic for discussion in FLIDA 101 since commerce and ethics also have a role in creating virtual worlds.

As these two examples illustrate, there are technological, ethical, and economic implications to design choices in virtual worlds, just as there are in real life. Again, like material life, the narrative, linguistic, and aesthetic choices in selecting SL as the course site call upon the histories and theories of the range of the humanities and the arts. In establishing the site, the professors would need to think through some key ideas in cultural studies, gender theory, critical race theory, and postcolonial theory to inform the class's thinking about the ethical and social questions arising from the built-environments in the virtual world. There are questions about where and what to build, whose avatar and by extension actual lives the class would be impacting. This entails surfacing questions of class, wealth and resource distribution, region, nation, neighborhood, access, sustainability, resource use, and so forth.

Significantly, these same implications pertain in the site of a course held in a conventional classroom at a traditional university. However, university instructors (the authors of this book included) more often than not take the material circumstances of education as a given and only rarely apply critical skills to understanding the underpinnings (in every sense) of the conditions of labor and resource distribution that underlie higher education.[12] As with the legal and intellectual property issues discussed earlier, a transitional moment often exposes assumptions held so long that participants no longer see them. The critical, ethical questions evoked by selecting a virtual learning environment holds up a mirror, making participants more aware of the questions that must be asked about everyday life.

Once the FLIDA class begins to build its futuristic learning institution in SL, a new roster of interconnected issues comes into play. Namely, what will the class itself look like? Collectively, what does it represent? What is the demography of the virtual collective class, both actually and avatar-virtually? Male or female? In SL, about 70 percent of the residents are male, 30 percent female. In undergraduate American university classrooms today, the split tends to be more like 45:55 in favor of women. Which ratio better represents the gender breakdown in the FLIDA classroom? Do the class's avatars even have gender, traditionally conceived? Should that gender be intergender, transgender, or no recognizable gender at all?

What about race, class, region, or national origin, the kinds of identity categories one checks off on census forms or are meaningful still to many? Typically, in SL, people choose and customize avatars that are remarkably like themselves only better—same race and gender but better looking, stronger, and sometimes with superhuman powers (e.g., an ability to fly). If the students in FLIDA come from a range of disciplines from computer science to art, are those particular skills, specializations, and affective issues also reflected in the avatars they create? How many of one's real-world characteristics are projected onto one's avatars? These are all questions of choice and selection that make for individual introspection as well as for stimulating classroom discussion. Imagine the class introductions, as participants proceed around the *room*. Indeed, what takes introductory precedence, the room or the *room*, a student's actual identity or his or her avatar? "I am so-and-so, and *I* . . . ?" The question of self, embodied in one way or another, is in question from the outset.

Indeed, any single one of these issues could be not only the motivation but the specific *content* of the group-generating syllabus of FLIDA 101. "Race in Virtual Worlds" is its own topic, with an increasingly extensive syllabus of secondary readings.[13] So also is "Gender and the Future of Learning."[14]

Class disparities emerge as students and professors set about creating their avatars.[15] If the class is working in SL, it needs Linden dollars to give the characters "skin." More Linden dollars are required to give them costumes and various mythical or whimsical physical characteristics and abilities. How are gender and race apportioned? Are all of the avatars even human? If not human, are they animals, droids, aliens, or superheroes? What capacities do animals have in this virtual world? Can they speak? What about the superheroes? Do superheroes ace all the tests? Do they fly? Are they geniuses? Is anyone in this virtual classroom overweight or disabled? Is every one young and good-looking? If so, what prompting relations are there between prevailing entertainment media and choice of avatar identity, between notions of beauty, embodiment, and virtuality?

These are all social and philosophical issues that take on a different urgency when students (and faculty) are both designing idealized avatars of themselves and face-to-face with one another. What is the definition and value attached to the self in a virtual classroom? What is the relationship between *self* and *avatar*, and where do collective concerns like privacy, gossip, reputation, and respect come into play in virtual worlds and how is this the same or different from actual environments?[16]

These are profound issues and the stakes of the discussion are higher when students are designing the virtual worlds that they embody. This integrated mode of teaching-and-doing (artistic and technological creativity paired with critical thinking) is the point. FLIDA 101 is not only thinking about the future of virtual learning institutions; it is thinking about them in the DIY customizing style that makes such virtual learning appealing, possible, and potentially rich for the current generation of students (and, not incidentally, their professors).

FLIDA's Community-Generated Syllabus

The FLIDA course will involve developing some technological and social knowledge, technical skills in computing and critical theory, and facilities of scientific and humanistic thinking. The point in proposing this pedagogical allegory is that, in addressing issues of the virtual, one *is* addressing the future of learning institutions, and that overlap means creating or revising an expanding range of courses across the curriculum, in and between the sciences, humanities, arts, and applied areas— the mechanisms for building the environments and avatars for the sort of digital institution characterized by FLIDA 101 are as much the medium for skill-building as the course content is the medium for knowledge formation.

Through class blogs and wikis, students will constantly challenge one another's assumptions and will be adding to an evolving class syllabus. Professors will vary as much as students in the SL skills to develop impressive avatars (some professors may even bear the brunt of student satire in this regard, but the capacity to handle derision with dignity may likewise offer lessons in social skill). Surely this model of learning together is preferable to the sort of self-proclaimed political policing of courseware and culture practiced today by the likes of Campus Watch. Other traditionalist or even reactionary organizations, too, seem determined to promote a nineteenth-century hierarchical pedagogy for higher education equivalent to the antiquated No Child Left Behind model[17] on the K–12 level, even though twenty-first century students come with new collaborative interests and skills and, equally, go out into a job market in which training in interdisciplinary teamwork is demanded.

Notwithstanding, professors can generate an extensive syllabus of secondary theoretical and historical readings to encourage students to think deeply about every term in our course title: *future, thinking, learning, institutions, digital,* and *age.* What constitutes a *digital age* and how is it different from other eras in the history of media and technology? What is the relationship of the future learning institution professors and students are cocreating to past experiments in utopian learning or in technologically enhanced learning, many of which failed dismally? What is learning, and what could it more effectively be? What is an institution, and how does virtualizing institutions alter their modus operandi, if not their definition (see chapter 5)?

Readings beginning at least with Plato and running to contemporary learning blogs would frame the course. For the course properly to fulfill its mission in moving from a hierarchical, one-to-many classroom to an interactive and socially networked classroom, the syllabus would also need to be constantly enlivened by the students' own curiosity and not just simply contributing to the development of a new technological formalism (see figures 4.7 and 4.8). Google jockeys set to searching and then reporting to the class on any idea that arises in the discussions would supplement reading materials.[18]

Students generally would be encouraged to propose readings for one another, based on what they find through their searches and from what they have read in their more standard courses. A wiki forum would enable those in the class to comment on each other's suggestions and on the reading materials themselves, producing a critical consensus of what is compelling and critical, what is informative and insightful, and what is misleading

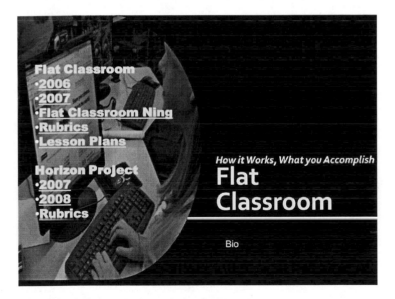

Figure 4.7
Image from Davis' slideshow on how to create a flat classroom, slide 1 (http://www.slideshare.net/coolcatteacher/flatclassroom-presen tation-il-tce, accessed July 5, 2009).

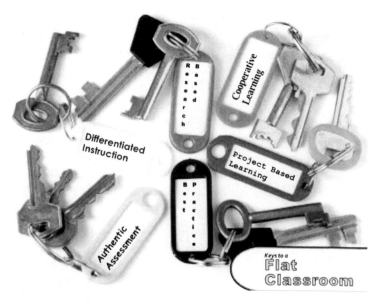

Figure 4.8
Image from Davis' slideshow on how to create a flat classroom, slide 2
(http://www.slideshare.net/coolcatteacher/flatclassroom-presen
tation-il-tce, accessed July 5, 2009).

or missing the point (see figure 4.9 for an example of how wikis
can be used in the classroom and figure 4.10 for a comical representation of how wikis are affecting our everyday lives).

In addition, the students' own weekly blog postings would
be part of the syllabus, and those postings would change
according to the reading but also according to what topics arose
from the SL building task at hand. One basic issue in thinking
about how learning should be structured and enabled by digital
technology concerns the function and organization of the
library as repository and medium of information for virtual

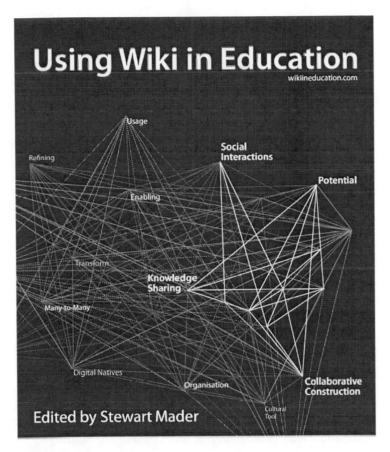

Figure 4.9
Cover reproduced by permission from Stewart Mader, ed., *Using Wiki in Education* (Lulu.com, 2008) (http://www.lulu.com/content/2175253, accessed July 5, 2009).

Figure 4.10
Wikis on Toilet (image taken from http://upload.wikimedia.org/wiki
pedia/commons/thumb/7/73/Warning_-_Wikis_on_toilet.svg/600px
-Warning_-_Wikis_on_toilet.svg.png, accessed July 5, 2009).

institutions of advanced learning. Should a virtual learning
institution such as FLIDA University have its own library that
only its "registered" students can use? Should that library emu-
late online how university libraries function in their material
manifestations? Or should the FLIDA class be working with
other SL inhabitants to build interoperable information systems where all the world's knowledge can exist in some open-
access knowledge nirvana where copyright no longer pertains,
all knowledge is coproduced, collaboratively vetted, loosely
structured to maximize alternative modes of presentation, and
readily available to all?

Potential students might think of this free-flowing world of ideas not as nirvana but as hell, as anarchic and too unformed to be useable, let alone useful. Too little informational structure and too much freedom of choice risks disorder, insecurity as a result of lack of predictability, and ultimately the incapacity to act because of the unreliability of information sources and the resulting failure of replicable experimentation. In a world where anything goes, one risks the danger that everything goes. Such a copyright-free world has the potential of depriving a would-be professional writer in the class of a livelihood. Why, she might ask, should the words and ideas that she generates be available without cost when nothing else is? If she must pay for all kinds of goods and services manufactured by people with MBA degrees, why do those same businessmen and women think they are entitled to her art for free? In discussing the mechanisms for dispersing the books and articles on the syllabus, yet another syllabus of readings on open access, open source, intellectual property, and other crucial issues will be generated. In short, the structure of knowledge on which learning is predicated implies a certain structure to the world; the world structured in certain ways entails that knowledge and learning will be tailored to inform such a world. World-making and world-learning go hand in glove.

In FLIDA 101, students and instructors learn by doing, and they learn from one another as they are doing. Class participants will use technology creatively *because* they are being critical and introspective about the technology itself. Participants are not simple consumers of SL or any other technology. They are using the experience of building a creative, digital learning environment to think deeply about the nature of all learning institutions, about the structure of knowledge, past and future.

Participants are solving problems as they arise but not reducing all learning to the solving of problems. We learn too from critical reflection, from cultural engagement, from failure. A philosophy of learning is implicit in and, in turn, shapes the nature of learning institutions. As learning and learning institutions go digital, it would be naïve to think how, what, when, and where one learns would not be dramatically transformed as a consequence.

FLIDA 101 is a pedagogical allegory, imagined to help us think about pedagogy in digital worlds and the way such courses might work in actual traditional and transitional institutions. Already, though, a growing number of creative courses dot the landscape of higher education and challenge institutional assumptions, including courses exploring the enhancing technologies of three-dimensional representation, the virtues of digital mapping and visualization technologies—whether to bring to life geographic references of literary classics or to make available to learners in dynamic ways historical archival content they can mine together—or that allow students to create and draw on laser-generated digital reproductions of works of art and architecture revealing features of those works otherwise hidden from view. Such ventures in cultural analytics not only make knowledge potentially more accessible, they also encourage and make possible productive new modes of participatory learning.[19] The pedagogical point of the FLIDA 101 allegory: New technologies can prompt genuinely new questions. In doing so, they promote the emergence of a genuinely new knowledge formation not otherwise within reach.

FLIDA 101 in the Traditional University

Clearly FLIDA 101 is a far-reaching course that raises many issues about both virtual and real worlds. The creation of such a course also poses important issues about institutions. How would such a course work in the most practical, curricular terms? How does it count toward that all-important degree?

A first issue might be disciplinary. In what department would a university offer such a course? As is often the case in team or cotaught courses, the FLIDA 101 professors each have multidepartmental and multidisciplinary home departments and affiliations. They teach at universities that encourage interdisciplinarity and consider it a hallmark of those institutions. The most likely host sites for FLIDA 101 in any institution would be nonstandard innovative programs. Trying to have FLIDA cross-listed in more traditional departments, even with the institutional flexibility at the professors' respective universities, would be challenging.

Since the range of bureaucratic issues is so different across institutions, this book will not belabor all of the discrete (and enervating) hurdles of departmental approval and counting that arise with any interdisciplinary course. Anyone who has ever tried to offer a team-taught and cross-departmental course runs into such issues. Faculty wanting to pursue digitally-enabled virtual team-teaching across institutions will confront issues faced by faculty wanting to team-teach across units within an institution to the power of 10. Different institutional and administrative cultures, different ways of assessing credit for cotaught courses, the divides between public and private institutions, different levels of student expectation and expertise, and different institutional levels of technological support and openness to technological as well as pedagogical experimentation. Such issues will frame the institutional conditions of success or failure.

The sort of course FLIDA represents poses special challenges, since it would involve students and professors from many fields—engineers, social scientists, artists, computer scientists who specialize in artificial intelligence (AI), philosophers who contest current (limited) definitions of AI, literature professors who understand narrative, anthropologists who can do ethnographies of game play, political theorists who can help understand the social rules of the constructed virtual environment, and law professors for the intellectual property issues, human rights issues, and highly contested issues of who is responsible for policing violence and other social misconduct in virtual worlds. One can add many more examples to this list. As exciting as such a course could end up being as a learning experience, it poses conceptual, architectural, and logistical challenges, too. And yet it is safe—and sorry—to say that many faculty and administrators in all of the departments listed above would not necessarily recognize the subject matter of FLIDA as their own. It is even possible that *no* department would find FLIDA comprehensible. That is the dilemma of innovation at the edge, to use John Seely Brown's term.[20] What happens then?

Many students might not be able to take FLIDA because such a course belongs in no single major, and students at most traditional universities are required to check off all the myriad requirements for general education and a major before they graduate. This is an "elective." But assuming there are adventurous students who want to take such a course even though it may not count institutionally, what happens when we go to the computer science department and find out that, at some of the most distinguished departments in the country, games are considered unworthy of scholarly attention—despite the fact that games require some of the most complex code writing? Who in the computer science department might want to join us in team-teaching the course?

Often the person most prepared to participate in an innovative course such as this is the brilliant adjunct professor, the non-tenure-track research professor who works in some full professor's lab, or the quirky but marginalized maverick professor in the department. That person may well be on unstable grant money, because she was not able to find a *real* job in a traditional computer science department or dismissed for doing work out of touch with mainstream *real* science. Grants likely do not cover teaching, and a side interest to departmental pedagogy may not count toward teaching credit. Such instructors would have to contribute to FLIDA for free, on their own time, at personal cost. The course, if it were to be offered at all, would likely run once, tolerated for its quirkiness but just as a one-time anomaly. This may be exciting for the student, surely, but it is not exactly in the best interest of a professor and not the best way to promote institutional change. And it is no way to have a lasting impact on the curriculum and on the future of learning institutions.

The silos that separate departments, disciplines, and divisions of universities are a problem well beyond the customized, collaborative, and collective form of participatory learning this book promotes for the digital age. However, the digital exacerbates the problems created by the existing silos that are so deeply entrenched within traditional universities.

Also entrenched are the specific systems of reward and recognition that have evolved at each university. If the FLIDA 101 professors wish to team-teach a cross-institutional course in a virtual environment, there are a host of other institutional issues that must be considered. An innovative institution such as the University of California's systemwide Humanities Research Institute (UCHRI), directed by one of this book's authors, is relatively rare in its spanning of the separate institutions within the vast University of California system encompassing 10 universities. UCHRI brings together faculty across the system for shared research. Yet, even as it can assist in setting up the virtual infrastructure for the course, UCHRI has no standing within the university administrative structure to offer accredited courses of any kind.

Some years ago, two colleagues at Duke University and the University of North Carolina decided to team-teach a graduate course. Only 11 miles separate the two campuses, so it was decided that half of the course would be conducted at one university and half at the other. However, working out the details of how the course would "count" turned into a nightmare. The challenges ranged from those of scheduling to grading and from course accreditation to faculty workload (not to mention insurance considerations for faculty and students traveling from one campus to another on university business). For example, the identical grade at the one institution did not necessarily count the same as it might at the other because of different gradations (pluses and minuses versus a numerical system) within grading structures.[21] In the end, the two professors decided to act as if they were not team-teaching at all, even though they happened to be meeting in the same classroom at the same time and teaching the same course—just filled half with students from Duke and half with students from the University of North Carolina. If the institutional obstacles were simply too difficult to negotiate for a course otherwise recognizably similar to regular college courses on each respective campus, how much more difficult for courses conducted largely, if not exclusively, in and through virtual environments, bicoastal and multi-institutional?

Virtual Learning, Traditional Institutions

It would be all too easy to end this allegory of participatory learning with a screed against the intransigence of the academy. In truth, the authors of this book have each spent a significant portion of their careers working against institutional barriers, as have many faculty now fueled by recognition of the dynamic possibilities for participatory learning that new media suggest. However, as frustrating as are the obstacles posed by the bureaucracies and silos in traditional universities, it is acknowledged that they will not go away any time soon. Indeed, as Craig Avery notes in a comment on the Institute for the Future of the Book site, one goes to college not only to learn but also to receive a degree. Avery asks: "What is (will be) the focus here regarding curriculum outcomes, outcomes assessment, skill sets, and professional certification? It seems to me that there are at least two forms of learning outcomes here—implicit 'discovery' models that encourage and facilitate students' ability to undertake open-ended personal searches and explicit "satisfy the gatekeeper" outcomes that meter out graduates subject to and capable of passing institutional review to enter business, medicine, law, and other professions."[22] From its inception in the West, these two functions—teaching to inspire and learning for learning's sake, on the one hand, and official certification, on the other—have operated simultaneously. Virtual learning may fulfill the first role but, if we are going to fulfill the second—of achieving a degree—then the virtual must recognize the way it nests within traditional universities.

It has long been the case that a degree is not just about knowledge. It is a certification that one is capable of performing long and complicated tasks, according to specific standards, along a strict timeline, fulfilling a range of requirements, adapting to the demands (hierarchy again) of various people in positions of power, and balancing institutional (or professional) demands with social life. It also indicates to some degree that one has the capacity to negotiate and execute an extremely complex and interconnected series of operations that require everything from time management to independent thinking to subordination to psychology (being able to understand and meet the expectations of various institutional officers). No wonder that those with an advanced degree have far greater earning capacity over the course of a lifetime! All of these skills are less about formal learning than about learning to succeed in an environment that looks a lot like middle-class occupational roles. To quote the droll title of writer Irvine Welsh's recent collection of short stories, *If You Liked School, You'll Love Work.*[23]

Virtual learning both resembles and is different from traditional institution-based learning. The idealistic rhetoric of many-to-many, smart mobs,[24] long tails, and Web 2.0 must be set against the realism of the myriad social norms that undergird the virtual. Here is an aphorism: Virtually nothing that happens virtually happens in a vacuum. When Clay Shirky announces "Here Comes Everybody!" and focuses on "The Power of Organizing Without Organizations," he highlights exactly the collaborative, adaptive, improvisational character of participatory learning that this book, too, embraces. At the same time, Shirky acknowledges the limits of this model: "The logic of publish-then-filter means that new social systems have to tolerate enormous amounts of failure. The only way to uncover and promote the rare successes is to rely, yet again, on social structure supported by social tools."[25] But often, too, the viability of virtual learning environments, of the conditions of possibility enabling virtual social arrangements and their institutional expression, is predicated on preexisting institutional arrangements that are willing, materially and discursively, to support or at least tacitly tolerate them.

FLIDA 101 has the potential to be effective as virtual learning precisely because of its uneasy, prickly, and nested relationship within traditional institutions. Virtual learning rarely exists without some kind of support from traditional institutions. Henry Jenkins reminds us that the digital divide is closing across class structure, but a significant gap in participatory learning online remains precisely because customizing and interacting virtually often requires (often personal) economic resources and the availability of technologies that may not be readily within reach for impoverished youth.[26] For example, the laptop of an enormously creative teenager at an after-school digital learning center on the south side of Chicago had been stolen. It was the only laptop in a household unable to afford a replacement, and he was able to continue his intensive experimental creative practice only by attending the after-school program every afternoon (figures 4.11 and 4.12). Economic class is one of those social structures, in Shirky's term, that order the virtual world.

Social structures and social institutions support virtual learning in myriad ways. Sometimes those institutions are corporate. Google's motto may well be "Don't Be Evil," but Google's initial public offering, in August 2004, netted $23 billion, and it is naïve to think that any corporation of that size manages always to be on the side of the angels. Google's brilliant idea was to make user preference the base of its search functions. *User preference* is a form of social networking and spontaneous organization. That does not make it free, democratic, or inherently not *evil* (whatever that word might mean in the Google economy).

Figure 4.11
See Cathy Davidson's HASTAC blog from June 15, 2008 (http://www
.hastac.org/node/1435, accessed June 15, 2008).

The point is that many creative sites, where learning is part
of social networking, thrive on user-generated content (UGC)
and generate enormous profits from that UGC for their corporate owners. SL, Facebook, MySpace, YouTube, and Flickr are all
virtual learning spaces in the sense that users create, customize,
share, exchange information, and socialize together. Meanwhile,
from all this participatory activity, corporations, shareholders,
investors, and entrepreneurs engage in a form of e-commerce
and global capitalism that coexists with traditional forms. Thus
a traditional media mogul like Rupert Murdoch can move
rather seamlessly from the acquisition of newspapers and tele-

Figure 4.12
See Cathy Davidson's HASTAC blog from June 15, 2008 (http://www
.hastac.org/node/1435, accessed June 15, 2008) .

vision to gobbling up MySpace. And then there is Google—
which voraciously feeds off everything else.[27]

Anne Balsamo reminds us of how, before the bursting of
the dot.com bubble in April 2002, there was considerable
rhetoric about the new Internet world operating according to
entirely new sets of rules and being beyond capitalism. The
emphasis on customizing, on user-generated content, and on
participatory learning, information exchange, and peer-to-peer
sharing (in sites such as eBay) meant we had moved into a
"post-Fordist organizational form."[28] The dot.com bust revealed
the hype and the myths. Virtual capitalism had little ability to

sustain itself outside the rules of corporate capitalism. In any case, capitalism's chameleonlike capacity to adapt to new circumstances is notorious. It is fueled, after all, by the drive to fashion new desires, as John Stuart Mill long ago observed. Underpinning e-commerce are the likes of Wall Street, and thus many of the spectacular successes (and failures) of the e-economy are bankrolled by conventional players in the global economy.

Yet there *is* something new about the participatory possibilities of the Internet, even with this realistic assessment of all the traditional institutions that undergird it. Some scholars, such as Michael Strangelove, steadfastly adhere to the utopian vision of an Internet culture that continues to exist outside the normal corporate capitalist hegemonies. [29] Strangelove focuses on hacker culture and other anarchic online communities that he believes continue to resist capitalism and globalization in all forms. This is the Internet as an alternate space dedicated to "anarchic freedom, culture jamming, alternative journalism, and resistance to authoritarian forms of consumer capitalism and globalization."

The potentials for collaborative, participatory learning that the Internet fosters are exciting, even if a more sober assessment of its revolutionary political potential is assumed. Thus, one can be frustrated with the sometimes knee-jerk resistance within traditional academic structures to new modes of creative learning and, at the same time, be suspicious of new technology utopianism that fails to attend to the traditional structures referenced above, whether those that thwart the new or those—wittingly or not—that support individuals (including the authors of this book) whose research, teaching, and practices push the conventional limits of the institution.

As the cotaught, cross-institutional FLIDA course makes clear (as does any course seeking to advance technology-centered collaborative learning), the virtual world exists in parallel and interdependence with the actual world. Participatory learning exists as an overlay on institutions that support and provide sustenance to "the new." Those servers that support the FLIDA course in SL are real. They cost real dollars, spew real toxins, and are manufactured by the standard principles of global commerce (including exploitation of workers). Real material conditions, in other words, undergird new media and, therefore, participatory learning. No rhetoric of democratization, participation, customization, or the many-to-many, nonhierarchical models of learning can erase real disparities and inequalities institutionalized beyond the computer screen or supporting the virtual environment.

The same institutions that frustrate innovators with their solidity support almost every aspect of the digital. Whether talking about legal and social institutions, cultural institutions, or learning institutions—family, state, and nation can serve as all three—each is part of the social fabric undergirding technology. Technology is not just software and hardware. It is also all of the social and human arrangements supported, facilitated, destabilized, or fostered by technology.

FLIDA 101, then, would be difficult to offer across Duke University and the University of California (or most any other institutions). There are numerous institutional barriers to be overcome or, for those that cannot be overcome, finessed or worked around. Yet, without these institutions, FLIDA 101 could not even exist. This point is important because far too much of the rhetoric of virtual learning, participatory learning, and customized learning is detached from real-world conditions and real-world disparities. New media (including participatory and democratized learning) are supported by the same material and social arrangements—including conditions of privilege or inequality—that support the most staid and traditional institutions of what, for now, seems like "old media."

Every aspect of this project (including the computers and networks and wireless systems over which the authors of this book have exchanged numerous drafts) is supported by an array of institutions, private and public, innovative and traditional. To believe that the digital and the virtual have no connection to the real, no foundation in complex institutional and commercial arrangements, is, we insist, one of the most insupportable and potentially dangerous fantasies of the digital age. Among other things, refusing to attend to the virtual's connection to the actual material arrangements of society plays into the Internet fantasy of its own free and open access at precisely the time when the Internet is being corporatized and regulated beyond recognition of its idealistic founders such as Tim Berners-Lee and other leaders of the W3C (World Wide Web Consortium).

Indeed, courses like FLIDA 101—courses in virtual learning based in virtual environments as well as courses enabling collaborative participatory learning enabled or enhanced by the unique social networking possibilities of today's digitalities—should be required of students because their virtuality helps to expose the tangible, persistent, and real institutional arrangements undergirding digital ones. At the same time, working through the thicket of rules and assumptions in order to make such a cross-institutional, cross-disciplinary course possible is an excellent way of promoting change within traditional institutions of higher learning.

This pedagogical allegory is one of change and resistance to change. The virtual is susceptible to the same tugs in opposite directions as brick-and-mortar learning environments, and good pedagogy means confronting both the traditions and the potential for transition within even the most stolid institutions. To that end, chapter 5 considers how digitally prompted and promoted prisms and practices of social networking suggest the need for a different conception of an institution as a learning environment.

5 Institutions as Mobilizing Networks: (Or, "I Hate the Institution—But I Love What It Did for Me")

Institution, n Origin: 1350–1400; ME<L institūtiōn- (s. of institūtiō). 1. an organization, establishment, foundation, society, or the like, devoted to the promotion of a particular cause or program, esp. one of a public, educational, or charitable character. 2. the building devoted to such work. 3. a public or private place for the care or confinement of inmates, esp. mental patients or other disabled or handicapped persons. 4. Sociology: a well-established and structured pattern of behavior or of relationships that is accepted as a fundamental part of a culture, as marriage: the institution of the family. 5. any established law, custom, etc. 6. any familiar, long-established person, thing, or practice; fixture. 7. the act of instituting or setting up; establishment: the institution of laws.

—*Random House Unabridged Dictionary*, © Random House, Inc., 2006

Institution-Building

In the standard *Random House* dictionary entry for *institution*, the word *established* (or *establishment*) occurs five times. Against innovation, virtuality, and the future, the institution stands as an anchor, a remnant that symbolizes the solidity of the past persisting through time and change into the present (*well-established, long-established*).

Yet in setting to work on the future of learning institutions in a digital age, an interesting challenge emerged. Institutions by conception are solid, slow moving, and even slower to change. They hold their members within their defined and refining boundaries, fashioning and reproducing habits, activities, and ways of being and doing. Connie Yowell of the MacArthur Foundation, the division director responsible for the Digital Media and Learning Initiative, wondered what would happen if a succinct definition of *institution* were developed, one more agile, placing less emphasis on what was established and more on the potentialities, on the ways that institutions could and do foster and not simply impede or provide obstacles to innovation.[1]

This is an intriguing concept. There is a familiar narrative of personal institutional history that goes something like: "I hated ____ , but in retrospect I learned from it." That blank might be filled in with anything: a Jesuit education, prep school, the military, any strong institutional enforcer of discipline that one survived but, somehow, against odds, learned from. Too often, this compensatory retrospection is tinged with nostalgia and conservatism—as if salvaging something from that despised past made the institution worth preserving.

Conserving institutional traditions for their own sake is not this chapter's aim. Instead, it explores the way change seeps through and gradually changes institutions, the way individuals and collectives can make institutional change, and also the way groups of individuals within institutions can sometimes become agents of change even within and around and, sometimes, supported by the institution that may name its own mission in different ways. Would a more agile comprehension of institutions promote innovation?

If, in fact, institutions change and adapt to changing environments as well as maintain their establishment as seemingly impervious to change, what could be gained by emphasizing the disruptions rather than the continuities? Instead of thinking conventionally of the medieval remnants in the contemporary institutions of higher education, what might emerge were one to think in terms of the range of options that learning institutions offer today? These range across research universities, liberal arts colleges, community colleges, distance-learning programs, global learning programs, universities in prisons or mental institutions, community-outreach and in-reach programs, Wikiversity, and whole campuses in Second Life. If there are structural features of the university that remain unchanged, other aspects often tend to be illegible if not invisible, incomprehensible if not threatening. Focusing on the permanence of institutions offers some conceptual and social gains, but would thinking of institutions in terms of what they change and how they change provide other forms of inspiration? It is an intriguing challenge.

In response to this challenge, the following definition is proposed:

Institutions are mobilizing networks.

This definition is deliberately provocative. The intention in proposing it is to see the effects of injecting a verb—*to mobilize*—into the traditional solidity (establishment) of *institution*. At the same time, holding on to something positive in the notion of an institution undermines a naïve, if utopian, fantasy of the Internet as a noninstitutional place of free-flowing choice.[2] Indeed, drawing here upon Michel Foucault, even the most powerfully repressive institutions (monarchies, prisons, the military, and so forth) themselves admit of both determination and choice, constraint and flow, and sites of hierarchy and resistance. *And networks do as well.*

This book's definition of *institution* is as concise as that of Avner Greif's magisterial yet quite different definition of institutions as "equilibria of rules, norms, and beliefs."[3] His definition arises from economic game theory. While appreciating Greif's metaphor of constant retuning, adjudicating, counterposing, and balancing, switching to the more active and agentive metaphor of "mobilizing" is preferable. Networks need mobilizing—they certainly neither occur nor can be sustained naturally, of their own accord, without effort—and, in turn, they mobilize the interactive to effective purpose or ends.

This book uses *networks* to gesture toward the complex, multiple, sometimes self-generating and sometimes contradictory connections, linkages, and flows that occur in all institutions, not to signal egalitarianism (i.e., networks are *not* purely or simply egalitarian).

Numerous scholars (at least as far back as Plato's exegesis of the state and justice in the *Republic*) have argued that institutional structures that seem permeable in their delineations as well as institutions that appear to be draconian and powerfully linear in their organization and administration all admit and (sometimes inadvertently) foster counter-forces and countertendencies. Yet, interestingly, historical definitions of *institution* have tended to privilege the foundational, static, formal, and regulatory aspects rather than the human flows within, into, and out of institutions.

This book's modification of classic definitions of *institution* (including rational choice theory definitions) is intended to elicit discussion concerning the differences between traditional and peer-to-peer or virtual institutions. What would it mean to start with a definition that emphasized social networks and the processes of creating those networks? In any new definition, something is gained and something is lost.

This book's definition deliberately builds upon and pushes at a classic definition of institution such as that offered by political scientist Robert Keohane, of "persistent and connected sets of rules (formal and informal) that, along with norms and beliefs, prescribe behavioral roles, constrain activity, and shape expectations."[4] Our intent is to help rethink the institution in terms of agency and movement as a way of making visible continuities and discontinuities between traditional and virtual institutions. The definition also helps us find points between the poles of organization and chaos—a way of thinking in *institutional terms* of what Howard Rheingold calls "smart mobs."[5]

An elaboration of the working definition of *institution* as a *mobilizing network* is provided below. A dozen subject-matter experts in as many fields offered insights, feedback, and exceptions that interject cautions (and terminologies) from various disciplinary perspectives, and that make clear that institutions, in and of themselves, are not intrinsically good or bad.[6] Their utility is a function of what they enable or disable and make possible or restrict. The definition is intended to apply to both traditional and peer-to-peer institutions.[7]

Institution: A Working Definition

Institutions are mobilizing networks They aggregate, coordinate, disperse, balance, and adjudicate complex flows of resources.

Institutions are also social, political, and economic structures prompting a culture of their own. They embody protocols of governance and varying degrees of control over their members. Institutions validate and impose norms, practices, and beliefs, seeking to ensure orderly interchange through normative interactions. However, intra-institutional conflict and complexity are not always susceptible to being managed by such norms.

Institutions sometimes disseminate products to a larger public. Institutional distribution of goods may be prompted and promoted for reasons of profit, influence, policy, institutional self-perpetuation and power, or the public good.

Institutions may occupy a primary site and exercise jurisdiction over constituents. Institutional sites may be concrete or virtual, and jurisdiction may be legal or social and ideological.

An institution is differentiated from other looser forms of affiliation by duration. Institutions are expected to include mechanisms for continuity over time, often seeking to provide an archive or repository of their own collective processes and history.

This working definition has been especially useful in thinking through the full implications of what a peer-to-peer institution might look like. Of key importance is its motivational premise pointing to the institution's role as a mobilizing network. In building the field of digital media and learning, for example, one must consider what it would take to form the kind of institutional base that will be responsible to its members in its role as a purveyor of cultural norms and protocols for wise decision-making across a distributed network.

An institutional base would also be a responsive builder of a common language and a set of creative translation functions capable nevertheless of being modified, riffed upon, and improvisationally put to practice. This base would also need to be an arbiter of social practices, an honest broker of financial resources, a resource for credentialing and reputation, and a repository or an archive of its own practices—while maintaining its core innovative function as a mobilizing network.

In other words, corporatizing the institution or even reverting to a conventional institutional model subverts the self-organizing operations of the field—those that are the most like the Linux model of self-motivated, open access, self-sourced, and self-resourced collaboration and creativity or the industrious and even playful collaborative operations that Yochai Benkler ascribes to Coase's penguin.[8] These kinds of peer-to-peer institutions are what promise to be most responsive to issues of innovative pedagogy. They are also most suited to a field whose goal it is to rethink the future of institutions for young and older people alike, teachers and learners, often the same person—whether schools and colleges (the traditional learning institutions) or an array of ancillary sites where learning also happens. These sites include civic centers, community centers, libraries, museums, after-school programs, and even playgrounds and coffee houses.

Although this book's focus has been primarily on higher education, it is important to underscore that learning, even within the grounds of the academy, does not happen only in the classroom or lab (or, indeed, within the walls, literally, of formal educational institutions). Peer-to-peer learning might happen as much in the social space on campus as in the classroom. Indeed, given the shape of the library in the digital age, the blurring of intellectual and social spaces is becoming increasingly important, with libraries often serving as hosting sites for an array of online learning. Thus, libraries as digital catalysts have manifested, in the simplest way, through wireless affordance as well as in more innovative and activist ways by becoming, on many campuses, the catalyst for innovative uses of technology for pedagogy, from creating digital archives to discussion boards or nodes to sites for collaborative virtual invention. The point is that, even within conventional institutions, there are a variety of other supporting sites of mobilization, and many of those have multiple (and sometimes unexpected) functions. The library-as-social-space plays as much an institutional role as the library-as-information source.

There are many additional examples bearing out the fruits of learning institutions as mobilizing networks. One exemplary model is the Urban Education Institute, part of the Chicago public school system located in Hyde Park and the University of Chicago (figure 5.1). The Institute sponsors four charter schools and offers a robust example of schooling for the future, a mobilizing network of the most imaginative sort. It serves as a community center, an after-school program, a teacher training and support facility, a meeting place for teachers and parents, a resource facility and library, a recording studio and "thinkering" space for local youth, an art gallery exhibiting many of the inventive products designed and produced by the children and instructional leaders, as well as a café and gathering space for local residents. It offers facilities and opportunities not otherwise available, bringing into creative play youth who would otherwise less likely interact to productive learning purpose, composing music and lyrics, designing board and video games, acquiring on-camera interview skills as they learn video production, elaborating complex social skills as well as fostering insight and capability in community and broader urban political knowledge ranging from the local community level to national presidential politics. Funded in part by the MacArthur Foundation Digital Media and Learning Initiative, it is a site also for teachers in training to observe and acquire experience in networked and networking learning practices as well as for program officers of the Foundation to extrapolate lessons learned from this mobilizing network in order to apply them to other locations.

While the Urban Education Institute offers a compelling example for how mobilizing learning networks as institutional sites are put in play, it is far from the only example of the complex relations between teachers, community organizers, uni-

Figure 5.1
Screenshot of the home page of the Urban Education Institute (http://uei.uchicago.edu/index.shtml, accessed July 5, 2009).

versity members, youth, family, and funding agency. Another good example of such a complex institutional partnership would be the Sustainable South Bronx project in New York City. This is a community network, drawing on local residents and youth, to mobilize both to learn and do something about the considerable environmental challenges facing residents of the South Bronx. In creating the toolset to collect and disseminate information, to mobilize politically around these counterknowledges, to design and build environmentally conscious tools to address issues of sustainable environmental practice, the Sustainable

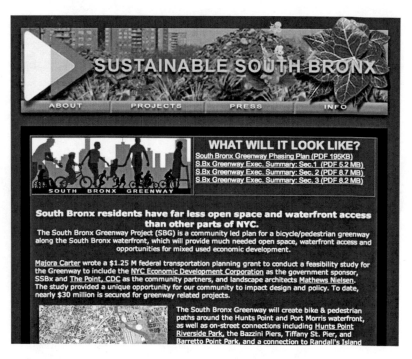

Figure 5.2
Screenshot of the Sustainable South Bronx project (http://www.ssbx.
org/greenway.html, accessed July 5, 2009).

South Bronx project offers a good example of how mobilizing
learning networks as institutional sites work (see figure 5.2).

Waag Society (http://www.waag.org), located in the historic
building at the center of Amsterdam, is dedicated to experimentation in and development of new technologies for healthcare,
education, and networked art and culture (figure 5.3). An independent nonprofit, the Waag Society partners with ordinary
people, corporations, schools, teachers and students, and univer-

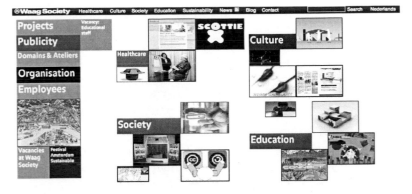

Figure 5.3
Screenshot of the home page for the Waag Society (http://www.waag
.org, accessed July 5, 2009).

sities to develop innovative products, such as applications
enabling those with demanding physical or mental challenges to
express themselves, communicate, and make their own choices
to sustain their independent living possibilities; mobile learning
games to explore the history of the cities, whether medieval
Amsterdam or "New Amsterdam" (Manhattan); digital story-
boards that enable the elderly to connect with youth through
imaginative photographic narratives recounting lived experiences and memory; or a software application to develop interactive symbol-based communication and educational materials.

Increasingly, museums are turning to digital media to provide learning tools connecting the public and, in particular,
the young public to the learning possibilities provided by these
institutional sites. This is particularly so for science and technology museums, though far from limited to them. Thus, the
Hayden planetarium of New York's Museum of Natural History
has developed a series of "educator's activities" to provide

students at all levels with access to astronomical data sets from their Digital Universe database (figure 5.4). When combined with Microsoft's recently released WorldWide Telescope (http://www.worldwidetelescope.org), educators, researchers, and self-learners are provided access to a powerful tool—a "virtual telescope" linked to real-time data provided by major observatories around the world—operating off their personal computers to explore the astronomical universe.[9] In these ways, traditional, conventional, and largely static institutions increasingly become mobilizing networks, engaging with schools, community groups, corporations, nonprofits, and individuals.

Even corporations, nongovernmental organizations, and workplaces in general can amount to mobilizing networks. They, too, can and do serve as learning institutions in various ways. They train and retrain those who work for them; they run internships and participate in service learning programs; and they occasionally offer learning possibilities for their clients and consumers. Consider Google, a corporation that offers learning possibilities that range from the traditional to the genuinely novel. Whatever one thinks about the drive to corporate dominance, and there is much to be concerned about, Google offers today what is probably the most compelling gateway to the most extraordinary range of information. It enables—*mobilizes*—the possibility of repeatedly retooling and resourcing production possibilities around the most open-ended informational access and circulation currently available to human beings on a mass and user-friendly scale. The Google Book Search program, in conjunction with an expanding group of major university and public libraries, seeks to digitize in searchable and ultimately publicly accessible form the full text of all published books in the libraries' collections. Google would like to offer a gateway to learning, dramatically expanding access to

Figure 5.4
Screenshot of Hayden Planetarium's Digital Universe Atlas (http://www
.haydenplanetarium.org/universe/products, accessed July 5, 2009).

Information, if not itself offering criteria for distinguishing
compelling from questionable sources. Its mobilizing capacity
and promise are borne out by the fact that its brand name has
become a widely invoked verb, even sometime imperative:
Googling, to Google, or just *Google (it)*! This is so much the case
that we now have the reverse formation, the fearful version,
as in what Siva Vaidhyanathan calls "The Googlization of
Everything."[10]

In all of these institutional instances, a form of learning radiates outward from traditional institutions and inward from other less-usual kinds, mobilizing and invigorating both in such creative ways that it is difficult to define the borders of one or another. Mobilizing learning institutions concerns eradicating some borders, manifesting others, and in all ways creating energies and interdependencies whereby learning is integrated into all aspects, operations, and active members of a larger community. Indeed, mobilizing institutions mobilizes collective activity and activates inspiring and productive resources and social relations.

There is another point here as well. The back-and-forth between the traditional or stable institutional role and the mobilizing role is every bit as complex and shifting as the relationship described for the cotaught, bicoastal, biuniversity FLIDA course described in chapter 4. And, viewed this way, almost every educational institution has, within it and in its relationship to the community beyond, some mobilizing and some (literally) immobilizing aspects. For higher education, the increasingly prominent role of interdisciplinary centers is one example of mobilizing within institutions. The center structure often allows for reaching across, through, and around traditional departments and even schools in order to focus on some specific topic, problem, or new swath through multidisciplinary terrains. Often, the center exists not within one institution but across multiple institutions that share a similar mission and, by the creation of a center, can broker faculty strengths, equipment, libraries, and other human and material resources.

What then of learning institutions as mobilizing networks in higher education? Driven by faculty and, to some extent, student interest and demand, more and more universities are creating dynamic centers and institutes cutting across disciplines and the institution as a whole, sometimes drawing together into interactive engagement universities across cities, regions, and countries. Building on digital humanities laboratories founded in the early 1990s such as IATH at the University of Virginia (http://www.iath.virginia.edu) or MITH at the University of Maryland (http://www.mith2.umd.edu) and on digital repositories such as PERSEUS at Tufts University (http://www.perseus.tufts.edu) or the Electronic Cultural Atlas Initiative (http://www.ecai.org), which started at the University of California at Berkeley, a newer generation of dynamic learning and research facilities has emerged, drawing on state-of-the-art high-performance computing.

At the University of California at Los Angeles, the Experiential Technologies Center (ETC) (http://www.etc.ucla.edu) creates three-dimensional models across a wide range of disciplines, including architecture, the performing arts, classics, archaeology, foreign language studies, and education. The Center is best known for its innovative work in creating compelling three-dimensional representations of historical sites around the world. Working closely with the University of California at Los Angeles's Center for Digital Humanities (http://www.humnet.ucla.edu/itc/resources/index.html), ETC has been widely used by scholars and students to explore such diverse topics as the structure of the human heart, the architectural and civic formation of the Roman Forum, medieval cities in Europe, or early modern cities in the Caribbean. The Pittsburgh Science of Learning Center (http://www.learnlab.org), run jointly by the University of Pittsburgh and Carnegie Mellon University, recreates learning environments in a laboratory setting so that students and researchers can examine the most effective digital learning instruments and practices. In Sweden, the University of Umea's HUMlab (http://www.humlab.umu.se/about) creates new institutional formations and dynamic cross-disciplinary partnerships to address human informatics, digital culture and art, and shifting conceptions of performance at the interface of the humanities, cultural studies, and information and media technology. It enables students and scholars to explore whether culture and history can be simulated, what can be learned from the visualization of large quantities of data, how modes of narration are altered by computer games, and more generally how modes of communication are transformed by new media.[11]

These are examples—there are many others—of scholars and students, often in partnership with community and corporate interests, mobilizing to develop or leverage existing technological innovation for the purpose of enhancing learning within and beyond the institutional boundaries.

At the same time, the complex bureaucracies that are contemporary universities, including increasing defensiveness and fear of litigation that give rise to procedures that can certainly be immobilizing, should be seen as one of the least savory aspects of modern learning institutions. The distribution of grant funding "indirect costs" is but one of the bureaucratized procedures universities use to systemize redistribution of resources in such a complex and competitive way that, in some instances, failure—or immobility writ large—is the result.

The tensions between the mobile and mobilizing tendencies and the tendencies of institutions toward reification and stasis are, perhaps, a hallmark of the traditional institution of higher education. There is another issue. If one is trying to mobilize effectively on behalf of a new participatory learning practice, if one requires crossing not only disciplinary boundaries but institutional ones, too, where does one begin? How are effective learning networks to be created that reach out to, across, and through all of these different functions and institutional manifestations?

Analogously, is there a way to sustain a learning network without creating fixed rules of organization that, inevitably, replicate exactly the institutional silos one is seeking to diminish as part of the process of reenvisioning learning? The standard organizational model of large academic associations such as the Modern Language Association or the Organization of American Historians has limited the reach of social networking to the one-on-one interpersonal or the anonymity of mass mailings. This seems in its lack of agility and relative immobility to run counter to the potentialities of Web 2.0 social networking and aggregating. What other models might there be?

What we see is a form of interactive learning that radiates outward from traditional educational institutions and inward from other kinds of learning institutions, mobilizing and invigorating both in such creative ways that it is difficult to define the borders of one or another. Mobilizing learning institutions are precisely about eradicating some borders, (re)making others, and in all ways creating energies and interdependencies whereby learning is integrated into all aspects and operations of the multiple lives of larger communities.

The concept of *emergence* is key to thinking through the future of learning institutions.[12] Emergence is the complex process of pattern formation that begins to take shape and evolve as a result of continuous interactions across and among more basic constituent parts or behaviors.[13] Emergence happens constantly in education. New fields emerge. Marginal or peripheral intellectual activity becomes central. Central concerns, likewise, become peripheral. Whole fields change in their focus, methodology, and emphasis. Concomitantly, institutions change as well, sometimes more gradually than one would like, but they do change.

Are there models or principles for how one creates emergent institutions for an emergent field? Contention and resistance are familiar models for field-transformation. And yet, at least as often, new fields emerge in ways that are taken up by and even substantively change the identities of the institution itself. So are there ways that learning institutions can be more innovative and aggressive in support of this latter process while still confident enough to be open to the innovative developments in field (trans)formation that may be a product of the former?

Over a decade ago, John Seely Brown and Paul Duguid suggested that the university of the future might not even look like a university. They proposed that higher education might itself become something more flexible, flowing, integrated, networked, distributed, inventive—something that "breaks down the monolith" of university credentialing, training, and (in all senses) disciplinary field-definition.[14] If one looked at universities from on high, one indeed would see many tentacles reaching out in complex new collaborative directions that seem to underscore the validity of Brown and Duguid's prediction. And yet there are other features of universities that resemble nineteenth-century Germany or medieval England far more than they do the networked, knowledge-sharing, global open learning models of the Net Age. This is not to say that the latter are all good, the former all bad. But to ignore the deep changes in conditions and structures of learning—in what and how learning takes place among and across and beyond learners today, when we learn and with and through whom, by what means and with what interest(s)—is to lose one of the most generative educational *opportunities* in recent history.

Institutions are mobilizing networks.

At the same time, we must use our networks to mobilize our institutions. That is the interactive imperative of the digital age.

6   HASTAC: A Case Study of a Virtual Learning Institution as a Mobilizing Network

Institutions are mobilizing networks. This is a provocative definition. It is also highly abstract. Just as it is useful to imagine a specific course (e.g., FLIDA 101) in order to address both the pedagogical potentials and institutional obstacles of digital learning, it is helpful to think about a specific mobilizing network in order to see the ways in which it operates. The most obvious candidate for this conversation is HASTAC, the virtual learning network that the authors of this book cofounded with several colleagues in 2002–2003 (figures 6.1 and 6.2).

What is HASTAC?

HASTAC is the Humanities, Arts, Science, and Technology Advanced Collaboratory, pronounced "haystack." The point in such an unwieldy name is to avoid privileging one discipline, field, or institutional faculty over another. The academy, if indeed there is just one these days, is considerably messier, more amorphous, and more heterogeneous than its post-eighteenth century composition.

HASTAC is a collaboratory. The term *collaboratory*, according to Wikipedia, was coined in 1989 by engineer William Wulf

Figure 6.1
Screenshot of HASTAC home page from 2008 (http://www.hastac.org, accessed June 15, 2008).

and is defined as a "center without walls, in which the nation's researchers can perform their research without regard to physical location, interacting with colleagues, accessing instrumentation, sharing data and computational resources, [and] accessing information in digital libraries."[1] HASTAC takes that science-prompted definition and expands it to include the humanities, social sciences, and the arts as well. What would an expansive, transdisciplinary collaboratory driven by common interests in engaging digital media to expand the boundaries of collaboratively produced knowledge formation look like? HASTAC is our response, at least at this slice of knowledge-creating history.

Primarily focusing on higher education, HASTAC also supports affiliated efforts in youth learning and K–12 education. The network has members who operate outside and beyond any formal educational institutions yet who remain actively engaged in all forms of digital learning. All share (in many different

Figure 6.2
Screenshot of HASTAC home page from 2009 (http://www.hastac.org,
accessed on July 31, 2009).

ways) the common dedication to using and developing the most creative learning and research technologies while, at the same time, thinking critically about the role of technology in learning and in society as a whole.

HASTAC has taken a leadership role in developing an interactive network for scholars engaged in the technological, pedagogical, humanistic, and sociocultural explorations central to Web 2.0 learning. As an institution, HASTAC is unusual, but its form is becoming increasingly common as more and more educators become familiar with social networking sites and what educators can both contribute and learn simply by participating.

HASTAC is a voluntary organization. To become a member, one simply registers to the HASTAC Web site. More than 2700 individuals were registered HASTAC members as of summer 2009.

To become a HASTAC leader, one volunteers what one has to offer in collaborative and complementary engagements with others in leadership roles. Contributions are open ended, ranging from posting blog entries or creating an affiliated HASTAC social network dedicated to a particular topic, to something more tangible such as holding a HASTAC conference.

The HASTAC Web site (http://www.hastac.org) promotes access that is as open as the community standards of the site can support, so long as participants are clearly serving HASTAC's overarching mission. It is loosely moderated to protect the network from commercial spammers and irrelevant, inappropriate, or offensive material.

In short, HASTAC is an information commons, a social network, and a blog-hosting Web site, with various events announced throughout the year. It operates as a network of networks, reaching expansively across existing or emerging networks. And, as such, it is also a partnering—a social networking—matchmaker. Not unlike Craigslist (http://www.craigslist.org), it matches researchers' interests, drawing into research partnerships humanistic content providers with high-level computer engineering or programming skills, students eager to learn collaboratively with experts thrilled to convey their knowledge interactively. The information commons is facilitated through an online bulletin board, called *Needle* (http://www.hastac.org/needle). *Needle* posts pertinent items as they become available, ranging from relevant news items to grants and fellowships, employment opportunities, book and research announcements, conferences, and workshops.

Examining what HASTAC is, how it operates, what ways it works to mobilize energies at and across institutions, and also the way it is supported by a variety of institutions adds specificity to the discussion of the future of learning institutions in a digital age. Like the peer-to-peer models of learning, social communication, publicity, and communitarian ranking, HASTAC provides a site and set of mechanisms where a loosely defined community of affiliates interacts through peer-to-peer connectivity. New offshoots (e.g., HASTAC teacher subgroup on Ning, "A Synergistic Symposium for the Cybernetic Age," which focuses mostly on K–12) emerge, organizing their own social networks as part of the larger HASTAC network.[2]

The HASTAC network often provides individuals who are isolated, marginalized, sometimes even underappreciated within their departments or institutions access to a distributed community. Of crucial importance, it is leading to the formative emergence of a complex interdisciplinary field within which present (and future) research can be assessed, evaluated, distributed, and utilized. HASTAC's partnering with the MacArthur Foundation has contributed to this catalyzing of a field which, for the academy, partly means forming cross-disciplinary networks of referees who can judge the quality of one another's

work (for hiring, tenure, promotion, or publication) while informing others (e.g., administrators) of the importance of this kind
of research, teaching, and writing.

HASTAC embraces a range of diversities as part of its mission
and encourages intellectuals at universities without adequate
resources to provide leadership grounded in, quite precisely, the
collaborative and community networking skills and ingenuities
required by the lack of resources. At the same time, these institutions can partake, through webcasts and collaboration, in
possibilities available at institutions with far greater financial
and technological resources and expertise. HASTAC's goal is to
establish the firm foundations for field-building by reaching
out across an extraordinarily wide constituency. In disciplinary
terms, this means drawing from humanities and arts institutes,
social science organizations, supercomputing and grid computing institutes, and technology and engineering centers. This
mix includes the leading institutions of their kind in the United
States and abroad as well as minority-serving organizations
designed to include less-advantaged learning institutions.

In its boldest vision, HASTAC aims to support an emerging
generation of scholars equally at ease with current (which is also
to say historical) knowledge in the humanities, arts, and social
sciences, on the one hand, and with the technological, scientific, and engineering knowledge, on the other. By identifying a
field, however loosely defined, HASTAC helps to certify a range
of skills, interests, and specializations that might otherwise
seem irrelevant to those in more traditional disciplines. Does it
matter that an English teacher knows hypertext markup language and teaches hypertext markup to students interested in
digital humanities? Does it count that a historian has created a
worldwide research network building a multinational and multilingual archive for the comparative study of the laws pertain-

ing to slavery and abolitionism? Is a monograph not the point of these professions? In short, what is the relevant range of content and technological knowledge to be reproduced in and across disciplines today? These are the kinds of issues that HASTAC addresses. By addressing these issues, HASTAC helps to expand the criteria for rewards and recognition. In so doing, it helps develop the institutional credibility of the field. Without such credibility, younger scholars entering into digital learning fields have little chance of success.

HASTAC represents different genres of interdisciplinary humanistic technology projects, with some coming down much more on the humanistic than the technological side of that term and others weighted in the opposite direction. HASTAC leader Anne Balsamo notes that the HASTAC taxonomy includes (but is not limited to): electronic literature, humanities computing projects, Web portals, cultural informatics, and multimodal publishing.[3] It also includes Global Position Survey projects focusing on political geography, access grid communication projects, visualization and sonification projects, digital archiving, research and learning in virtual environments, multimedia exhibits and concerts, and a range of other endeavors across interdisciplinary spectrums as well as deep within disciplines and subdisciplines.

Finally, in terms of audience, Patricia Seed notes that HASTAC also serves two quite different audiences with different needs and skill levels. She notes that "the first audience consists of scholars and potential scholars who have or can acquire technological, scientific, and engineering skills. They need a support network where they can find a community that can critique their projects, inform them of related work occurring in their fields(s), and at best locate potential collaborators." HASTAC has a second audience of academics and academics-in-training who do not have the skills to advance or create technical, scientific, and engineering tools in a particular area but who are comfortable with the existing tools (e.g., blogging, distributed applications such as Google Maps). They are eager to incorporate these tools into college and general education. This audience needs user-friendly how-to directions with varied successful examples, online help sources, and discussion boards for solutions to problems.[4]

These characteristics exist at the level of ideas. This chapter focuses on the more material, infrastructural supports and costs to HASTAC. HASTAC could not exist without financial and technical support from the University of California and Duke University and without leadership and assistance of the staff at the interdisciplinary centers at those two institutions, UCHRI, physically located in Irvine, and the John Hope Franklin Humanities Institute within the larger John Hope Franklin Center for Interdisciplinary and International Studies at Duke.

A Web 2.0 Institution

Tim O'Reilly's optimistic definitions of Web 2.0—*many-to-many collaborating* and *customizing together*—need to be reexamined. As corporations such as Google (the largest Web 2.0 corporation) control and data mine more and more of the world's personal, corporate, institutional, and national information, one must be concerned about unregulated sharing, and when user-generated content becomes someone else's source of profit. What happens the day Google buys Wikipedia, a colleague's digital archive of Ancient Rome 3D, or early Portuguese maps of West Africa?[5]

Yet even though the concept is vague or open to exploitative, monopolistic, or oligopolistic practices, Web 2.0 is a convenient way of signaling a new type of institution. It is one where contributions are distributed rather than coming from a single physical location and where ideas are shared outside the normal rules of tenure, credentialing, and professional peer review. HASTAC is an institution where the knowledge sharing is based on peer-to-peer interactivity rather than hierarchical peer certification.

These new learning communities embody a range of distributed diversities—in networking skills, ingenuities, and facilities, as well as in resources and background experience. They represent robust interdisciplinarity and expansive virtual heterogeneity, as well as an equal ease with their more or less specialized fields of knowledge and with their knowledge of technology.

The challenge is to devise institutional learning structures to facilitate, accommodate, and accredit these new learning forms and their outcomes. The other challenge is to use HASTAC's success and its remarkable global reach to be precisely that institution (however virtual) that is also a mobilizing network.

If we do, indeed, live on the long tail, then virtual institutions such as HASTAC may be the long virtual tail that wags the dog of the traditional educational institutions without which it could not exist.

HASTAC: A History

In 2001, the Mellon Foundation held a workshop to help invigorate leadership at humanities centers. In the course of the meeting, it became clear that the group at the very least had not yet awakened to the pull of new digital media, perhaps implicitly even seeing it as a (potential) threat to the humanities. By contrast, a small minority understood new media not as threat but as an affirmation and reinvigoration of the oldest traditions of the humanities. In particular, new digital media were seen to raise anew concerns with human life, human rights, human ideas, and human communication. Notions of property and

privacy, identity and community, long key concerns of humanistic inquiry and commentary across human history, take on
new resonance when considered as newly applicable to the present social and academic arrangements.

The repeated lament about the "crisis in the humanities" is a
tiresome and outmoded approach. *If the humanities themselves
understood their full power,* they would reassume a central place
not only in the academy but in a society confused over these
myriad new developments. In the wake of these developments,
other like-minded humanists, artists, social scientists, scientists, and engineers with a similarly broad and complementary
vision were identified.[6] Some were new to thinking about the
application of digital technology to the humanities; others had
been long at work on the movement that had started out as
humanities *and* computing. A network of fellow practitioners
quickly materialized, drawing into the fold a newly emergent
paradigm of those concerned with analyzing and utilizing the
new possibilities of the digital era. Thus began HASTAC.

HASTAC is not traditional humanities computing or even
traditional digital humanities. While supportive of traditional
humanities computing (at least initially largely text-based digi-
tization projects), HASTAC's mission is in the codevelopment
and analysis of new learning and research technologies and
their implications for individuals and societies. The focus has
been on novel and inventive ways of learning with, through,
and about new media.

HASTAC is *not* an organization in any traditional sense. It is
a voluntary networked consortium of individuals and the
institutions represented—a mobilizing network or peer-to-peer
institution. It is committed to a different, interdisciplinary, collaborative view of higher education and, by extension, of education more generally in the digital world. It is as committed to

issues of social equity as to technological innovation and as committed to theory as practice (and vice versa). At present, social credit (not capital) is the main cost of admission to HAS-TAC. Those who do the work, who produce, and who contribute effectively lead the network.[7]

While HASTAC has completed many projects to date (e.g., a toolkit of software and other resources created collaboratively), one of its most dramatic public outcomes is the shared, distributed, coordinated In|Formation Year (2006–2007) (figure 6.3). This field-building year offered one public conference or mediated event per month, sponsored by several centers or institutes at one geographical location, then offered up to a global public via webcasts, podcasts, vodcasts, and even cell phone distribution. At the individual sites, courses, programs, seminars, and workshops focused on the site's particular In|Formation theme. In aggregate, the In|Formation Year was a way of gathering together those scholars and students dedicated to rethinking what constitutes learning in a digital age.

The In|Formation Year began with a graduate-student conference, "Thinking Through New Media" in June 2006. The conference was cosponsored by the Information Studies+Information Science (ISIS) program at Duke University and the Renaissance Computing Institute (a high-performance supercomputing organization based at the University of North Carolina and serving the entire state). This graduate-student conference had a limited registration of 65 (because of space restrictions). Many who would have liked to participate had to be turned away.

Starting in September 2006 and ending in May 2007, HASTAC hosted a full academic year of collaborative productions of face-to-face events at the host site and then webcast to a larger audience. For the hosting site, the events required new intellectual

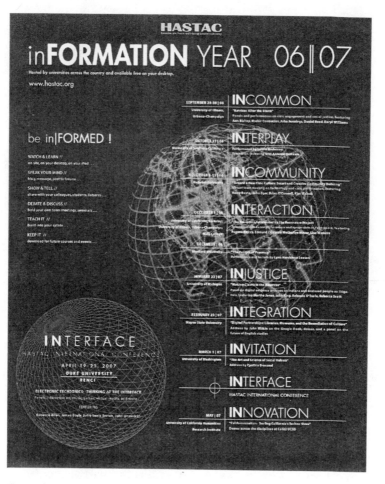

Figure 6.3
HASTAC In|Formation Year poster (http://hastac-new.aas.duke.edu/events/information-year-integration, accessed July 29, 2009.

boundary crossing, administrative buy-in to a new concept of what *technology* is and means, and an expansive sense of the arts, humanities, and social sciences assuming a leadership role in the production of novel kinds of content and innovative technologies for both the larger community and for an international virtual audience. Each site bore the cost of its own event, and each decided upon its own level of involvement and institutional commitment. This ranged from a simple webcast or podcast panel discussion to a full-out conference with elaborate technological innovation.

All of the events centered on In|Formation themes. The point was that information is not just about hardware and software, nor just about data in a narrow reductive sense. In|Formation indicates the complex ways in which information is produced at the interface of conceptual ordering and technological production, between data, its conceptual layering, instrumentation, and effective use. Information, in short, is always complexly in formation. Learning is in good part coming to an understanding of the intricate and interactive processes by which information is always in formation, today not least as a result of the overdetermining applications of new information technologies, of new media. With this comprehensive understanding of information in mind, the themes selected for the year were: In|Common, Interplay, In|Community, Interaction, Integration, Injustice, Invitation, Interface, and Innovation. The In|Formation Year was designed as a field-building enterprise that demonstrated the power of peer-to-peer institution-building on local and global levels.

This year of exciting, collaborative events, taken together, illustrated the possibilities for e-enabled interactive collaborative learning across traditional institutions. At once structured and improvisational, fueled by sustained knowledge of deep structures and by innovative experimentation, this form of networked learning required trust and risk-taking, individual and interactive effort, shared knowledge and committed resources, and recourse to the tried and tested plus openness to the new, no matter the source. It required the recognition that theory without embodiment can be alienating, but that data or content or embodiment without the structuring of theoretical principle can be simplistic, ungrounded, and confusing. It involved the drive to succeed and a willingness to learn from failure and knowing when to push and when the game is up. And it meant being open to the fact that no matter how tough the going gets, learning and teaching should be fun all around.

The first HASTAC conference took place at Duke in April 2007 as part of the Interface events. "Electronic Techtonics: Thinking at the Interface" welcomed 150 participants and consisted of plenary sessions by visionary engineer and self-styled "Chief of Confusion," John Seely Brown; by legal scholar (a cofounder of Creative Commons and the Center for the Study of the Public Domain) James Boyle; by new media artist Rebecca Allen; and by humanities computing pioneer and leader of the American Council of Learned Society's Commission on Cyberinfrastructure for the Humanities and Social Sciences, John Unsworth. "Electronic Techtonics" also held a digital poster hall, virtual reality exhibits and a sensor-space interactive museum of the history of the Information Age, a multimedia dance concert, and numerous panels of refereed papers and public forums. The conference was videotaped and is viewable on the HASTAC Web site; the papers from the refereed panels have been published in a volume issued under Creative Commons by Lulu, the open-source press.[8]

An important component of "Electronic Techtonics" was a forum on "The Future of Learning" addressed to the general public, to schoolteachers, and to academics (figure 6.4). The

Figure 6.4
The Future of Learning Poster (http://www.hastac.org/blogs/cathy
-davidson/who-our-role-model-future-learning,   accessed   July   29,
2009).

focus was on "what the digital future holds for learning and
education," and thus provided an explicitly pedagogical imperative to the experimental, technical, legal, social, artistic, and
critical issues raised by the other sessions.

The final event of the HASTAC In|Formation Year ended,
appropriately, with Innovation. This closing event of the series,
held at Calit2 at the University of California at San Diego in
conjunction with UCHRI, included state-of-the-art demo projects at the interface of humanities–arts–social sciences, and the
digital presentation of work across the University of California.
The afternoon consisted of demonstrations of innovative arts-
related projects, designed to inspire new projects, not close off

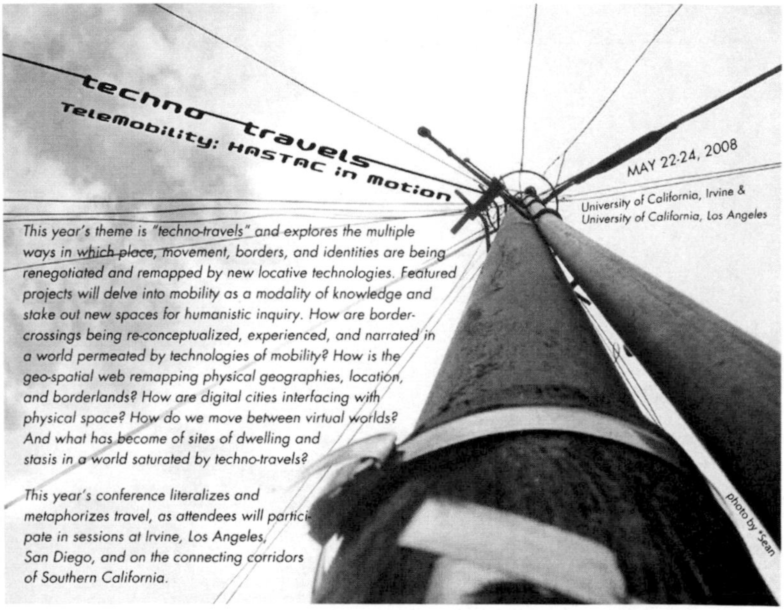

Figure 6.5
Poster for the 2008 HASTAC Conference in California (http://www.
hastac.org/forums/conference-announcements-and-calls-papers/cfp
-fourth-international-conference-foundations-dig, accessed July 29,
2009).

the activity of the year. These included SPECFLIC, artist Adriene Jenik's new-media project, and the use of multispectral
imaging and analytical tools to reveal hidden histories in major
artworks, with potentially revolutionary implications for their
interpretation and understanding. The latter is innovative work
being conducted by Calit2's new Center of Interdisciplinary
Science for Art, Architecture and Archaeology (CISA3), directed
by Maurizio Serracini (figure 6.5).[9]

HASTAC has been actively engaged in training activities for graduate students and faculty across the digital humanities. As part of the In|Formation Year activities, UCHRI, the San Diego Supercomputing Center, and the educational division of the national TeraGrid initiative funded by the National Science Foundation offered a one-week skills-building, hands-on workshop, "Cyberinfrastructure for the Humanities, Arts, and Social Sciences" in July 2006. The workshop, repeated in summer 2007, introduced scholars to an array of learning technologies from global positioning system and various visualization technologies to semantic Web, database conception, construction, searches, gaming, and other applications widely used in the sciences and beneficial to educators and learners across all domains as well.

In August 2006, UCHRI ran a visionary and ambitious two-week-long intensive workshop, "technoSpheres: futureS of Thinking." Coconvened by David Theo Goldberg and University of Southern California professor (and HASTAC coleader) Anne Balsamo, the event was part of UCHRI's annual Seminar in Experimental Critical Theory (SECT). It was attended by approximately 65 people, along with the almost 40 instructing participants. There were backchannel conversation and daily blogging on the HASTAC Web site, as well as on an even more ambitious UCHRI gaming site that was finalized, collaboratively, and put to hard use by the sophisticated SECT fellows during the two-week workshop. Most of the fellows were graduate students or young professionals, although several full professors also participated as "students."

Through the two weeks, word got around and some notable names in the field—John Seely Brown, Lev Manovich, Katherine Hayles, George Lewis, Craig Calhoun, Saskia Sassen, Larry Smarr, Geert Lovink, Lynn Hershman, and Guillermo Gomez-Pena—stayed around or dropped in to feel the pulse of an extraordinary

set of events. As with the previous activities, nearly all participants in the SECT group self-identified as loners within their
home institutions. Many joked that they were scholars in search
of a field. SECT provided a cohort for most of its multidisciplinary and multitasking fellows. It was an exhilarating two
weeks of ideas and interchange; it was, in short, both a glimpse
of and planning for the future. Each day began with a panel of
paired thinkers from different fields: technology leaders, media
artists, game designers, electronic publishers, social scientists,
and humanists, all dedicated to and with significant experience
in practicing new ways of thinking. Afternoons were spent with
hands-on project development and breakout groups. Evenings
(usually lasting until late at night—organizers sent participants
home at 11:00 p.m.) were dedicated to demonstrations, media
projects, screenings, and other multimedia events.[10]

Since he started running the Institute for Computing in the
Humanities, Arts, and Social Sciences for the National Center
for Supercomputing Applications at the University of Illinois in
2007, Kevin Franklin has expanded the number of training
workshops in cyberinfrastructure for humanities, arts, and
social sciences. He has also worked to encourage the adoption
by HASTAC scholars of high-performance computing facilities
at major national computing laboratories to advance research
in humanities, arts, and social sciences.

Separately, HASTAC has also initiated a HASTAC Scholars
Program (http://www.hastac.org/scholars). The program, begun
in 2008, recognizes graduate and undergraduate students
engaged in innovative work across the areas of technology, the
arts, the humanities, and the social sciences. This group of
HASTAC Scholars from institutions across the nation form a
virtual network, bringing the work happening on their campuses and in their regions into interactive engagement and to

international attention. The Scholars spend the year as part of a virtual community of 50–100 students creating, reporting on, blogging, vlogging, and podcasting events related to digital media and learning for an international audience. The HASTAC Scholars also orchestrate a regular discussion forum on the HASTAC Web site featuring their own ground-breaking research and interests alongside those of leaders and innovators in the digital humanities, such as social networking pioneer Howard Rheingold or Brett Bobley, the director of the Office of Digital Humanities for the National Endowment for the Humanities.

HASTAC/MacArthur Foundation Digital Media and Learning Competition

After completing the In|Formation Year, HASTAC embarked on a partnership with the John D. and Catherine T. MacArthur Foundation to run the Digital Media and Learning Competition (http://www.dmlcompetition.net). The MacArthur Foundation established a $2 million prize to be distributed among 15 to 20 winning projects to reward innovative work in digital media and learning. The competition serves to surface the extraordinary activity taking place in these areas that neither the MacArthur Foundation nor HASTAC might have identified previously, to network winning projects, and to share solutions and best practices in the most open-source environment possible.

Since the opening of the competition's first round in August 2007, the interest has been intense. Web site activity for the first year of the competition received nearly 60,000 visits, approximately 30,000 occurring in the "absolute unique visitor" category. The average visitor clicked through 6.24 pages, indicating serious interest. Visitors came from 139 countries and used 55 languages, even though the first year's competition required a U.S.-based principal investigator. But even with so much activity, no one expected the final tally. When the competition closed in mid-October 2007, 1,010 applications had been filed. The second year of the competition accordingly narrowed its focus to participatory learning prompted and enabled by digital media. Eligible participation was expanded to include 10 countries in addition to the United States, where the MacArthur Foundation and HASTAC had working relations. A unique category was added aimed at youth innovators, specifically 18- to 25-year-olds, interested in facilitating the development of innovative digital media learning projects from the garage to a broader theater of adoptability. In the second year, almost 700 applications were filed, 33 in the youth category and 133 from countries outside the United States. The third year will open the competition internationally, with no geographic restrictions.

Clay Shirky writes of the common Internet experience of the "crisis of success."[11] He describes numerous stories of stunning victories that went bust, precisely because the virtual can be built on so little with so little and then, in a heartbeat, be called upon to deliver so much. There are many such allegories in other fields (publishing best sellers at small presses can similarly spell disaster), but the Internet seems to spawn such stories daily. A couple of street dancers create a dance and a song and upload it to YouTube. Suddenly, Soulja Boy is everyone, everywhere. Prisoners in the Philippines are doing the dance (and uploading their video to YouTube). Television appearances, a record deal, a release, and, by their second single, the kids from Atlanta are moaning about paparazzi and con men and lack of privacy. Who knows what the end of this story will be? In the virtual city, fame and fortune comes, and just as fleetingly goes. And sometimes it comes again.

Because so much of what happens on the Internet happens for the first time and without expectation or preparation, because there are so many new things to try and so many complex viral ways of communicating them, one never knows if 10 people or 10,000 or 1 million will show up at the flash mob experience or for the virtual party. Many an Internet business has collapsed because too many people appeared at the door. There were too many visitors for the hardware, software, and, most important, the human support could not keep up with demand.

HASTAC is in something of this situation now. With pride at its accomplishments in helping to create the architecture for and administering the Digital Media and Learning Competition, HASTAC is also now attempting to manage the "crisis of success." With HASTAC team members focusing on running the Digital Media and Learning Competition, there is little time for actual fundraising to support HASTAC's other operations or to expand its staff so that future competitions are not overwhelmed by so much success. More to the point, networks rarely perpetuate themselves. Unless they are populated, active, and exciting, fickle participants move on. That has not yet happened at HASTAC, which continues to grow, but it is a source of anxiety.

This is, after all, the parable and peril of every virtual organization. Many-to-many can be a gold rush or an avalanche. Choose your metaphor! In either case, it is easy to overwhelm a small, dedicated team, comprised mostly of volunteers. It is easy for a virtual institution's goals to be swamped by its own success.[12]

One more consideration: HASTAC is not just a virtual network but a network of networks. That compounds both the possibilities and the challenges of sustainability. The possibilities are fueled by the inputs from the individual networks that make up its membership, most if not all of them institutionally based. The activities of local networks become aggregated into the network of networks, fueling the latter in and through their own activities. The activities of local networks get added to the network of networks, while drawing on resources available from the super-aggregation of effort, people, and resources. But where the benefits to local networks are seen to lag, where local networks are absorbed in their own activities without perpetual prompt or pull into the larger network, the likelihood of continued engagement or contribution will lag, if not recede. A network of networks like HASTAC, a mobilizing network, accordingly requires constant attendance and attention, investment, encouragement, and publicity as reminders of the benefits of continued effort and engagement. But absent continued effort and engagement, the benefits are likely to dissipate. Once again, this is the challenge of the commons.[13]

HASTAC as a Trust Network

Unlike most organizations, HASTAC has no formal rules—only action items. Loyalty is based on a shared mission, passion for the play of ideas and practices, and on clear, observable follow-through and deliverables.[14] As many commentators have noted, "developing a high-trust virtual community is no easy task."[15] HASTAC has succeeded where many more formal organizations have failed, at least partly through what Hassan Masum and Yi-Cheng Zhang call the "interconnected ecology of socially beneficial reputation systems." [16] And yet HASTAC is a tiny mobilizing network in a vast system of higher learning, which, in too many instances, is characterized by lockbox knowledge, competitive Internet protocol interests, disciplinary silos, and other subtle and explicit ways of keeping learning local. Sadly, this is as true of public institutions as it is of private institutions; in any case, it is a distinction increasingly breaking down today (many large public institutions, such as the University of California and the University of Michigan, receive significantly less than 25 percent of their annual budgets from local state treasuries, and this percentage is declining).

The challenge is how to move to a more "open" idea of learning. It is a challenge, too, to move to a new definition of *institution* that both recognizes the constituencies that every university needs to address and offers its constituencies the best possibilities for collaborative learning suitable to the Net Age. The In|Formation Year was intended to form new networks and to inform the public, educators, administrators, and students about potentials for cross-institutional and cross-interdisciplinary e-learning in an In|Formation Age that is as much about injustice as it is about innovation.

HASTAC has existed as something like an emergent institution, and its constituents and its mission are far from monolithic. HASTAC leaders at the distributed sites learn with and from each other. They determine in practice and in situ what works and what does not. Each is a mobilizing network and distributed center of learning. HASTAC's events are inherently collaborative undertakings; they are experimental ventures, with shared failures *and* productive outcomes (e.g., see figures 6.2 and 6.3).

New models for peer-to-peer institutions and mobilizing networks are needed. At present, there are many routes to stabilization: individual memberships, collective memberships, external grant funding, commercialization, or absorption into a larger, commercially-viable nonprofit organization such as EDUCAUSE. None of these models on its own is a sufficient condition for the creation of a field. It is possible that a hybrid model will prove productive in cementing and sustaining a field with sufficient flexibility to accommodate the rapidly transforming conditions of digital learning. This book seeks to help discover what other models exist, which are the most feasible, and what are the true potentialities for the institution as a mobilizing network.

Other Models, Other Possibilities

What other models are there? That is not a rhetorical question but an actual one. When this question was posed to readers of the draft of this book on the Institute for the Future of the Book Web site, numerous responses were received, several of which have been incorporated into this chapter. Steve Jones noted that one element is missing in this discussion of institutions: the personal element. "Where are the people?" he asks, "They seem implicit in this discussion but oddly removed."[17]

This is a completely valid point. In fact, it is actual people— whether face-to-face or in virtual environments—who are responsible for mobilizing networks. And one issue that HAS-TAC has not yet confronted is what happens when there is a change in leadership? What happens when the current enthusiasm of the leaders wanes? In business, there is much discussion of "the crisis of the third generation." Those in the first generation—those who found a business—give it all of their attention. Even the second generation, who typically were there at the founding, continue to be invested. However, by the third generation, there is enough distance between the zealous or enthusiastic founding vision—the mobilizing energy of mobilizing networks—and the everyday life of cranking out a productive operation. As a result, enthusiasm if not attention often flags. For many in the third generation, the business is no longer a point of personal pride and identification but is, basically, a cash cow. Often the business runs aground because of infighting among too many heirs, disputes in how the company should be run, lack of energy by the new directors, or a cultural conflict in the day-to-day sensibilities of the place as it has come to be and how it is thought it ought to be by new management. Virtual institutions, like actual businesses, face the same issues of leadership and succession. And, as Clay Shirky notes, for virtual businesses—especially those that have no profit to offer to those who work hard on their behalf—the human failures are far more catastrophic and the potential for failure even greater than in the so-called real world.

HASTAC as a 501(c)(3)

One reason for the difference is, precisely, institutional grounding. Without that real institutional identity, the role of individuals—even networked individuals—is far more important than it probably should be to ensure long-term survival. As Mike Roy notes in this regard, it is "hard to underestimate the force of the support provided by the traditional institutions involved in this work. While clearly we don't here propose the disbanding of all institutions of higher education in favor of these informal, ad hoc, emergent entities, the faculty who do this work are (we assume) largely paid their salaries and medical benefits and retirement contributions by these old-fashioned bricks and mortar (or bricks and clicks) schools that charge tuition, have endowments, etc. and therefore are powerful enablers of this work. The money matters."[18]

This statement could not be more true. HASTAC's support comes from universities, foundations, and government grant-making institutions. Costs for events by individual organizations are borne by those organizations. Infrastructure is largely born by the two pillar institutions, Duke University and the University of California. How long can this last? How long will it hold? Those are questions that can not be answered for a variety of reasons. Perhaps most important and least tangible is the idea of respect, reputation, and credit. Why should a traditional institution support a virtual institution, however successful, whose credit is dispersed? Traditional institutions do not always like to support that which does not prominently bear their name; a network cannot hold and gain members if some institutions are more prominently advertised than others. Altruism is not the best business practice for ensuring sustainability.

Yet all of the normal roads to sustainability point up the significance of actual institutions for supporting virtual ones. For example, in exploring the possibility of pursuing 501(c)(3) status[19] for HASTAC, it became clear just how much HASTAC owes its supporting institutions, Duke University and the University of California. For example, the infrastructural and especially technological support for HASTAC is all located at one of those two institutions. Although a number of staff are paid solely or partly on grants, others are not. All staff, even those on grant funding, receive pension, health care, and other benefits from one of those two institutions. As a 501(c)(3), HASTAC would not be eligible to be part of these pension programs. It would have to find other ways to pay benefits, outside the umbrella, shield, and collective pools of Duke University and the University of California.

Other factors would also come into play. If HASTAC were a totally separate corporation, it would have to pay rent for office space. It would have to hire technology support. It would, in other words, have to pay for all that Duke University and the

University of California now give as in-kind support to HAS-TAC. HASTAC would have to purchase insurance against possible liabilities that are now assumed by the universities that employ and certify HASTAC's staff.

By the rules of Duke University and the University of California, if HASTAC were an independent 501(c)(3), the amount of time its staff spent contributing to HASTAC would be limited. The salaries of its staff are paid by the institutions, and the staff members are paid to do primary work on behalf of and representing those institutions. Even though the University of California and Duke University are not part of the HASTAC brand name, the names of those respective institutions supporting this innovative virtual one are evident (http://www.hastac.org). There is a luster to innovation, and presumably HASTAC sheds some of that back on the universities. As a 501(c)(3), everyone would have to be careful to keep HASTAC at arms' length from the two universities, and the universities would do the same. There would be limits on how much of the staff's time could be spent consulting for this private nonprofit. Although it would only cost about $3,000 or $4,000 to incorporate in one state, to do this across states is difficult. The taxation rules for independent nonprofits are notably tricky. In any state, filing for this status and working it through all the state approval processes can take a lot of time and attention.

Nor are the legal matters over once such status is granted. One next needs to apply for 501(c)(3) status with the Internal Revenue Service, which requires more forms and more legal bills, which can run in the thousands if not tens of thousands of dollars for the entire process. Again, operating between two states has specific complications. Factoring in 80 or more centers and institutes across many states and in different countries would add to the complications.

Added to the other duties of overseeing a social network and a communications node in a network of networks, HASTAC's administrators suddenly would be responsible for an array of bureaucratic tasks such as running the payroll and obtaining support from local civic authorities (which would need a plan for appropriate management systems for payroll, health, and retirement benefits). These various forms of approval would be required, as would the creation of bylaws, a formal corporate board, a dues structure, liability and fiduciary legal structures, and the kinds of structures and governance of such major professional associations as the Modern Language Association or the Anthropological Association of America.

The Bottom Line Is Not Just the Bottom Line

Institutions are not just about economic supports, nor are the seemingly free worlds of the Internet beyond institutions or beyond economics. The bottom line is that, like many virtual institutions, HASTAC is supported by its institutional homes in myriad ways. The actual financial support to HASTAC (which is modest, since most of HASTAC is accomplished by voluntary, pro bono, and distributed labor) may well be less significant than the infrastructural supports these institutional homes provide to a virtual network of networks. HASTAC's independence as a virtual network would, ironically, be more limited were we to try to be institutionally separate and *independent*.

The emphasis on the word *independent* is meant to signal a larger point: The virtual and the real, the digital institution and the traditional one, are entwined in innumerable and complex ways. It is one role of a virtual learning network such as HASTAC to make those ways as visible and as productive as possible.

As Yochai Benkler emphasizes in *The Wealth of Networks: How Social Production Transforms Markets and Freedom*, there are many economic forms that are not strictly about proprietary motivations, profit, or market appropriations, and yet they are economic nonetheless.[20] Such things as reputation and credit are the intangibles exchanged between major, traditional institutions and upstart and start-up virtual ones such as HASTAC. Each institutional form has something to offer, something to gain from, and something that counterbalances the other. It is certainly not an equal exchange, but it is one that needs to be factored into the definition of *institution*. The institution as a stable social establishment and the institution as an organizing and mobilizing social network are both key now. As Benkler notes, "It is a mistake to think that we have only two basic free transactional forms—property-based markets and hierarchically organized firms. We have three, and the third is social sharing and exchange. It is a widespread phenomenon—we live and practice it every day with our household members, coworkers, and neighbors. We coproduce and exchange economic goods and services. But we do not count these in the economic senses. Worse, we do not count them in our institutional design."[21]

These transactional forms need to be counted in institutional design, because, in every way, these nonmaterial forms of exchange need to count.

7 (In)Conclusive: Thinking the Future of Digital Thinking

A 1998 report by Robert Kraut at the Carnegie Mellon University indicated that the chief reason people turn to social networking on the Internet is because they are "lonely."[1] A few years later, this study was revisited. It turns out that Internet online social networkers are not that lonely after all. Rather, they are people who enjoy communicating with others. They like sharing their specific intellectual or social interests, they like talking about them, and they like meeting people who share these interests, even if they might be far removed from them geographically. They are more interested in creating communities of common concern and interest, and the Internet enables them to ignore physical distance. New studies indicate that Internet use correlates with other forms of sociality and other forms of literacy.[2]

The gap between these two studies is intriguing for the future of learning institutions. It is indubitably the case that many who seek new knowledge networks and virtual affiliations do so because they are isolated—but not in the way that Kraut's 1998 report suggested. They may well be isolated within their disciplines and departments, on their home campuses or more broadly. They may well have few, if any, other colleagues within their institutions who share their vision. They could be described as "lonely," at least intellectually, but not with the implication of being self-isolating "loners." Quite the contrary, they may well be lonely in the sense of pioneers, lonely because they are staking out a new field.

Such a questing state of intellectual loneliness may be a mark of the early stage of an emergent field. Individuals have insights, work on developments, breaking with the given and well established. They may find their work greeted with skepticism or dismissed as peripheral and their findings rejected as anomalous or irrelevant. Over time, they discover others working in similar directions who find the intellectual lines of development they are pursuing to be productive, and they begin to communicate and then collaborate with these new colleagues. Prior to the availability of social networking tools, and indeed of the Internet in a broader sense, the development of this second phase of intellectual field-building would have taken longer. Their work would first have to appear in journals or be presented at conferences, for others, usually at different institutions, to recognize commonalities.

Social networking applications have now quickened this dynamic of intellectual exchange and perhaps even transformed it. One of the first things inquiring people do is to search out productive lines of investigation by others in the field or area in which they are (or are thinking about) working. Colleagues committed to expanding the ways in which new media technologies could be put to productive purpose in pedagogy and research turn to each other for guidance and for collaborative engagement. The physical and metaphoric walls containing and constraining emergence and development of new intellectual directions are more quickly shattered. Representation is key to recognition; recognition is key to change.

Institutions are mobilizing networks. And, conversely, mobilized networks change institutions.

New digital tools have the potential to make group participation more mobile, global, and powerful than in previous decades. In *Here Comes Everybody,* Clay Shirky notes:[3]

> We are so natively good at group effort that we often factor groups out of our thinking about the world. Many jobs that we regard as the province of a single mind actually require a crowd. Michelangelo had assistants paint part of the Sistine Chapel ceiling. Thomas Edison, who had over a thousand patents in his name, managed a staff of two dozen. Even writing a book, a famously solitary pursuit, involves the work of editors, publishers, and designers; getting this particular book into your hands involved additional coordination among printers, warehouse managers, truck drivers, and a host of others in the network between me and you. . . . The centrality of group effort to human life means that anything that changes the way groups function will have profound ramifications for everything from commerce and government to media and religion.[4]

Shirky's point is that our long history of emphasizing individual achievement can make us blind to all the ways brilliant thinkers have collaborated in the past and make us resistant to all new ways that digital tools offer us for collaborating in the present and anticipated in the future. To Shirky's excellent lists of group social endeavors that stand to be enhanced and even transformed by the new collaborative possibilities of the Internet—commerce, government, media, religion—one must add *learning.* Learning has always been better as a group enterprise. New digital tools promise to make the potential of collective, collaborative learning still greater and more inventive and interesting.

Participatory learning changes not just how we learn but the institutions in our society dedicated to the art and practice of learning. It is not a matter of when such a change will happen.

The change is happening now, everywhere, on small and large levels, and these transformations will no doubt continue, sustained by their own momentum.

Learning happens in many places and in many ways, including but not limited to a conventional classroom in a single, fixed, preidentified, or static institutional setting. This is not new, though the tensions between formal, institutionalized education and the more diverse, distributed, and dispersed practices of learning may have become especially acute and may even have reached a *tipping point*, in Malcolm Gladwell's sense of the term.[5]

That tipping point might be schematized as a shift from older models of nationalist education to a new model of networked education. At least since the time of the American Revolution, American public education has been promoted as a key mechanism for instilling and promoting a national culture, with ideals of citizenship embedded deep within the pedagogy and practice of public schooling.[6] The nationalist imperative in public education, throughout much of the nineteenth and twentieth centuries through the present, concerned itself with establishing a common national culture, supported by basic educational principles, common national expectations, and even a broadly common curriculum. American public education has been heavily concerned with character and moral development, intellectual discipline, civics and citizenship, and universal literacy to enable dissemination of information as the basis for individual and collective decision-making in a democracy. Education for most was centered in public schools, and, later, for the qualified, in public universities, supplemented by after-school character-building activities such as sports, clubs, and scouting arrangements.

Since the late nineteenth century and the emergence of the Humboldtian model of professional education, there has been a tension between the civic function of national education and the technical, professional, or skills-building function. Educational institutions have become wedded to ensuring technological knowledge and an expanding array of literacies, including linguistic, technical-scientific, cultural, and civic. In many ways, the United States, as elsewhere, still faces a tension between a national educational model and a professional model, a tension exacerbated by a combustible mix of globalizing conditions in economic and sociocultural practices fueled by a deeply transformative technological revolution.

Caught in this complicated mix of objectives, where might learning institutions go next? Available evidence to date points to the fact that a mix of deep cultural and technological change has already begun to presage a shift in learning practices behind which national and local educational institutions are sadly lagging—and in some cases are fiercely resisting. What would it mean to switch the terms of institutional educational culture away from both a national model and skills-based preprofessional model to what we might call *global learning*, global in both literal and metaphoric senses of being international and also intellectually expansive?

Global learning requires both leadership and shaping in its emergence, which, in turn, requires comprehending its conditions, possibilities, and implications. It is global in its reach, both in the sense of learning robustly about the world in its specificities and connectivities, about the deep connectedness of our place to (most) every other place, *our* impact on *them* and *theirs* on *us*. While globalizing economic and cultural conditions are creating commonalities across cultural differences, the generalities of globalizing practice are nevertheless almost always given local resonance, understanding, and expression.

Global learning requires coming to an understanding not just of the general principles but of their local conditions and expression.

Global learning is global through the connectivity and cultural generation that technological developments have produced. It is global both in what the learning is about and in the new media of learning and the media's attendant cultures of practice. Global learning signals that while local educational institutional arrangements are important, indeed crucially so, they can and often do fail to adapt to quickly changing learning practices and learning trajectories across all generations but especially among youth.

As Tara McPherson has argued, it is standard for reformers in any era to comment on the mismatch between the restricted form of learning that occurs within formal institutions and the more creative learning happening beyond the walls of the schoolhouse.[7] Yet, even with this historical caveat in mind, it is nonetheless significant to recognize how the emergence of new digital media and massive, global social networking practices in our era challenge traditional educational forms and purposes. Practices of engagement with the media, as well as civic engagement through new media, of cultural creation and knowledge formation, gathering, and response, not only look dramatically different from even 15 years ago, they have tended to loosen and sometimes to undercut epistemological authority, the traditional sense of expert knowledge, and authoritative sources of reference (see chapter 3). As new digitally-mediated practices have not only quickened but also expanded the sources and reach of communication, they have democratized the production of, access to, and circulation of information. This is not to say that all forms of participation are available to everyone globally. Inequalities most certainly continue to exist, deeply and profoundly.[8] Nonetheless, learning has become more networked with the networking of knowledge creation, circulation, and accreditation.

As learning is taking place through online facilitation, the shortcomings of public educational institutions become more glaring. Even public higher education has lost some of its sparkle, dulled by the soaring cost of tuition, as well as a shift of resources from public to private institutions as tax reductions have dried up public support.[9] Virtual learning environments—games, social networking sites, and collaborative online and mobile applications, and so forth—increasingly command learners' attention, most notably, but far from only, for youth. Universities are struggling to keep up, even against economic obstacles and shortfalls, as more and more classes become organized around available hardware and software, from academic podcasting to facilitation of collaboration through proprietary instructional software systems such as Blackboard. Universities are attempting to plug students into a world of global learning that is unavailable to students without such technology.

All this is relatively recent. These global learning developments emerged after World War II in a long, slow, steady shift. They exploded into visibility with the advent of the Internet in the 1990s and especially the rapidity of Web 2.0 social networking developments in the past decade.

The potentials for learning and exchange across the bounds of time and space, across the obstacles of discipline and institution, consequently are almost limitless. The limits are largely socially manufactured. One significant concern has to do with the fact that the same networking technology that makes knowledge creation and learning so flexible, appealing, and robust has the potential to circulate more quickly truth claims that turn out to be misguided, socially disturbed, or false. Credibility has always been a concern of those charged with the instruction of youth, but the ubiquity of information—reliable and not— makes credibility a central concern of responsible pedagogy.[10] It is not just that a free flow of information can turn a virtue into a vice; it is that the vice of unreliable information can take hold of a broad swath of the population quickly and potentially pro- duce serious damage before assessment mechanisms are able either to catch or mitigate the more extreme effects.

At the same time, globally networked and participatory learn- ing does not happen by accident. As a result of all the work in the past decade or so, it may be that a corner has been turned. Universities now see a need to provide learning technologies and instruction to students along with pedagogies designed to make students more canny about issues of reliability, credibil- ity, access, security, privacy, intellectual property, and so forth. Driven by a mix of market demand and comprehension of the learning potential of new media, universities are coming to embrace new modes and forms of learning. National agencies that once might have been skeptical about the impact of tech- nology, such as the National Endowment for the Humanities and the Institute for Museum and Library Services, as well as national foundations such as the MacArthur and Hewlett foun- dations, have been exemplary in leading the way in technologi- cal applications to the fields they serve and to learning and education more generally. But for every visionary, there has also been a skeptic and for every innovator a gatekeeper.

In short, this is a transitional moment. At this particularly crucial transitional moment in global learning, then, it is imperative for those dedicated to the most expansive forms of learning to be critical activists within whatever institutions they occupy. Indeed, this book's definition of institutions as mobilizing networks is intended to offer a challenge to the insularity of lockbox education, libraries, community centers, or any other civic organizations that define their mission exclusively in terms of their limited, physical turf. It is intended to highlight the possibilities of institutions grounded in distributed and virtual social networks, geographic and national boundaries notwithstanding.[11]

So what is the future of higher learning institutions in a digital age? Learning institutions *should* change and *can* change by building upon the digital affordances of the twenty-first century as well as upon the skills that most students entering universities now have already attained. Will the university survive as a hybrid of medieval structure and national ideological apparatus even in this global, interlinked, participatory digital world of informal and global learning? Or, as has happened so often in the history of technology, will the new digital learning arrangements simply be absorbed into existing and traditional institutions?

No one knows. But what is known is that the virtual and the material both support and destabilize one another. One cannot consider the digital without the real, and vice versa. Even Second Life, among the most virtual of virtual environments, predicates its virtuality on recognizable features of material life, as its name suggests. Studying the digital or the real helps to make visible the hidden or implicit arrangements of the other. That revelation, in itself, is important to the future of participatory learning. But, in any case, digitally-enabled participatory learning has already transformed how we learn and, in many ways, what we learn, and has impacted institutions of learning. There is no going back to the status quo ante.

The challenges to reimagining institutional configurations are considerable. Discovering how to support the imaginative possibilities of smart mobs, as Howard Rheingold insists, and to avoid merely replicating older, proprietary institutional models is no simple task. Yet, now is the time to do precisely that. As in any transitional moment, any time the paradigms are shifting, *how* one learns becomes as central an issue as *what* one learns.

Will the future of learning occur in virtual spaces or face-to-face, in traditional classrooms? The answer is likely not one or the other but both. Where the learning happens is less important than how and why and, still more important, what one does with what one learns.

The single most important real estate for the future of learning is that of the *imagination*. Larry Smarr, a pioneering figure in the development of the Internet, currently Director of the California Institute for Telecommunications and Information Technology (Calit2) and an early participant in HASTAC activities, poses two insistent questions: How do we "live the future" and "live in the future"?[12] There are no clear, short, or simple answers to those interlinked questions, except to underscore that imagining better worlds, better futures, has to be the ultimate goal of all who are dedicated to and engaged in participatory learning in the digital age. Better futures mean better links, networks, interactions, and engagements with others elsewhere, wherever those elsewheres may be.

To that end, we offer the following 10 principles as foundational to rethinking the future of learning institutions.[13] We see these principles as riders, both as challenges to and as the general grounds upon which to develop creative learning practices, both transformative and transforming as new challenges emerge and new technological possibilities are fashioned.

Ten Principles for the Future of Learning Institutions

1. Self-Learning

Self-learning has bloomed, across all generations, early in childhood until late in life. Both online reading and writing have become collaborative, as has composition—the making of things—more generally. Mash-ups and comments redo texts. Some poets—for example, Millie Niss—compose exactly with this in mind.[14] And the likes of Google Docs encourage collaborative composition, the sharing of products in the process of making them. While common social networking distribution sites like Flickr and YouTube circulate ready-mades, their existence prompts people to post their productions close to instantaneously. The time from manufacture to market and the resources needed to manufacture have shrunk.

2. Horizontal Structures

Learning has become increasingly horizontal, rather than hierarchical. Lateral learning—peer-to-peer rather than teacher to student—requires rearrangement of learning institutions—schools, colleges, universities, and their surrounding support apparatuses. The latter have tended to be authoritative, top-down, standardized, and predicated on individuated assessment measured on standard tests. At the workplace, teamwork today is increasingly valued over spectacular performance, even if our culture rewards the latter disproportionately and (as we have seen in the recent financial debacle) with sometimes disastrous impact. The volume and range of information now available in almost any domain more or less requires collaborative engagement across all performative aspects of work, from decision-making to actual production. Learning strategy thus commands shifts from information acquisition—it is widely available to anyone who knows how to look and comprehend—to judgment concerning reliable information, from memorizing information to how to find reliable sources—in short, from learning *that* to learning *how*, from knowledge content to the processes of its formation.

3. From Presumed Authority to Collective Credibility

Learning is shifting from issues of authoritativeness to those of credibility. A major part of the future of learning is in developing critical methods, often collective, for distinguishing sources of good knowledge from those that for a variety of reasons are problematic. What experienced knowers have to offer those less experienced or less in the know are the subtleties in what knowing—the process—involves and entails; it is the making of wise judgments and choices—about sources, information architecture, and who and what to trust, especially in robustly interdisciplinary and multidisciplinary environments.

4. A Decentered Pedagogy

Many education administrators and individual teachers have taken to limiting or restricting use of collectively and collaboratively crafted knowledge sources to complete formal assignments. Such restrictions have focused especially on Wikipedia. This is a deeply misguided reaction to networking knowledge making in a global era.

To ban or even vigorously to restrict sources such as Wikipedia is to miss the importance of a collaborative knowledge-making impulse in humans who are willing to contribute, correct, and collect information without remuneration: Definitionally, this *is* education. To miss how much such collaborative, participatory learning underscores the foundations of learning is defeatist, unimaginative, even self-destructive.[15]

The opportunity and challenge now exist for leaders at learning institutions to adopt a more inductive, collective pedagogy that takes advantage of the extraordinary range of technological resources that are available. John Seely Brown has noted that it took professional astronomers many years to realize that the benefits to their field of having tens of thousands of amateur stargazers reporting on celestial activity far outweighed the disadvantages of unreliability. This was a colossal commitment, a leap of scientific faith into what could have turned into a proverbial black hole, given that among the cohort of amateur astronomers were some who believed it was their duty to save the earth from martians. In other words, professional astronomers faced large issues of credibility that had to be counterpoised to the compelling issue of wanting to expand the knowledge base of observed celestial activity.[16] In the end, it was thought that "kooks" would be sorted out through Web 2.0 participatory and corrective learning.

The result has been a far more robust and expansive body of knowledge, amassed by means of this participatory method, than anyone had dreamed possible. Faith in networking paid off and then some! Amateur publics have long participated in data collection in the expansion of scientific knowledge. Tidal data, for example, were long collected by local publics, such as fishermen, before such data collection became an institutionalized, professionalized activity. Such more or less informal data collection has long been balanced by collective and professional procedures for sorting through the data for obviously wrong or misguided reportings. If professional astronomers can adopt such a decentered method for assembling information, certainly college and high school teachers as well as collective encyclopedias can develop reliable methods based on collective checking, inquisitive skepticism, group assessment, best community practices, and informed instruction in what wise decision-making amounts to.

5. Networked Learning

In a world increasingly ordered by complex, multifaceted problems, the likelihood of working out solutions, resolutions, or work-arounds is heightened by drawing on the intersection of different specializations and forms of expertise rather than on the brilliance of a single know-all individual. This is the case no matter the field or domain—from the natural sciences to computing technology, from social and political issues to humanistic challenges. The complex, invariably multidimensional nature of the issues confronting us scientifically and politically today call for multiple modes of expertise to address them successfully. But networked learning is not just about a number of discrete contributors arithmetically adding their contributions to solving problems, challenges, or even threats. Networked knowledge, by contrast, takes the power of its interactive engagements around any issue from the algorithmic, multiplier impact working together contributes to resolving any issue.

So it is with learning. One can learn alone, seeking out solutions through solitary effort. Invariably that will overlook key dimensions to addressing issues. Individuals learn not only content from others but process. Another's insight or explanation reveals, opens one up to a different way of looking not only at this but at a range of other issues, too. Interaction with others teaches how to ask revealing questions, how to address features of the general question hitherto hidden from view. The enthusiasm of others in one's learning circle is likely to rub off, too. As trust builds up, one hesitates less in asking help or for an explanation, or indeed offering it when in a position to do so.

In that sense, networks are synergistic, as much for learning as for doing. They challenge as they support. Members who take without contributing will soon develop a reputation for not pulling their weight; those who are rude or arrogant or unhelpful will likely be shunned. So learning networks contribute to lessons in civility and sociality alongside those in process and content. Networked learning operates on the logic of participation, expecting interaction, correcting through exchange, deepening knowledge through extended engagement. Networked learning likewise offers lessons in negotiating complexity. Thus, they are likely to promote nonauthoritarian modes of knowledge formation, nuance over dogmatic assertion, critical challenge over blind or even rote acceptance of authority.

6. Open-Source and Open-Access Education

Networked learning and, open-source and open-access culture are mutually reinforcing. The drive to produce and promote freely available applications, tools, and learning resources encourages their circulation and use. The more information that can be easily accessed, the more likely it is to be vetted, tested, revised, and remixed to collective benefit. Applications and information that prove most successful and reliable are likely to be most widely circulated, shared, applied, and improved. Their availability and popularity become virally self-promoting; their shortcomings and failures are quickly discovered. This can apply to applications and programs that may involve distasteful elements also. But openness is more likely to reveal the shortcomings, and to do so more quickly, than imposing top-down applications and programs.

Open-source learning trades on the *many-to-multitudes model*. A group that has access to resources, including information, makes it virally available to widening circles of engagement.

The many feed the multitudes, some subset of whom, in turn, take up the baton of informational and resource provision, of the nourishing of learning. Many international social movements—such as those focused on Darfur or Tibet—operate from this many-to-multitudes interactivity, where financial resources on one end are balanced by local expertise and human investment and labor on the other, for interchanges that are rich and socially valuable for all participants. Many-to-multitudes does not erase the digital divide but, rather, acknowledges its material reality and provides a more collective model of economic and human capital to promote interchange. The desire (on all sides) for interactivity fuels this digitally driven form of social networking, as much in learning as in economic practices, enlarging the possibilities of successful innovation and the circles of those likely to learn from the inevitable, necessary, and, in the end, productive failures.

There are challenges, magnified as they are by the relational, interactive commitments of digital, of participatory learning and an inordinate expansion of scope and reach. Just as the challenges can make spectacular the successes, they have the possibility to magnify dramatically if not disastrously the potential failures. They are better weathered together, interactively, with the experience of working collectively and in participatory fashion rather than discretely, individually, and separately.

7. Learning as Connectivity and Interactivity

Notwithstanding open source and access, digitally enabled social networking applications make possible increasingly robust connectivities and interactivities not otherwise available and are enlarging and expanding them as well. They serve to produce learning environments and ensembles in which participants both enable and elaborate each others' learning inputs, practices, and products. Participatory learning ecologies establish environments, virtual and face-to-face, that dispose participants to support and sustain contributions from others. Learning challenges and problems are faced collectively and collaboratively, not simply individually. This tends to undercut frustrations, encouraging the development of work-arounds where direct resolutions seem distant or impossible. The challenges tend to be mutually shared and distributed across the learning community. Accordingly, they are faced, redefined, solved, resolved, or worked around—together.

There are a growing range of applications now enabling users to unite and synchronize their devices and applications into a seamless web of interactivity. We are able not only to share work instantaneously with others at a distance but to work with them simultaneously on a common, mutually shared document. File and data sharing with other users in remote locations is now more or less matter of course and increasingly gravitating to the ubiquity of mobile devices. Massively multiplayer online games have made possible robust interactivity, sharing decision-making, online communication, and movement, and exchange and conjoint creation. Working environments are no different. Technological architecture thus is fast making net-*working* the default, rather than isolated, individualized working. The organizational architecture of educational and learning institutions and pedagogical delivery should be no different and are just awakening to that fact. The administration of President Barack Obama in the United States promises surer and swifter developments along these fronts.

8. Lifelong Learning
Participatory learning suggests a different disposition to knowledge making, acquisition, and sharing. It means that there is no

finality to learning. We learn throughout life, through formal institutions or, far more readily and repeatedly, informally, from each other. The new technological developments and the rapid transformation in knowledge across almost every field as a result makes lifelong learning all the more a condition of contemporary life, whether it concerns staying healthy, physically and financially, comprehending the quickly shifting world politically, addressing the profound social or environmental challenges globally, considering the recreational options available, or simply for the sheer pleasure of it.

Institutions of higher learning, especially in the United States, have seen the average age of their students increase. This has been fueled in considerable part by the interests of 40- and 50-year-olds to improve their employment prospects and earning power. It has been driven, in part, by retirees pursuing areas of knowledge they discover to be fascinating but never quite had the time to attend while balancing busy working lives and child-raising or parental care. Networked culture afforded by plugging in digitally has made so much more readily possible not just informing oneself on one's own but fashioning virtual learning communities, drawing on expertise and companionship virtually, and transforming the social conditions of ongoing knowledge development as it shifts the grounds of sociality.

With this developing self-consciousness about lifelong learning, there have emerged opportunities alongside it to contribute to knowledge formation across all sorts of even more traditional knowledge domains. Thus, formal university-based knowledge communities have begun to draw on the affordances of digital technology and new media to engage interested parties across the population, locally and globally, to contribute to the development of expanding and important data sets in well-established and academically grounded domains. Thus, publics, young and old, can contribute to developing data sets on all of life's species, or to those on every known bird species sighted, or to astronomical observations. Johannes Kepler's formalization of tidal readings made so painstakingly in the early seventeenth century are now potentially the contributions of everyman across many, if not all, domains. Lifelong learning is also now lifelong contribution to knowledge production and expansion, collaboratively conceived. Means and ends are mutually remaking.

9. Learning Institutions as Mobilizing Networks
Collaborative, networked learning consequently alters also how one thinks about learning *institutions*, and network culture alters how to conceive of institutions more generally. Traditionally, institutions have been thought about in terms of rules, regulations, and norms governing interactivity, production, and distribution within the institutional structure. Network culture and associated learning practices and arrangements suggest that one thinks of institutions, especially those promoting learning, as mobilizing networks. The networks enable mobilization that stresses flexibility, interactivity, and outcome. And mobilizing, in turn, encourages and enables networking interactivity that lasts as long as it is productive, opening up or giving way to new interacting networks as older ones ossify or emergent ones signal new possibilities. Institutional culture thus shifts from the weighty to the light, from the assertive to the enabling. With this new formation of institutional understanding and practice, the challenges faced include such considerations as reliability and predictability alongside flexibility and innovation.

10. Flexible Scalability and Simulation
Finally, networked learning both makes possible and must remain open to various scales of learning possibility, from the

small and local to the widest and most far-reaching constituencies capable of productively contributing to a domain, subject matter, and knowledge formation and creation. New technologies allow for small groups whose members are at considerable physical distance from each other to learn collaboratively, together and from each other; but they also enable larger, more anonymous yet equally productive interactions. They make possible, through virtual simulation for instance, to learn about large-scale processes, life systems, and social structures without either having to observe or recreate them in real life.

The scale is driven by the nature of the project or knowledge base. The scope may range from a small group of students working on a specific topic together to open-ended and open-sourced contributions to the Encyclopedia of Life, Wildlab (a comprehensive database of bird life based at Cornell University), Digital Oceans (a comprehensive database of ocean life based at the University of California at Santa Barbara), or to Wikipedia. Learning institutions must be open to flexibility of scale at both ends of the spectrum. The most effective institutions will acknowledge and reward appropriate participation in and contributions to such collective and collaborative contributions, on scales small and large, rather than too readily dismissing them as easy, secondary, or insufficiently individualistic or idiosyncratic to warrant merit.

Challenges from Past Practice, Moving Fast Forward

The range of opportunities and the transformative possibilities for learning at all levels as a result of readily available and emergent digital technologies are broad. The transformation in knowledge conception and production as a result of these new technological practices must be considered.

There are challenges, limitations, and misdirections—in short, opportunity costs—resulting from these developments. Some of the concern no doubt relates to technological overreach, underdevelopment, or underperformance. But some anxiety results inevitably from the unsettlement of long-established ways of doing things. When well-established modes of knowledge making and acquisition stagnate, they can become restrictive, if not unproductive. As new modes emerge, those responsible for sustaining traditional institutional structures can either dig in and refuse to respond other than to dismiss the new modes, or they can seek to work out renewed and renewing regimes to take advantage of new productive elements and possibilities.

The challenges offered by digitally enhanced participatory learning to institutional order in higher education (and in other educational levels and formations) range from the banal to the constitutive. They reach likewise from the disciplining of behavioral breaches of protocol and expectation to normative conceptions of what constitutes knowledge and how it is authorized. In short, the challenges posed by participatory, global learning threaten established orders and practices as well as settled modes of being and doing. They portend significant shifts of authority, credibility, individuality, and hierarchy. Their promise is discounted by the attendant costs, their benefits discounted by the losses following from practices taken for granted, and the advantages from innovative modes of thinking and execution discounted by the drawbacks always attendant to the novel and insurgent.

That is not a good argument to dismiss the innovative, to ignore its developmental possibilities, or even to be driven by a cost-benefit calculus. Quite the contrary, it is to recognize that the enormously productive power of participatory and collaborative work will be uncontained and, in the end, unbounded by the individualizing boundaries of the given and established. Rather than dismiss the shortcomings as the inevitable cost of innovation, the shortcomings should encourage us to pay special attention to failures, to learn how they occur, to learn what we can from their occurrence.

The source of failure may vary. Is it a failure of the technology as such, of the incapacity to address the problem at hand, or is it a failure resulting from the overreaching of an application unintended for that technology? Is it a failure from underestimating the projected attendant costs demanded by the application or the ongoing commitment to service the infrastructure or human attention to sustain it? Or, yet again, is it a failure to have thought about the technological–human interface, the ways human beings interact with hardware or software, that the design has ignored or inadequately attended?

The failure in the latter case may have to do with the inability of the technology in question to deliver the kind of knowledge needed or sought or to frame that knowledge in ways deemed difficult to use. It may turn out that the application is more time-consuming than older modes of knowledge creation, or less enlightening, or more awkwardly framed. Implementing a technological solution, for example, may require a greater commitment to new modes of social networking than one finds productive. It may require practices less pleasing or more demanding than is acceptable. Each of these possible modes of failure informs us, makes us less likely to simply give in to a technological determinism or a naïve idea that the most technologically complex solution is the best solution. To fully radicalize learning in a digital age requires serious, creative, and sustained comprehension of the outcomes one wishes and the pedagogical process one desires, and then a realistic accounting of all of the available learning possibilities—virtual, real, or in some visionary (because appropriately circumspect) combination.

Conclusion: Yesterday's Tomorrow

It would be easy to fall into hand-wringing, to say that our institutions of education are antiquated and, therefore, doomed. In fact, their persistence suggests that, outmoded as they may be, they are not only not doomed—they are thriving. At present, the baby boom of the baby boom, makes admission to a college or university more competitive than it has ever been. A college degree is still the key to success as all comparative studies of income levels and educational attainment attest. Rather than dismiss, excoriate, or condemn our learning institutions, this book examines sites where institutions *are* and inventively *could be* changing in order to provide examples for those innovative educators, administrators, students, and parents who wish to promote productive change and seek models to guide the process and support their endeavor.

Digital learning pioneer Henry Jenkins has argued for the importance of the convergence resulting from networking a culture of new models, forms, and contributions with older models. The convergence is not just the new working on and around older forms but thoroughly remixing and modding them, transforming them piecemeal, and expanding and enlarging access to them.[17] So, too, is the charge and challenge to the immediate future of learning institutions. Remix learning institutions may well be the model of the future. Modding and remix are the moving modalities of institutions as mobilizing networks.

This book's portfolio of models for institutional remix (laid out at the close of chapter 2), in both practice and form, allows one to imagine anew what remix educational enterprises might aspire to, what practices they might draw on, and what trajectories of being and doing they might take up and push. One must challenge institutional changes not just in the tools of the trade of education—but to the trade itself. How successful these experiments in new institutional formations will be remains in question. The following concluding examples are included to provoke thought, not to foreclose it, to prod imagination, and to refuse to accept the given as the limit of the possible.

The dominant disposition in modern higher education has been to center the individual as the problem solver. Technology labs are now drawing on more collective modes of working toward problem solving. Someone facing a significant problem poses it to the relevant network to which she or he is connected. Others in the network suggest possible responses, solutions, or productive ways to address the problem. Out of the ensuing discussion, a working group of interested contributors forms and starts working together to resolve the problem posed. Knowledge networking tools make it highly likely that the working group will be physically distributed. The group remains open enough that others may keep abreast of the progress in resolving the challenge and be called on where their expertise might be needed. This way of working suggests, in turn, different work virtues and values to be inculcated in the learning process. The transformation of learning institutions likewise will involve their practical inculcation.

Similarly, a social networking tool such as Twitter can be put to brainstorming use. Instead of social twittering, the tool can be used for idea or concept twittering. Promising suggestions can be quickly migrated or hyperlinked to a more sustaining application such as a wiki more conducive to sustained exploration or development. It also allows those with access to institutionalized forms of learning to share that knowledge more broadly with those who cannot afford formal education. In short, ubiquitous computing suggests the instantaneous capacity both to generate and develop germinal ideas in or across any field, within communities and to more general, distributed publics. There are downsides: the instant "tweet" can stall out, just as the romance with novelty and the next cool application can push users to ignore deeper development and more sustained or more subtle spirals of knowledge formation. Yet, the sociality of networking dimensions suggests that brakes will be built into even the most headlong push into innovation for its own sake.

The proliferation of collective learning applications, practices, and communities signal an emergent mode of knowledge production called *networking knowledge*. Networking knowledge, as the ambiguity is intended to suggest, includes two considerations. It involves knowledge of how networks and networking tools operate. At the same time, it conveys the possibilities and the profile that these new applications give to knowledge itself, shaping knowledge in genuinely innovative ways, and stressing the relational and social dimensions to the process of knowledge making.

The pressing question is how educational institutions self-consciously embed these new applications and practices and new epistemologies and pedagogies and how they institutionalize these new modes of learning and are remade in so doing.

In thinking together, we engage a process, together, of envisioning better ways to rethink the future of learning institutions in our digital age.

Notes

1 Introduction and Overview: The Future of Learning Institutions in a Digital Age

1. Washington Irving, "The Legend of Sleepy Hollow," in *The Sketch Book of Geoffrey Crayon* (New York: C. S. Van Winkle, 1820).

2. "Wikipedia," on Wikipedia, http://en.wikipedia.org/wiki/Wikipedia :About.

3. The initial posting of the draft manuscript of this book on the Institute for the Future of the Book's Web site in January 2007 amassed over 350 registrants. It has since changed considerably to take the comments and suggestions of these registrants into consideration. All comments through March 2008 have been taken into consideration in this printed book.

4. An excellent example of an interactive hybrid is the multiple publication sites for the proceedings of our first HASTAC conference (May 2007). *Electronic Techtonics: Thinking at the Interface*, edited by Erin Ennis, Zoë Marie Jones, Paolo Mangiafico, Mark Olson, Jennifer Rhee, Mitali Routh, Jonathan E. Tarr, and Brett Walters, was published under Creative Commons licensing by Lulu, an open-source venture founded by Red Hat CEO Bob Young. The book is available for purchasing as a printed volume or by free digital download. Additionally, a multimedia version is available on the HASTAC Web site (http://www.hastac.org),

and edited talks from the conference appear on the HASTAC YouTube channel (http://www.youtube.com/user/video4hastac). Finally, the interactive data visualization experiment collaboratively produced for the conference has contributed to the nonprofit research Web site SparkIP (http://www.sparkip.com), which also has an online for-profit component. All of these various forms of content creation constitute "publishing" in the digital age.

5. For more information on the history of the book, see Cathy N. Davidson, ed., *Reading in America: Literature and Social History* (Baltimore: Johns Hopkins University Press, 1989).

6. Roland Barthes, *Image-Music-Text* (New York: Hill and Wang, 1978).

7. Mark Granovetter, "The Strength of Weak Ties: A Network Theory Revisited," *Sociological Theory* 1 (1983): 201–233.

8. Following this success, the MacArthur Foundation funded two subsequent competitions. The second focused on participatory learning; at press time, the third had not yet been defined.

2   Customized and Participatory Learning

1. Anderson, *The Long Tail: Why the Future of Business Is Selling Less of More.* (New York: Hyperion, 2006).

2. Jason Mittell of Middlebury College wittily notes that using the phrase *smash bestseller* for a book about the long tail is a bit of a contradiction (Jason Mittell, comment on "Future of Learning Institutions in a Digital Age," Institute for the Future of the Book, http://futureofthebook.org). This is true: books, in general, are such a niche market that even bestsellers reach only a small segment of the population. Even in the case of *The Long Tail*, there has been relatively little academic or educational use of the book.

3. Erik Brynjolfsson, Yu Jeffrey Hu, and Duncan Simester, "Goodbye Pareto Principle, Hello Long Tail: The Effect of Search Costs on the Concentration of Product Sales" (2007), http://ssrn.com/abstract=953587.

4. For more information, see: http://www.softwaretime.com.

5. No Child Left Behind Act of 2001, Public Law 107–110, 107th Congress, (January 8, 2002).

6. House Committee on Health, Education, Labor, and Pensions, *NCLB Reauthorization: Modernizing Middle and High Schools for the 21st Century*, 2007. See also Deborah Meier et al., *Many Children Left Behind: How the No Child Left Behind Act Is Damaging Our Children and Our Schools* (Boston: Beacon Press, 2004); Paul E. Peterson and Martin R. West, eds., *No Child Left Behind? The Politics and Practice of School Accountability* (Washington, DC: Brookings Institute Press, 2003).

7. K. G. Schneider and Becky Kinney rightly point out in their comments on the Institute for the Future of the Book that many demographic factors contribute to dropout rates. Kinney notes, however, that, for some dropouts, there are strong preferences for video gaming (sometimes accompanied by recreational drug use) over attending class. Some educators have addressed this issue by experimenting with gaming environments and whole gaming schools for kids, including those deemed at risk for dropping out of school entirely. See Bibliography II in this book for some models for using virtual environments for alternative education in formal educational settings. K. G. Schneider, comment on "Future of Learning Institutions in a Digital Age," Institute for the Future of the Book, comment posted on February 10, 2007, http://www.futureofthebook.org/HASTAC/learningreport/i-overview; Becky Kinney, comment on "Future of Learning Institutions in a Digital Age," Institute for the Future of the Book, comment posted on February 19, 2007, http://www.futureofthebook.org/HASTAC/learningreport/i-overview.

8. Some of the most dedicated researchers of social networking sites like Facebook and MySpace are adamantly opposed to using these sites for formal education. In a debate in *The Economist*, danah boyd protests, "I have yet to hear a compelling argument for why social network sites (or networking ones) should be used in the classroom. Those tools are primarily about socializing, with media and information sharing there to prop up the socialization process (much status is gained from knowing about the cool new thing). I haven't even heard of a good reason why social network site features should be used in the classroom."

See Wikipedia for a brief history of Facebook and a summary of some of the arguments surrounding it: http://en.wikipedia.org/wiki/Facebook.

9. For more information, see: Bibliography II in this book; http://hastac .ning.com; http://www.classroom20.com; and http://www.shapingy outh.org.

10. http://digitalyouth.ischool.berkeley.edu/user/5.

11. A more self-conscious hybrid is McKenzie Wark's publication of his new book, *?GAM3R 7H30RY?* (Gamer Theory), on a collaborative software environment sponsored by the Institute for the Future of the Book (http://www.futureofthebook.org/gamertheory), a project designed to bring readers into the creation of the book (Andrew Richard Albanese, "The Social Life of Books," *Library Journal* [2006]) and offering readers one-click preordering of the next iteration of the book (to be published by Harvard University Press). New projects such as the Wikiversity Learning Project (http://en.wikiversity.org) are designed to support collaborative models of knowledge sharing. Excellent discussions of the impact of open-source and Creative Commons licensing on discourse, scholarship, creativity, and media are provided by James Boyle, *The Public Domain: Enclosing the Commons of the Mind* (New Haven, CT: Yale University Press, 2008) and Lawrence Lessig, *Free Culture: The Nature and Future of Creativity* (New York: Penguin, 2005).

12. Alex Reid, comment on "Future of Learning Institutions in a Digital Age," Institute for the Future of the Book, comment posted on March 31, 2007, http://www.futureofthebook.org/HASTAC/learningre port/i-overview.

13. For an excellent overview of some of the key issues of open source, see Christopher M. Kelty, *Two Bits: The Cultural Significance of Free Software* (Durham: Duke University Press, 2008).

14. Itzkoff, Dave. "A.P. Says It Owns Image in Obama Poster," *New York Times*, March 11, 2009, http://artsbeat.blogs.nytimes.com/2009/03/11/ associated-press-files-countersuit-over-obama-poster/.

15. Creative Commons allows knowledge producers to license their published material in a broad spectrum of possibilities between full copyright and the public domain (http://creativecommons.org).

16. In 2008, at least two prominent universities, Harvard and the University of California, Berkeley, each made well publicized (if partial) experiments into open-access publishing; MIT joined this movement in 2009. Harvard now requires its faculty to republish any scholarship that appears in a subscription-only journal into an open-access archive supported by the Harvard University Library. Harvard pays publishers a fee to offset potential lost revenue from this republication. Since this only applies to Harvard faculty, it addresses the issue of access but replicates the problem of site-specific (rather than seamlessly interoperable) silos at libraries. The University of California at Berkeley has gone a different route with its experiment, subsidizing its faculty to publish original scholarship in open-access journals. For an analysis of potentials and problems and of the necessity for rethinking the entire publishing cycle as an interrelated continuum (author, publisher, distributor, reader), see "Open Access and Its Costs," March 13, 2008, http://www.hastac.org/node/1263.

17. Henry Jenkins, comment on "Recut, Reframe, Recycle: An Interview with Pat Aufderheide and Peter Jaszi (Part Two)," The Confessions of an Aca-Fan: The Official Weblog of Henry Jenkins, comment posted February 8, 2008, http://www.henryjenkins.org/2008/02/recut_reframe_recycle_an_inter.html.

18. Keith Aoki, James Boyle, and Jennifer Jenkins, *Tales from the Public Domain: Bound by Law?* (Durham, NC: Duke University Center for the Study of the Public Domain, 2006).

19. *Eyes on the Prize: America's Civil Rights Years (1954–1965)*, produced by Henry Hampton (Boston: Blackside, 1987).

20. For an analysis, see, for example, Immanuel Wallerstein's *The Uncertainty of Knowledge* (Philadelphia: Temple University Press, 2004).

21. In some modest way, the experiment of "The Future of Learning Institutions in a Digital Age" should be useful to others who are pursuing new forms of writing and new kinds of collaborative projects.

3 Our Digital Age Implications for Learning and Its (Online) Institutions

1. Wheat, comment on "Future of Learning Institutions in a Digital Age," Institute for the Future of the Book, comment posted on August 6, 2007, http://www.futureofthebook.org/HASTAC/learningreport/i-overview.

2. No Child Left Behind Act of 2001, Public Law 107–110, 107th Congress (January 8, 2002).

3. Philomena Essed and David Theo Goldberg, "Cloning Cultures: The Social Injustices of Sameness," *Ethnic and Racial Studies* 6, no. 1 (2002): 1066–1082.

4. A trenchant analysis of the ways these factors in the lives of youth merge in U.S. national policy and ideology is provided by Lawrence Grossberg, *Caught in the Crossfire: Kids, Politics, and America's Future* (Boulder, CO: Paradigm, 2005).

5. The Education Trust, "Getting Honest about Grad Rates: Too Many States Hide Behind False Data," June 23, 2005, http://www2.edtrust.org/EdTrust/Press+Room/HSGradRate2005.htm.

6. *Cities in Crisis: A Special Analytic Report on High School Graduation*, released April 1, 2008, chaired by Alma J. Powell of America's Promise Alliance and prepared by Editorial Projects in Education Research Center, reveals that "in the metropolitan areas surrounding 35 of the nation's largest cities, graduation rates in urban schools were lower than those in nearby suburban communities. In several instances, the disparity between urban-suburban graduation rates was more than 35 percentage points." http://www.americaspromise.org/Our-Work/Dropout-Prevention/Cities-in-Crisis.aspx.

7. See the Prison University Project, http://www.prisonuniversityproject.org/resources.html, and the Correctional Education Facts from the National Institute for Literacy, http://www.nifl.gov/nifl/facts/correctional.html.

8. Human Rights Watch, "U.S.: Prison Rates Hit New High," (Washington, D.C: Human Rights Watch, 2008), http://www.hrw.org/english/docs/2008/06/06/usdom19035.htm.

9. Douglas Thomas and John Seely Brown, "The Play of Imagination: Beyond the Literary Mind," working paper, August 22, 2006, http://www.johnseelybrown.com/playimagination.pdf.

10. Although many people use the phrase *Net Age* as shorthand for *Internet Age*, this book uses John Seely Brown's particular use of the term to signal both the Internet and networking, the specific combination that Tim O'Reilly calls *Web 2.0* and that seems a vastly rich model for learning and a specific challenge to most existing forms of learning institutions (Tim O'Reilly, "What is Web. 2.0: Design Patterns and Business Models for the Next Generation of Software" (Cambridge, MA: O'Reilly Media, Inc., 2005), http://www.oreillynet.com/pub/a/oreilly/tim/news/2005/09/30/what-is-web-20.html.

11. James Boyle, "A Closed Mind about an Open World," *Financial Times* (August 7 2006): 20–24.

12. Since 1994, Alan Liu has been the "weaver," of The Voice of the Shuttle: Web Page for Humanities Research, http://liu.english.ucsb.edu/the-voice-of-the-shuttle-web-page-for-humanities-research.

13. Ron Rosenzweig, "Can History Be Open Source? Wikipedia and the Future of the Past," *Journal of American History* 93, no. 1 (2006): 117–146, http://chnm.gmu.edu/resources/essays/d/42.

14. "Peopling the Police: A Social Computing Approach to Information Authority in the Age of Web 2.0," Alan Liu, 2008, http://liu.english.ucsb.edu/peopling-the-police-a-social-computing-approach-to-information-authority-in-the-age-of-web-20-drha-2008/.

15. Perhaps the best article available on the advantages and the shortcomings of Wikipedia as a collaborative knowledge site and as a reference work is the entry on "Wikipedia" on Wikipedia, http://en.wikipedia.org/wiki/Wikipedia:About. See also Cathy N. Davidson, "We Can't Ignore the Influence of Digital Technologies," *Chronicle of Higher Education Review* 53 (2007): B20, http://chronicle.com/weekly/v53/i29/29b02001.htm.

16. For an excellent discussion of the value system implicit in open-source culture, see Kelty, *Two Bits*, 2008. On networked individualism and society, see Barry Wellman et al., "The Social Affordances of the

Internet for Networked Individualism," *Journal Of Computer Mediated Communication* 8, 3 (2003). http://jcmc.indiana.edu/vol8/issue3/well man.html.

17. For an extended discussion of how collaborative knowledge making exposes assumptions in what academics call *peer review*, see Cathy N. Davidson, "Humanities 2.0: Promise, Perils, Predictions," *PMLA* 123, no. 3 (2008): 707–717.

18. HASTAC has taken an active role in exploring a variety of electronic publishing forms. In addition to helping to support Kelty's online version of *Two Bits* (as a free download that can be remixed and commented upon) and to publishing the first draft of this book on a collaborative writing site, HASTAC has published the proceedings of its first annual conference with Lulu, a self-publishing site that allows users to purchase a book or to download it for free as well as in a multimedia form. The proceedings of the second conference combine multimedia (audio-video) as well as multiauthored live blogging of talks, exhibits, and events combined as an online archive of the event. Discussions with various academic presses about contemporary electronic publishing initiatives as the future direction of academic publishing are ongoing.

19. MILLEE, http://www.cs.berkeley.edu/~mattkam/millee.

20. One implication of this is that the "English Only" movement— whether as administrative vernacular or more pointedly here as medium of instruction—fails dismally to comprehend the hybrid histories of the formation and transformation of the language of English over time.

21. Persuasive Games, http://www.persuasivegames.com.

22. AgoraXChange, http://www.agoraxchange.net.

23. Virtual Peace, http://www.virtualpeace.org.

24. Black Cloud, http://studio.berkeley.edu/bc.

25. "Law Professors Rule Laptops Out of Order in Class," http://chroni cle.com/article/Law-Professors-Rule-Laptops/29745.

26. C. Avery, comment on "Future of Learning Institutions in a Digital Age," Institute for the Future of the Book, comment posted on March 18, 2007, http://futureofthebook.org.

27. Mark Bauerlein, *The Dumbest Generation: How the Digital Age Stupefies Young Americans and Jeopardizes Our Future (or Don't Trust Anyone Under 30)* (New York, NY: Jeremy P. Tarcher/Penguin, 2008); "8 Reasons Why This Is the Dumbest Generation," *The Boston Globe Online*, http://www.boston.com/lifestyle/gallery/dumbestgeneration, accessed July 31, 2009.

28. Elizabeth Gudrais, "Unequal America: Causes and Consequences of the Wide—and Growing—Gap Between Rich and Poor," *Harvard Magazine* 110, no. 6 (2008): 22–29, http://harvardmagazine.com/2008/07/unequal-america.html; Claudia Goldin, *The Race Between Education and Technology* (Cambridge, MA: Belknap Press, 2008); Bill Readings, *The University in Ruins* (Cambridge, MA: Harvard University Press, 1996); Mark Gibson and Alec McHoul, "Interdisciplinarity," in *A Companion to Cultural Studies*, ed. Toby Miller (Oxford: Basil Blackwell, 2006); David Theo Goldberg, "Enduring Occupations," *The Threat of Race* (Oxford: Wiley-Blackwell, 2008).

29. This is the title for the keynote address that John Seely Brown delivered at the first international conference of HASTAC, "Electronic Techtonics: Thinking at the Interface," April 19, 2007, at the Nasher Museum of Art at Duke University. A webcast is available at http://www.hastac.org. Some schools, including public schools, are just coming online and seek to institutionalize these newly emergent models of networked learning practices.

4 FLIDA 101: A Pedagogical Allegory

1. According to the *Guinness Book of World Records*, the title of "oldest" university is a matter of dispute, but, generally, the order is accepted as: University of Al-Karaouine, in Fes, Morocco (859); Al-Azhar University in Cairo, Egypt (975); the University of Bologna, Italy (1088); the University of Paris (1150); and Oxford (1167). http://www.guinnessworldrecords.com/, accessed July 31, 2009.

2. This hypothetical course highlights the issues raised by virtual learning for traditional institutions and underscores the real, material conditions supporting digital interaction. Currently, there are many existing experimental team-taught, cross-institutional courses, offered in the United States and abroad, that combine face-to-face and virtual environments. A number of these are discussed by John Seely Brown and Richard P. Adler, "Minds on Fire: Open Education, the Long Tail, and Learning 2.0," *Educause Review* 43, no. 1 (2008), 16–32.

3. Steve Anderson and Anne Balsamo, "A Pedagogy of Original Synners," in *Digital Youth, Innovation, and the Unexpected*, ed. Tara McPherson (Cambridge, MA: MIT Press, 2008), 241–259. Anderson and Balsamo use, as an example, an interesting experiment in SL conducted by the Harvard Law School and the Harvard Extension School in fall 2006 called *CyberOne: Law in the Court of Public Opinion*. Harvard law students could enroll in the course at Harvard Law School and attend the class in person; non-law students could enroll through the extension program and could take the class and interact with other students and the professors in SL; and non-Harvard students could review all the materials for the course online for free.

4. http://en.wikiquote.org/wiki/William_Gibson.

5. On March 31, 2008, a start-up called Vivaty announced a three-dimensional virtual chat room that can be added to the Web pages and social networking profiles on sites such as MySpace and Facebook, which are purported to have over 100 million and 65 million registered users, respectively, compared to SL's 13 million accounts. Some predict that Vivaty's or a similar three-dimensional live chat feature could radically diminish SL's appeal, especially in areas where it has extensive traffic, such as gambling and online sex. See Brad Stone, "Online Chat, as Inspired by Real Chat," *New York Times,* March 31, 2008. Croquet is another imminently emergent possibility. For an extended critical ethnography of SL, see Tom Boellstorff's recent book, *Coming of Age in Second Life: An Anthropologist Explores the Virtually Human* (Princeton, NJ: Princeton University Press, 2008).

6. For an example of what SL can do, see: http://www.youtube.com/watch?v=bQL8_HB1HtQ).

7. David Silver comments on "The Future of Learning Institutions in a Digital Age," Institute for the Future of the Book, comment posted on January 23, 2007, http://www.futureofthebook.org/HASTAC/learning report/i-overview:

> The events that HASTAC has organized, or is currently organizing, are really inspired. That said, I strongly believe that engaging undergraduates in digital media and culture is so much more productive than engaging graduate students. I am not suggesting either/or. However, I would like to hear more about how peer-to-peer learning affects undergraduate digital literacy and digital creation. Conferences that attract faculty and graduate students already exist. What we need, I think, are massively distributed digital projects designed and built by massively distributed undergraduates.

Many such undergraduate courses exist. Funding an undergraduate conference is a bigger proposition, and the authors of this book are currently working with HASTAC affiliates to see about taking on this challenge. As Steve Jones at the University of Illinois at Chicago notes in response to Silver's comment, it is not "massively distributed" undergraduate projects that are needed but rather mechanisms for making any kind of peer-to-peer exchange (even between two students on different campuses) work. Steve Jones, comment on "Future of Learning Institutions in a Digital Age," Institute for the Future of the Book, http://www.futureofthebook.org/HASTAC/learningreport/i-overview. The issue is not size but new intellectual possibility, at any scale. At HASTAC, the authors of this book are experimenting with the "HASTAC Scholars" program, where 50 to 60 undergraduates and graduate students nominated by HASTAC steering committee members take a leadership role not only in reporting on events in their region and at their institutions but in weekly discussion forums, virtual book groups, and in networking together and organizing HASTAC events (including nonhierarchical student-run "un-conferences" and BarConferences).

8. For a recent example of just such an exercise in the deconstructive reconsideration of familiar terms that this book advocates, see the extended list of definitions of *hard drive* in Matthew G. Kirschenbaum's *Mechanisms: New Media and the Forensic Imagination* (Cambridge, MA: MIT Press, 2008), 86–92. A hard drive is "random access . . . a signal processor . . . differential . . . volumetric . . . rationalized," and

so on. There is virtually no hardware, software, programming, or Internet terminology that would not benefit from this level of deconstructive scrutiny.

9. SL's home page (http://secondlife.com/whatis) includes statistics, charts, and graphs about all aspects of the virtual environment. Katie Salen, ed., *The Ecology of Games: Connecting Youth, Games, and Learning* (Cambridge, MA: MIT Press, 2008), is the best volume by far on the learning potential of games and is part of the pathbreaking MacArthur Foundation book series on Digital Media and Learning. For an excellent analysis of teaching in SL, see Cory Ondrejka's contribution to that volume, "Education Unleashed: Participatory Culture, Education, and Innovation in Second Life," 229–252. Ondrejka was so-called Employee Number 4 at Linden Labs (developers of SL), the first person hired there and one of its leaders until December 2007. He worked at Linden Labs when he wrote this essay.

10. See Shira Boss, "Even in a Virtual World, 'Stuff' Matters," *The New York Times*, September 9, 2007, and Richard Siklos, "A Virtual World but Real Money," *The New York Times*, October 19, 2006.

11. For more information on Evan Donahue's contributions to SL and HASTAC, see http://www.hastac.org/blogs/evan-donahue/times-they -are-changin.

12. One of the best assessments of the political geography and cultural studies implications of contemporary universities comes from the 3Cs, the Counter-Cartographies Collective at the University of North Carolina, http://www.countercartographies.org.

13. For a superb collection of essays on race and digital media, see Anna Everett, ed., *Learning Race and Ethnicity: Youth and Digital Media* (Cambridge, MA: MIT Press, 2007), another volume in the MacArthur Foundation series on Digital Media and Learning. See also Lisa Nakamura, *Digitizing Race: Visual Cultures of the Internet* (Minneapolis: University of Minnesota Press, 2007).

14. An excellent overview of some of the issues around gender and technology is Justine Cassell and Meg Cramer, "High Tech or High Risk: Moral Panics about Girls Online," in McPherson, *Digital Youth,*

53–76. See Yasmin Kafai, Carrie Heeter, Jill Denner, and Jennifer Sun, eds., *Beyond Barbie to Mortal Kombat: New Perspectives on Gender and Computer Games* (Cambridge, MA: MIT Press, 2008); Anne Balsamo, *Technology of the Gendered Body: Reading Cyborg Women* (Durham, NC: Duke University Press, 1996).

15. Grossberg, in *Caught in the Crossfire*, is one of our most powerful commentator on economic disparity, political rhetoric, and the disturbing demonizing of youth in contemporary America.

16. Daniel J. Solove, *The Future of Reputation: Gossip, Rumor, and Privacy on the Internet* (New Haven: Yale University Press, 2007).

17. No Child Left Behind Act of 2001, Public Law 107–110, 107th Congress (January 8, 2002).

18. "Google jockeying—search engines in the classroom," *Pandia Search Engine News*, July 3, 2006, http://www.pandia.com/sew/237 -google-jockeying-%E2%80%93-search-engines-in-the-classroom.html.

19. Lev Manovich directs the Software Studies Initiative at the University of California at San Diego and is the most important proponent of what he terms *cultural analytics*. See Kevin Franklin and Karen Rodriquez, "The Next Big Thing in Humanities, Arts, and Social Science Computing: Cultural Analytics," *HPC Wire*, July 29, 2008, http:// www.hpcwire.com.

20. http://www.johnseelybrown.com/speeches.html.

21. Such issues seem trivial until one realizes that, on the graduate level, a plus or a change in half a point can constitute being put on probation in a program. *God is in the details*, architects like to say—and sometimes demons reside in details, too.

22. Avery, comment on "Future of Learning Institutions in a Digital Age," Institute for the Future of the Book, comment posted on March 18, 2007, http://www.futureofthebook.org/HASTAC/learningreport/ i-overview.

23. Irvine Welsh, *If You Liked School, You'll Love Work* (New York: W.W. Norton, 2007).

24. Howard Rheingold, *Smart Mobs: The Next Social Revolution* (Cambridge, MA: Perseus Publishing, 2002).

25. Clay Shirky, *Here Comes Everybody: The Power of Organizing Without Organizations* (New York: The Penguin Press, 2008), 233.

26. Henry Jenkins, with Katie Clinton, Ravi Purushotma, Alice J. Robison, and Margaret Weigel, "Confronting the Challenges of Participatory Culture: Media Education for the 21st Century," http://www.digital learning.macfound.org/atf/cf/%7B7E45C7E0-A3E0-4B89-AC9C -E807E1B0AE4E%7D/JENKINS_WHITE_PAPER.PDF; Henry Jenkins, *Convergence Culture: Where Old and New Media Collide* (New York: New York University Press, 2006).

27. Siva Viswanathan, *The Googlization of Everything*, book in progress, http://www.googlizationofeverything.com.

28. Anne Balsamo, comment on "Future of Learning Institutions in a Digital Age," Institute for the Future of the Book, comment posted on August 31, 2007, http://www.futureofthebook.org/HASTAC/learnin greport/i-overview. See Balsamo, *Technology of the Gendered Body*; Balsamo, *Designing Culture: The Technological Imagination at Work* (forthcoming), for critiques of actual, if hidden, labor under the utopian mythology of the "virtual." For another point of view, see Rob Latham's *Consuming Youth: Vampires, Cyborgs, and the Culture of Consumption* (Chicago: University of Chicago Press, 2002), and his return to Marx's idea of the vampiric nature of commodity capitalism that pretends to be giving life to workers while actually sucking away their life blood.

29. Michael Strangelove, *The Empire of Mind: Digital Piracy and the Anticapitalist Movement* (Toronto: University of Toronto Press, 2005).

5 Institutions as Mobilizing Networks: (Or, "I Hate the Institution—But I Love What It Did for Me")

1. Connie Yowell's request came in conjunction with MacArthur Foundation President Jonathan Fanton's talk on "The Importance of Institutions," at the John D. and Catherine T. MacArthur Foundation Chicago

Donor's Forum Luncheon, June 22, 2006, http://www.macfound.org/
site/apps/nlnet/content2.aspx?c=lkLXJ8MQKrH&b=1054955&ct=
5124893. Fanton's argument is that institutions provide overt and
sometimes hidden supports that undergird transformation as well as
tradition. This chapter's definition of *institution* is partly inspired by
these remarks. Additionally, Sarita Yardi has urged an emphasis on the
role of individuals and groups in the constitution and in the revision-
ing of institutions. The point is well taken, and this version underscores the role of humans—individual and collective—in the shaping
of institutional structures.

2. Rcsha (username only, no information on true identity), responds to
this definition in a comment on "Future of Learning Institutions in a
Digital Age," Institute for the Future of the Book, comment posted on
June 15, 2007, http://www.futureofthebook.org/HASTAC/learningre
port/i-overview: "What are institutions as mobilizing networks mobilizing people to do? While I like the plasticity of mobility, I worry that
like the slipperiness of signs, slipperiness works both for and against
one's position."

3. Avner Greif, *Institutions and the Path to the Modern Economy* (Cambridge: Cambridge University Press, 2006).

4. Robert O. Keohane, *International Institutions and State Power: Essays
in International Relations Theory* (Boulder, CO: Westview Press, 1989), 3;
Keohane, email to authors, September 24, 2006. In correspondence
over this definition of *institution*, Keohane indicated that he has modified his 1989 definition, inserting the phrase "along with norms and
beliefs" into the original.

5. This definition complements but is to be distinguished in emphasis from Actor Network Theory. The latter emphasizes the ways in
which people interact with one another to individualized ends. This
book's concept of institutions as mobilizing networks focuses by contrast on the outcomes of interactive arrangements among individuals.
For further discussion of interactive arrangements, see Howard Rheingold, *Smart Mobs: The Next Social Revolution* (New York: Basic Books,
2003).

6. This definition is itself collaborative and was written with feedback, input, and constructive (and vigorous) disagreement from many colleagues: Anne Allison (Anthropology), Srinivas Aravamudan (English), Anne Balsamo (Interactive Media), James Boyle (Law), Rachael Brady (Electrical and Computer Engineering), Jonathon Cummings (Marketing), Neil DeMarchi (Economics), Kevin Franklin (Education and Grid Computing), Lawrence Grossberg (Communications and Cultural Studies), Harry Halpin (Philosophy and Computer Science), Andrew Janiak (Philosophy), Robert Keohane (Political Science), Julie Klein (English and Interdisciplinary Studies), Timothy Lenoir (History and New Technologies and Society), David Liu (Religion), Dana D. Nelson (American Studies and Political Theory), Mark Olson (New Media and Communications), Kenneth Rogerson (Public Policy), Kristine Stiles (Art History), and Kathleen Woodward (English). Lawrence Grossberg offered the most extended and persistent critique of this definition. He will not agree with the final version but his critiques allowed the clarification of a number of points.

7. Eileen McMahon, comment on "Future of Learning Institutions in a Digital Age," Institute for the Future of the Book, comment posted on March 20, 2007, http://www.futureofthebook.org/HASTAC/learningreport/i-overview. McMahon notes that there are a number of institutions that are not modeled after patriarchal hierarchies and that may well be models for participatory learning institutions: New England Shaker communities, computer/technical user groups like MSMUB, ACM SIGs, MUDS/Moos, yoga organizations such as Syda, and quilting circles. Contributor David Silver underscores the importance of libraries as a model for the networked, circulating learning center operating both within and across, inside and outside, of traditional learning institutions. Steve Jones notes, on the other hand, that students themselves find and make learning spaces within traditional institutions (including libraries) and make networks and learning communities in cafeterias, lounges, and computer labs, repurposing an institution's nooks and crannies as learning spaces.

8. James Boyle, "Mertonianism Unbound? Imagining Free, Decentralised Access to Most Cultural and Scientific Material" (Indiana University: The Digital Library of the Commons, 2006); Yochai Benkler,

"Coase's Penguin, or Linux and the Nature of the Firm," *Yale Law Journal* 112, no. 3 (2002).

9. Microsoft is releasing WorldWide Telescope free of charge to the astronomy and educational communities (though open-source release of the code would go a step further and be even more appealing).

10. Siva Vaidhayanathan's Web site and forthcoming collaborative book are both entitled *The Googlization of Everything: How One Company is Disrupting Culture, Commerce, and Community—and Why We Should Worry,* http://www.googlizationofeverything.com

11. For more information on these centers and organizations, see Bibliography II: Resources and Models.

12. Rishab Aiyer Ghosh, ed., *CODE: Collaborative Ownership and the Digital Economy* (Cambridge, MA: MIT Press, 2005).

13. Jochen Fromm, *The Emergence of Complexity* (Germany: Kassel University Press, 2004); Steven Johnson, *Emergence: The Connected Lives of Ants, Brains, Cities, and Software* (New York: Scribner, 2001).

14. John Seely Brown and Paul Duguid, "The University in the Digital Age," *Times Higher Education Supplement,* May 10, 1996: 1–4; Jonathon Cummings and Sara Kiesler, "Collaborative Research Across Disciplinary and Organizational Boundaries," *Social Studies of Science* 35 (2005): 703–722.

6 HASTAC

1. William Wulf, "The National Collaboratory," in *Towards a National Collaboratory* (unpublished report of a National Science Foundation invitational workshop, Rockefeller University, New York, March 1989).

2. Mechelle de Craene volunteered in fall 2007 to host a site primarily for others in K–12 education. HASTAC on Ning, "A Synergistic Symposium for the Cybernetic Age" (http://hastac.ning.com), is now an exceptionally active and physically beautiful site that feeds onto the HASTAC home page and is featured in *Needle,* the HASTAC Information

Commons. Additionally, blogs from the HASTAC page are automatically fed via Really Simply Syndication (RSS) to the HASTAC on Ning site.

3. Anne Balsamo, comment on "The Future of Learning Institutions in a Digital Age," Institute for the Future of the Book, comment posted on August 31, 2007, http://www.futureofthebook.org/HASTAC/learnin greport/i-overview.

4. Patricia Seed, comment on "Future of Learning Institutions in a Digital Age," Institute for the Future of the Book, comment posted on May 11, 2007, http://www.futureofthebook.org/HASTAC/learningre port/i-overview.

5. On Ancient Rome 3D, see http://www.google.com/educators/rome contest.html; on Portuguese maps of West Africa, see http://www.neh .gov/news/humanities/2008-11/ConeOfAfrica.html.

6. For example, some of the fundamental features of HASTAC were presaged by the 1999 establishment of Information Science + Information Studies, http://www.isis.duke.edu. ISIS is a certificate program designed to teach those who will be creating the next generation of technology to think creatively, critically, and in a socially responsible manner about its use and application. It is a program where students both analyze and create collaboratively and across disciplines.

7. Though this book does not address the legal rights and responsibilities of virtual institutions, legal theories being developed for online multiplayer games and their applicability to other forms of distribution and adjudication of virtual real estate, including peer-to-peer institutions, raise interesting issues. See F. Gregory Lastowka and Dan Hunter, "The Laws of the Virtual Worlds," *Legal Theory Research Paper Series, University of Pennsylvania Law School* 26 (2003).

8. Erin Ennis, Zoë Marie Jones, Paolo Mangiafico, Mark Olson, Jennifer Rhee, Mitali Routh, Jonathan E. Tarr, and Brett Walters, eds., *Electronic Techtonics: Thinking at the Interface* (lulu.com, 2008). See also videos of the conference on the HASTAC Web site, http://www.hastac.org/video/ archives.

9. http://www.hastac.org/node/1532.

10. Many of the days at SECT were blogged on the HASTAC Web site, http://www.hastac.org. Webcasts of the events are also available at http://www.uchri.org.

11. Shirky, *Here Comes Everybody: The Power of Organizing without Organizations* (New York: Penguin Press, 2008).

12. The bicoastal HASTAC team for the first HASTAC/MacArthur Foundation Digital Media and Learning Competition included: at Duke University, Cathy N. Davidson, Jason Doty, Erin Ennis, Mark Olson, Jonathan Tarr, and Brett Walters; and at UCHRI, David Theo Goldberg, Suzy Beemer, Khai Tang, Annette Rubado-Mejia, and Jenifer Wilkens.

13. Michael Hardt and Antonio Negri, *Commonwealth*, (Cambridge: Harvard University Press, 2009)

14. Thomas Finholt and Gary Olson, "From Laboratories to Collaboratories: A New Organizational Form for Scientific Collaboration," *Psychological Science* 8, no. 1 (1997): 28–36.

15. Hassan Masum and Yi–Cheng Zhang, "Manifesto for the Reputation Society," *First Monday* 9, no. 7, July 5, 2004, http://firstmonday.org/htbin/cgiwrap/bin/ojs/index.php/fm/article/view/1158/1078.

16. Masum and Zhang, "Manifesto for the Reputation Society."

17. Steve Jones, comment on "The Future of Learning Institutions in a Digital Age," Institute for the Future of the Book, comment posted on February 3, 2007, http://www.futureofthebook.org/HASTAC/learningreport/i-overview.

18. Mike Roy, comment on "The Future of Learning Institutions in a Digital Age," Institute for the Future of the Book, comment posted on March 27, 2007, http://www.futureofthebook.org/HASTAC/learningreport/i-overview.

19. 501(c) is a provision of the United States Internal Revenue Code (26 U.S.C. 501[c]) listing 26 types of nonprofit organizations exempt from some federal income taxes.

20. Yochai Benkler, *The Wealth of Networks: How Social Production Transforms Markets and Freedom* (New Haven: Yale University Press, 2006): 460–461.

21. Benkler, *The Wealth of Networks*, 463.

7   (In)Conclusive: Thinking the Future of Digital Thinking

1. Robert Kraut, M. Patterson, V. Lundmark, S. Kiesler, T. Mukhopadhyay, and W. Scherlis, "Internet Paradox: A Social Technology That Reduces Social Involvement and Psychological Well-Being?" *American Psychologist* 53, no. 9 (1998): 1017–1032.

2. Robert Kraut, Sara Kiesler, Bonka Boneva, Jonathon Cummings, Vicki Helgeson, and Anne Crawford, "Internet Paradox Revisited" *Journal of Social Issues* 58 no. 1 (2002): 49–74. See also Mizuko Ito et al., *Living and Learning with New Media: Summary of Findings from the Digital Youth Project*, (Cambridge, MA: MIT Press, 2009).

3. Shirky, *Here Comes Everybody*, 16.

4. Shirky, *Here Comes Everybody*, 16.

5. Malcolm Gladwell, *The Tipping Point: How Little Things Can Make a Big Difference* (New York: Little, Brown, 2002).

6. Lawrence Cremins and Freeman Butts, *A History of Education in American Culture* (New York: Holt, Rinehart and Winston, 1961). *A History of Education* is an early and generally positive account of the transformation from the religious-based colonial school to the nationalist model of public education. As many subsequent historians have noted, this account simplifies the ways that gender, race and ethnicity, class, region, country-of-origin, language, political persuasion, and religious differences have all, in different ways, been inflected as un-American within public education in an attempt to instill a unified, homogenous nationalist identity on a diverse and ever-changing population. For one of many critiques of nationalist educational policy, see David L. Angus and Jeffrey E. Mirel, *The Failed Promise of the American High School, 1890–1995* (New York: Teachers College Press, 1999). See also

Cathy N. Davidson, "Literacy, Education, and the Reader," in *Revolution and the Word: The Rise of the Novel in America* (New York, NY: Oxford University Press, 1986), 121–50; Dana Nelson Salvino, "The Word in Black and White: Ideologies of Race and Literacy in Antebellum America," in *Reading in America*, ed. Davidson, 140–156; Christopher Newfield, *Ivy and Industry: Business and the Making of the American University, 1880-1980* (Durham, NC: Duke University Press, 2004); Newfield, *Unmaking the Public University: The Forty-Year Assault on the Middle Class* (Cambridge, MA: Harvard University Press, 2008).

7. Tara McPherson, "A Rule Set for the Future," in *Digital Youth*, ed. McPherson, 1–26.

8. "Internet World Stats: Usage and Population Statistics," which records world Internet user numbers, indicates that, in 2009, Internet penetration was 74.4% of North Americans and only 5.6% of the population of Africa, with wide-ranging disparities by country, economic status, and region within those continents as well. Africa and the Middle East are seeing the most rapid new adoption of digital technologies worldwide but the numbers still lag far beyond those in the developed world, http://www.internetworldstats.com/stats.htm.

9. Andy Kroll, "Gated Communities of Learning," April 3, 2009, http://www.salon.com/news/feature/2009/04/03/kroll/index.html. Kroll notes: "Over the past 30 years, the average annual cost of college tuition, fees, and room and board has increased nearly 100 percent, from $7,857 in 1977–78 to $15,665 in 2007–08 (in constant 2006–07 dollars). Median household income, on the other hand, has risen a mere 18 percent over that same period, from about $42,500 to just over $50,000. College costs, in other words, have gone up at more than five times the rate of income."

10. For an excellent discussion, see Miriam J. Metzger and Andrew J. Flanagin, eds., *Digital Media, Youth, and Credibility*, (Cambridge, MA: MIT Press, 2008).

11. Barry Wellman, Janet Salaff, Dimitrina Dimitrova, Laura Garton, Milena Gulia, and Caroline Haythornthwaite, "Computer Networks as Social Networks: Collaborative Work, Telework, and Virtual Community,"

Annual Review of Sociology 22 (1996): 213–238. Mike Roy asked: "can you actually organize emergent behaviors? What motivates people to contribute to these sorts of projects? What does the reward structure for contributing look like? (It should be noted that one of the main reasons for Linux achieving its remarkable success is that IBM dedicated serious resources to transforming it into production-level code as a means of avoiding having to pay license fees for its servers.)" Mike Roy, comment on "The Future of Learning Institutions in a Digital Age," Institute for the Future of the Book, comment posted on March 27, 2007, http:// www.futureofthebook.org/HASTAC/learningreport/i-overview.

12. http://lecturecast.sdsc.edu/16114.ram and http://lecturecast.sdsc .edu/16115.ram.

13. For an excellent analysis of the pedagogical requirements for a digital age, see Steve Anderson and Anne Balsamo, "A Pedagogy for Original Synners," in McPherson, ed., *Digital Youth*, 241–259; Jenkins, *Confronting the Challenges of Participatory Culture*. Both of these works offer prescriptions for new forms of learning in a digital age, at points similar and in other ways different from the forms presented in this book but with similar goals and objectives.

14. See, for example Millie Niss, *Oulipoems*, http://www.uiowa.edu/ ~iareview/tirweb/feature/sept04/oulipoems/index.html.

15. See the entry on "Wikipedia" on Wikipedia, http://en.wikipedia .org/wiki/Wikipedia.

16. For a concise collection of essays addressing explicitly the issue of credibility in collaborative learning environments, see Metzger and Flanagin, eds., *Digital Media*.

17. Jenkins, *Convergence Culture*, 257.

Bibliography I: Selected Books, Articles, and Reports

Digital Learning, Technology, and Education

Brabazon, Tara. *The University of Google: Education in the (Post) Information Age.* Aldershot: Ashgate Press, 2007.

Brown, John Seely, and Richard P. Adler. "Minds on Fire: Open Education, the Long Tail, and Learning 2.0." *Educause Review* 43, no. 1 (2008): 16–32.

Brown, John Seely, and Allan Collins. "Situated Cognition and the Culture of Learning." *Educational Researcher* 18, no. 1 (1989): 32–42.

Brown, John Seely, and Paul Duguid. "The University in the Digital Age." *Times Higher Education Supplement* (May 10, 1996): 1–4.

Chun, Wendy Hui Kyong, and Thomas Keenan, eds. *New Media, Old Media: A History and Theory Reader.* London: Routledge, 2005.

Clark, Andy. *Natural-Born Cyborgs: Minds, Technologies, and the Future of Human Intelligence.* Oxford: Oxford University Press, 2003.

Cole, Jonathan, Elinor Barbar, and Stephen Graubard, eds. *The Research University in a Time of Discontent.* Baltimore: Johns Hopkins University Press, 1993.

Cuban, Larry. *Oversold and Underused: Computers in the Classroom.* Cambridge, MA: Harvard University Press, 2003.

Davidson, Cathy N. "Humanities 2.0: Promise, Perils, Predictions," *PMLA* 123, no. 3 (2008): 707–717.

———. "Teaching the Promise: The Research University in the Information Age." In *A Digital Gift to the Nation: Fulfilling the Promise of the Digital and Internet Age*, edited by Lawrence K. Grossman and Newton N. Minow. New York: The Century Foundation Press, 2001.

———. "We Can't Ignore the Influence of Digital Technologies." *Chronicle of Higher Education Review* 53, no. 29 (2007): B20.

———. "What if Scholars in the Humanities Worked Together in a Lab?" *Chronicle of Higher Education* (May 28, 1999).

Davidson, Cathy N., and David Theo Goldberg. "Engaging the Humanities." *Profession* (2004).

———. "Managing from the Middle." *Chronicle of Higher Education* (May 2, 2005).

———. "A Manifesto for the Humanities in a Technological Age." *Chronicle of Higher Education* (February 13, 2004).

diSessa, Andrea A. *Changing Minds: Computers, Learning, and Literacy.* Cambridge, MA: MIT Press, 2000.

Freedman, Terry, ed. *Coming of Age: An Introduction to the New World Wide Web.* Ilford, England: Terry Freedman Ltd., 2006, http://edu.blogs.com/edublogs/files/Coming_of_age.pdf.

Fromm, Jochen. *The Emergence of Complexity.* Germany: Kassel University Press, 2004.

Grabe, Mark, and Cindy Grabe. *Integrating Technology for Meaningful Learning.* New York: Houghton Mifflin, 2001.

Harley, Diane, Jonathan Henke, and Michael W. Maher. "Rethinking Space and Time: The Role of Internet Technology in a Large Lecture Course." *Innovate* 1, no. 1 (2004), http://cshe.berkeley.edu/publications/publications.php?id=34.

————. With Jonathan Henke, Shannon Lawrence, Ian Miller, Irene Perciali, and David Nasatir. "Use and Users of Digital Resources: A Focus on Undergraduate Education in the Humanities and Social Sciences." University of California, Berkeley: Center for Studies in Higher Education, 2006.

————. "Why Study Users? An Environmental Scan of Use and Users of Digital Resources in Humanities and Social Sciences Undergraduate Education." *First Monday* 12, no. 1 (2007), http://www.firstmonday.org/issues/issue12_1/harley/index.html.

Herz, J. C., ed., *The Internet and the University*. Boulder: EDUCAUSE, 2001.

Hiltz, Starr Roxanne. *The Virtual Classroom: Learning Without Limits via Computer Networks*. Norwood, NJ: Ablex: Human-Computer Interaction Series, 1994.

Jenkins, Henry. *Convergence Culture: Where Old and New Media Collide*. New York: New York University Press, 2006.

Jenkins, Henry, with Katie Clinton, Ravi Purushotma, Alice J. Robison, and Margaret Weigel. "Confronting the Challenges of Participatory Culture: Media Education for the 21st Century." Chicago, Illinois: The John D. and Catherine T. MacArthur Foundation, 2007, http://www.digitallearning.macfound.org/atf/cf/%7B7E45C7E0-A3E0-4B89-AC9C-E807E1B0AE4E%7D/JENKINS_WHITE_PAPER.PDF.

Johnson, Kay, and Elaine Magusin. *Exploring the Digital Library: A Guide for Online Teaching and Learning*. San Francisco, CA: Jossey-Bass, 2005.

Kellner, Douglas, and Jeff Share. "Critical Media Literacy is not an Option." *Learning Inquiry* 1, no. 1 (2007).

Kress, Gunther. *Literacy in the New Media Age*. London: Routledge, 2003.

Lave, Jean, and Etienne Wenger. *Situated Learning: Legitimate Peripheral Participation*. Cambridge: Cambridge University Press, 1991.

Merrill, Duane. "Mashups: The New Breed of Web App." IBM Developer-Works, 2006, http://www.ibm.com/developerworks/library/x-mashups.html

Minielli, Maureen C., and S. Pixy Ferris. "Electronic Courseware in Higher Education." *First Monday* 10, no. 9 (2005), http://www.uic.edu/htbin/cgiwrap/bin/ojs/index.php/fm/article/view/1279/1199.

O'Reilly, Tim. "What is Web. 2.0: Design Patterns and Business Models for the Next Generation of Software." O'Reilly Media, Inc., 2005, http://www.oreillynet.com/pub/a/oreilly/tim/news/2005/09/30/what-is-web -20.html.

Philip, Donald. "The Knowledge Building Paradigm: A Model of Learning for Net Generation Students." *Innovate* 3, no. 5 (2005), http://www.innovateonline.info/index.php?view=article&id=368&action.

Schank, Robert C. *Virtual Learning: A Revolutionary Approach to Building a Highly Skilled Workforce.* New York: McGraw Hill, 1997.

Schonfeld, Roger C. *JSTOR: A History.* Princeton, N.J.: Princeton University Press, 2003.

Shaffer, David Williamson, and Katherine A. Clinton. "Why all CSL is CL: Distributed Mind and the Future of Computer Supported Collaborative Learning." Proceedings of the 2005 Conference on Computer Support for Collaborative Learning: *Learning 2005: The Next 10 Years!* In Taipei, Taiwan, http://portal.acm.org/citation.cfm?id=1149371.

———. "Toolforthoughts: Reexamining Thinking in the Digital Age." *Mind, Culture, and Activity* 13, no. 4 (2006): 283–300, http://epistemic games.org/cv/papers/toolforthoughts-sub1.pdf.

Shaffer, David Williamson, and James J. Kaput. "Mathematics and Virtual Culture: An Evolutionary Perspective on Technology and Mathematics." *Educational Studies in Mathematics* 37, no. 2 (1998): 97–119, http://www.springerlink.com/content/h64180777736562t.

Shaffer, David Williamson, and Michael Resnick. "'Thick' Authenticity: New Media and Authentic Learning." *Journal of Interactive Learning Research* 10, no. 2 (1999): 195–215.

Szep, Jason. "Technology Reshapes America's Classrooms." *New York Times* (July 7, 2008).

Thomas, Douglas, and John Seely Brown. "The Play of Imagination: Beyond the Literary Mind." Working paper. August 22, 2006, http://www.hastac.org/system/files/The+Play+of+Imagination+Beyond+the+Literary+Mind.doc.

Warschauer, Mark. "The Paradoxical Future of Digital Learning." *Learning Inquiry* 1, no, 1 (2007): 41–49.

Wilson, Edward O. *Consilience: The Unity of Knowledge*. New York: Alfred A. Knopf: Distributed by Random House, 1998.

Young, Jeffrey R. "Browser-Based Software Will Help Scholars Organize Information Found Online, Researchers Say." *The Chronicle of Higher Education* (December 6, 2005), http://www.chronicle.com/daily/2005/12/2005120602t.htm.

Zemsky, Robert, and William F. Massy. *Thwarted Innovation: What Happened to e-Learning and Why*. The Weatherstation Project of The Learning Alliance at the University of Pennsylvania in Cooperation with the Thomson Corporation (2004), http://www.thelearningalliance.info/Docs/Jun2004/ThwartedInnovation.pdf.

Institutions

Benkler, Yochai. "Coase's Penguin, or Linux and the Nature of the Firm." *Yale Law Journal* 112, no. 3 (2002): 369–446.

———. *The Wealth of Networks: How Social Production Transforms Markets and Freedom*. New Haven: Yale University Press, 2006.

Bleecker, Samuel E. "The Virtual Organization." *The Futurist* 28, no. 2 (1994): 9–14.

Davidow, William H., and Michael S. Malone. *The Virtual Corporation: Structuring and Revitalizing the Corporation for the 21ˢᵗ Century*. New York: Harper Collins, 1992.

DeSanctis, Gerardine, and Janet Fulk, eds. *Shaping Organization Form: Communication, Connection, and Community*. Newbury Park, CA: Sage, 1999.

DeSanctis, Gerardine, and Peter Monge. "Communication Processes for Virtual Organizations," *Organization Science* 10, no. 6 (1999): 693–703.

Fanton, Jonathan. "The Importance of Institutions." Speech, John D. and Catherine T. MacArthur Foundation Chicago Donor's Forum Luncheon, Chicago, IL, June 22, 2006, http://www.macfound.org/site/c.lkLXJ8MQKrH/b.1054949/apps/nl/content2.asp?content_id=%7BADB530B0-BDC7-430E-B0C7-80DFD44658FF%7D&notoc=1.

Gibson, Mark, and Alec McHoul. "Interdisciplinarity," in *A Companion to Cultural Studies*, Toby Miller, ed., Oxford: Basil Blackwell, 2006.

Greif, Avner. *Institutions and the Path to the Modern Economy*. Cambridge: Cambridge University Press, 2006.

Gudrais, Greif. "Unequal America: Causes and Consequences of the Wide—and Growing—Gap Between Rich and Poor," *Harvard Magazine* 110, no. 6 (2008): 22–29, http://harvardmagazine.com/2008/07/unequal-america.html.

Goldberg, David Theo. "Enduring Occupations," in *The Threat of Race*. Oxford: Wiley-Blackwell, 2008.

Goldin, Claudia. *The Race between Education and Technology*. Cambridge, MA: Belknap Press, 2008.

Klein, Julie. *Crossing Boundaries: Knowledge, Disciplinarities and Interdisciplinarities*. Charlottesville: University of Virginia Press, 1996.

———. *Interdisciplinarity: History, Theory, and Practice*. Detroit: Wayne State University Press, 1990.

Lattuca, Lisa. *Creating Interdisciplinarity: Interdisciplinary Research and Teaching Among College and University Faculty*. Nashville: Vanderbilt University Press, 2001.

No Child Left Behind Act of 2001, Public Law 107–110, 107th Congress (January 8, 2002).

Newfield, Christopher. *Ivy and Industry: Business and the Making of the American University, 1880-1980*. Durham, NC: Duke University Press, 2004.

──────. *Unmaking the Public University: The Forty-Year Assault on the Middle Class*. Cambridge, MA: Harvard University Press, 2008.

Readings, Bill. *The University in Ruins*. Cambridge, MA: Harvard University Press, 1996.

Shirky, Clay. *Here Comes Everybody: The Power of Organizing Without Organizations*. New York: The Penguin Press, 2008.

Wellman, Barry, Anabel Quan-Haase, Jeffrey Boase, and Wenhong Chen. "The Social Affordances of the Internet for Networked Individualism." *Journal Of Computer Mediated Communication* 8, no. 3 (2003), http://jcmc.indiana.edu/vol8/issue3/wellman.html.

Social Networking and Knowledge Sharing

Angus, David L., and Jeffrey E. Mirel. *The Failed Promise of the American High School, 1890-1995*. New York: Teachers College Press, 1999.

Axelsson, Sofie, and Tim Regan. "How Belonging to an Online Group Affects Social Behavior—A Case Study of Asheron's Call." Microsoft: Microsoft Technical Report, 2002, http://research.microsoft.com/apps/pubs/default.aspx?id=69910.

Barab, Sasha A., Rob Kling, and James H. Gray, eds. *Designing for Virtual Communities in the Service of Learning*. Cambridge: Cambridge University Press, 2004.

Barabasi, Albert-Laszlo. *Linked: How Everything Is Connected to Everything Else and What It Means*. New York: Plume, 2003.

Black, Rebecca W. "Access and Affiliation: The New Literacy Practices of English Language Learners in an Online Animé-Based Fanfiction Community." *Journal of Adolescent & Adult Literacy* 49, no. 2. (2005): 118–128.

boyd, danah m., and Nicole B Ellison. "Social Network Sites: Definition, History, and Scholarship." *Journal of Computer-Mediated Communication* 13, no. 1, article 11 (2007), http://jcmc.indiana.edu/vol13/issue1/boyd.ellison.html.

Brown, John Seely, and Paul Duguid. *The Social Life of Information*. Boston: Harvard Business School Press, 2002.

Cremins, Lawrence, and Freeman Butts. *A History of Education in American Culture*. New York: Holt, Rinehart and Winston, 1961.

Cummings, Jonathon. "Work Groups, Structural Diversity, and Knowledge Sharing in a Global Organization." *Management Science* 50, no. 3 (2004): 352–364.

Cummings, Jonathon, Brian Butler, and Robert Kraut. "The Quality of Online Social Relationships." *Communications of the ACM* 45, no. 7 (2002): 103–108.

Cummings, Jonathon, and Sara Kiesler. "Collaborative Research Across Disciplinary and Organizational Boundaries." *Social Studies of Science* 35 (2005): 703–722.

Cummings, Jonathon, John B. Lee, and Robert Kraut. "Communication Technology and Friendship: The Transition from High School to College." In *Computers, Phones and The Internet: Domesticating Information Technology*, eds. Robert Kraut et al., 265–278. New York: Oxford University Press, 2006.

Finholt, Thomas, and Gary Olson. "From Laboratories to Collaboratories: A New Organizational Form for Scientific Collaboration." *Psychological Science* 8, no. 1 (1997): 28–36.

Franklin, Kevin, and Karen Rodriguez. "The Next Big Thing in Humanities, Arts, and Social Science Computing: Cultural Analytics." *HPC Wire* (July 29, 2008), http://www.hpcwire.com.

Fulk, Janet, and Charels Steinfield, eds. *Organizations and Communication Technology*. Beverly Hills, CA: Sage, 1990.

Gladwell, Malcolm. *The Tipping Point: How Little Things Can Make a Big Difference*. New York: Little, Brown, 2002.

Guernsey, Lisa. "Cyberspace Isn't So Lonely After All." *New York Times* (July 26, 2001).

Hargittai, Eszter. "Whose Space? Differences Among Users and Non-Users of Social Network Sites." *Journal of Computer-Mediated Communication* 13, no. 1, article 14 (2007), http://jcmc.indiana.edu/vol13/issue1/hargittai.html.

Hesse, Bradford W., and Charles E. Grantham. *Electronically Distributed Work Communities: Implications for Research on Telework*. Working Paper. Washington, DC: Center for Research on Technology, American Institute for Research, 1991.

Hildreth, Paul M., and Chris Kimble, eds. *Knowledge Networks: Innovation Through Communities of Practice*. Hershey, PA: Idea Group Publishing, 2004.

Hiltz, Starr Roxanne, and Murray Turoff. *The Network Nation: Human Communication via Computer*, rev. ed. Cambridge, MA: MIT Press, 1993.

Ito, Mizuko, Sonja Baumer, Matteo Bittanti, danah boyd, Rachel Cody, Becky Herr-Stephenson, Heather Horst, Patricia G. Lange, Dilan Mahendran, Katynka Z. Martinez, C. J. Pascoe, Dan Perkel, Laura Robinson, Christo Sims, and Lisa Tripp. *Living and Learning with New Media: Summary of Findings from the Digital Youth Project*. Cambridge, MA: MIT Press, 2009.

Jarillo, J. Carlos. *Strategic Networks: Creating the Borderless Organization*. Oxford: Butterworth-Heinemann, 1995.

Jenkins, Henry, and danah boyd. "Discussion: MySpace and Deleting Online Predators Act (DOPA)." May 30, 2006, http://web.mit.edu/cms/People/henry3/myspaceissues.htm.

———. *Confronting the Challenges of Participatory Culture*. Cambridge, MA: MIT Press, 2009, http://www.digitallearning.macfound.org/atf/cf/%7B7E45C7E0-A3E0-4B89-AC9C-E807E1B0AE4E%7D/JENKINS_WHITE_PAPER.PDF.

Kraut, Robert, Sara Kiesler, Bonka Boneva, Jonathon Cummings, Vicki Helgeson, and Anne Crawford. "Internet Paradox Revisited." *Journal of Social Issues* 58.1 (2002): 49–74.

Kraut, Robert, M. Patterson, V. Lundmark, S. Kiesler, T. Mukhopadhyay, and W. Scherlis. "Internet Paradox: A Social Technology That Reduces Social Involvement and Psychological Well-Being." *American Psychologist* 53, no. 9 (1998): 1017–1031.

Latour, Bruno. *Science in Action: How to Follow Scientists and Engineers Through Society.* Milton Keynes, UK: Open University Press, 1987.

Lipnack, Jessica, and Jeffrey Stamps. *Virtual Teams: People Working Across Boundaries with Technology.* Hoboken, NJ: Wiley & Sons, 2000.

Marcus, George E. "Notes on the Contemporary Imperative to Collaborate, the Traditional Aesthetics of Fieldwork That Will Not Be Denied, and the Need for Pedagogical Experiment in the Transformation of Anthropology's Signature Method." Original text released as part of The Anthropology of the Contemporary Research Collaboratory (http://www.anthropos-lab.net), http://anthropos-lab.net/wp/publications/2007/01/arc-aaa-2006-marcus.pdf.

Nakamura, Lisa. *Digitizing Race: Visual Cultures of the Internet.* Minneapolis: University of Minnesota Press, 2007.

O'Hear, Steve, and Richard MacManus, eds. "Elgg—Social Network Software for Education." *Read/Write Web* (2006), http://www.readwriteweb.com/archives/elgg.php.

Renninger, K. Ann, and Wesley Shumar, eds. *Building Virtual Communities: Learning and Change in Cyberspace (Learning in Doing: Social, Cognitive and Computational Perspectives).* Cambridge: Cambridge University Press, 2002.

Rheingold, Howard. *The Virtual Community: Surfing the Internet.* London: Minerva, 1994.

Rosenzweig, Ron. "Can History Be Open Source? Wikipedia and the Future of the Past." *Journal of American History* 93, no. 1 (2006): 117–146, http://chnm.gmu.edu/resources/essays/d/42.

Ruhleder, Karen, and Michael Twidale. "Reflective Collaborative Learning on the Web: Drawing on the Master Class." *First Monday* 5, no. 5 (2000), http://firstmonday.org/issues/issue5_5/ruhleder/index.html.

Shaffer, David Williamson. "When Computer-Supported Collaboration Means Computer-Supported Competition: Professional Mediation as a Model for Collaborative Learning." *Journal of Interactive Learning Research* 15, no. 2 (2004).

Solove Daniel J. *The Future of Reputation: Gossip, Rumor, and Privacy on the Internet.* New Haven: Yale University Press, 2007.

Stone, Brad. "Online Chat, as Inspired by Real Chat," *New York Times* (March 31, 2008).

Stuckey, Bronwyn, and John D. Smith. "Building Sustainable Communities of Practice," in Paul M. Hildreth and Chris Kimble, eds., *Knowledge Networks: Innovation Through Communities of Practice*, Idea Group Publications (2004).

Watts, Duncan. "Six Degrees of Interconnection." *Wired* 11, no. 6 (2003), http://www.wired.com/wired/archive/11.06/relation_spc.html.

Wellman, Barry, Janet Salaff, Dimitrina Dimitrova, Laura Garton, Milena Gulia, and Caroline Haythornthwaite. "Computer Networks as Social Networks: Collaborative Work, Telework, and Virtual Community." *Annual Review of Sociology* 22 (1996): 213–238.

Welsh, Irvine. *If You Liked School, You'll Love Work.* New York: W.W. Norton, 2007.

Wulf, William. "The National Collaboratory," in *Towards a National Collaboratory* (unpublished report of a National Science Foundation invitational workshop). New York: Rockefeller University, March 1989.

Gaming and Virtual Worlds

Adams, P. C. "Teaching and Learning with SimCity 2000." *Journal of Geography* 97. no. 2 (1998): 47–55.

Aldrich, C. *Simulations and the Future of Learning.* New York: Pfeiffer, 2004.

Barab, S. A., K. E. Hay, M. G. Barnett, and K. Squire. "Constructing Virtual Worlds: Tracing the Historical Development of Learner Practices/ Understandings." *Cognition and Instruction* 19, no. 1 (2001): 47–94.

Boellstorff, Tom. *Coming of Age in Second Life: An Anthropologist Explores the Virtually Human.* Princeton, NJ: Princeton University Press, 2008.

Boss, Shira. "Even in a Virtual World, 'Stuff' Matters," *New York Times* (September 9, 2007).

Castronova, Edward. *Synthetic Worlds: The Business and Culture of Online Games.* Chicago: University of Chicago Press, 2006.

———. "Virtual Worlds: A First-Hand Account of Market and Society on the Cyberian Frontier." *The Gruter Institute Working Papers on Law, Economics, and Evolutionary Biology* 2.1 (2000), http://www.bepress.com/ giwp/default/vol2/iss1/art1.

Clinton, K. A. "*Embodiment in Digital Worlds: What Being a Videogame Player Has to Teach Us About Learning.*" Paper, annual meeting of the American Educational Research Association, San Diego, CA, April 2004.

Ennis, Erin, Zoë Marie Jones, Paolo Mangiafico, Mark Olson, Jennifer Rhee, Mitali Routh, Jonathan E. Tarr, and Brett Walters, eds., *Electronic Techtonics: Thinking at the Interface.* Proceedings of the First International HASTAC Conference, Duke University, Durham, North Carolina, April 19–21, 2007. Lulu.com: 2008, http://www.lulu.com/content/ paperback-book/electronic-techtonics-thinking-at-the-interface/ 2124631.

Figueiredo, Antonio D. de, and Ana Paula Afonso, eds. *Managing Learning in Virtual Settings: The Role of Context.* Hershey, PA: Information Science Publishing, 2005.

Frye, B., and A. M. Frager. "Civilization, Colonization, SimCity: Simulations for the Social Studies." *Learning and Leading with Technology* 24 (1996): 21–23.

Games-to-Teach Team. "Design Principles of Next-Generation Digital Gaming for Education." *Educational Technology* 43, no. 5 (2003): 17–33.

Gee, James Paul. "Learning by Design: Games as Learning Machines." March 24, 2004, http://www.gamasutra.com/gdc2004/features/20040324/gee_01.shtml.

————. *What Video Games Have to Teach Us About Learning and Literacy.* New York: Palgrave Macmillan, 2003.

————. "Why Are Video Games Good For Learning?" Madison, WI: Academic ADL Co-Lab, 2006.

————. *Why Video Games are Good for Your Soul: Pleasure and Learning.* Melbourne: Common Ground, 2005.

Halverson, R. "What Can K-12 School Leaders Learn from Video Games and Gaming?" *Innovate* 1, no. 6 (2005), http://www.innovateonline. info/index.php?view=article&id-81.

Kolbert, Elizabeth. "Pimps and Dragons: How an Online World Survived a Social Breakdown." *The New Yorker* (May 28, 2001): 88.

Lenoir, Timothy. "All But War is Simulation: The Military-Entertainment Complex." *Configurations* 8, no. 3 (2000): 289–335.

Media-X Conference. "Gaming to Learn." September 5, 2003, http://mediax.stanford.edu/news/sep05_03.html.

Poster, Mark. "Theorizing Virtual Reality: Baudrillard and Derrida." In *Cyberspace Textuality: Computer Technology and Literary Theory,* ed. Marie-Laure Ryan. Bloomington: Indiana University Press, 1999.

Prensky, M. *Digital-Game-Based Learning.* New York: McGraw Hill, 2001.

Salen, Katie, ed. *The Ecology of Games: Connecting Youth, Games, and Learning.* The John D. and Catherine T. MacArthur Foundation Series on Digital Media and Learning. Cambridge, MA: MIT Press, 2008.

Shaffer, D. W. "Epistemic Games." *Innovate* 1, no. 6 (2006), http://www.innovateonline.info/index.php?view=article&id=79&action=synopsis.

Siklos, Richard. "A Virtual World but Real Money," *New York Times* (October 19, 2006).

Squire, Kurt D. "Changing The Game: What Happens When Video Games Enter the Classroom?" Academic ADL Co-Lab, 2005.

———. (in press). "Civilization III as a World History Sandbox." In *Civilization and its Discontents: Virtual History, Real Fantasies*. Milan, Italy: Ludilogica Press.

———. (in press). "Game Cultures, School Cultures." *Innovate*.

———. "Sid Meier's Civilization III." *Simulations and Gaming* 35, no. 1 (2004).

———. "Video Games in Education." *International Journal of Intelligent Simulations and Gaming* 2, no. 1 (2003).

Squire, Kurt, and Giovanetto, L. (in press). "The Higher Education of Gaming." *eLearning*.

Squire, Kurt, and Jenkins, Henry. "Harnessing the Power of Games in Education." *Insight* 3, no. 1 (2004): 5–33.

Steinkuehler, C. A. "Cognition and Learning in Massively Multiplayer Online Games: A Critical Approach." Unpublished PhD diss., University of Wisconsin-Madison, 2005.

———. "Learning in Massively Multiplayer Online Games." In *Proceedings of the Sixth International Conference of the Learning Sciences*, Y. B. Kafai, W. A. Sandoval, N. Enyedy, A. S. Nixon, and F. Herrera, eds., 521–528. Los Angeles: University of California, Los Angeles, 2004.

Taylor, T. L. "Living Digitally: Embodiment in Virtual Worlds." In *The Social Life of Avatars: Presence and Interaction in Shared Virtual Environments*, ed. Ralph Schroeder. London: Springer-Verlag, 2002.

———. *Play Between Worlds: Exploring Online Game Culture*. Cambridge, MA: MIT Press, 2006.

Wark, McKenzie. *Gamer Theory*. Cambridge, MA: Harvard University Press, 2007.

Young, Michael. "An Ecological Description of Video Games in Education." In *Proceedings of the Annual Conference on Education and Information Systems: Technologies and Applications*, Orlando, FL, 203–209. 2004.

Ethics, Law, Politics, and Activism

Anderson, David M., and Michael Cornfield, eds. *The Civic Web: Online Politics and Democratic Values.* Lanham, MD: Rowman & Littlefield, 2003.

Appiah, Kwame Anthony. *Cosmopolitanism: Ethics in a World of Strangers.* New York: Norton, 2006.

Armstrong, Jerome, and Markos Moulitsas Zúniga. *Crashing the Gate: Netroots, Grassroots, and the Rise of People-Powered Politics.* White River Junction, VT: Chelsea Green, 2006.

Barefoot, John C., and Lloyd H. Strickland. "Conflict and Dominance in Television-Mediated Interaction." *Human Relations* 35, no. 7 (1982): 559–566.

Barlow, John Perry. *A Declaration of the Independence of Cyberspace.* Electronic Frontier Foundation, 2006, http://homes.eff.org/~barlow/Declaration-Final.html.

Bimber, Bruce. *Information and American Democracy: Technology in the Evolution of Political Power.* New York: Cambridge University Press, 2003.

Boyle, James. "A Closed Mind about an Open World." *Financial Times* (August 7, 2006): 20–24.

———. "Mertonianism Unbound? Imagining Free, Decentralised Access to Most Cultural and Scientific Material." In *The Digital Library of the Commons,* Indiana University, 2006, http://dlc.dlib.indiana.edu/archive/00001259.

———. *Shamans, Software and Spleens: Law and the Construction of the Information Society.* Cambridge, MA: Harvard University Press, 1996.

Burris, Beverly H. *Technocracy at Work.* Albany, NY: State University of New York Press, 1993.

Caron, Paul. "The Long Tail of Legal Scholarship." *The Pocket Part: A Companion to the Yale Law Journal* (2006), http://www.thepocketpart.org/2006/09/06/caron.html.

Chesbrough, Henry W., and David J. Teece. "Organizing for Innovation: When is Virtual Virtuous?" *Harvard Business Review* (August 1, 2002): 65–73.

Chun, Wendy Hui Kyong. *Control and Freedom: Power and Paranoia in the Age of Fiber Optics*. Cambridge, MA: MIT Press, 2006.

Dartnel, Michael Y. *Insurgency Online: Web Activism and Global Conflict*. Toronto: University of Toronto Press, 2006.

Fried, Charles. *Modern Liberty: And the Limits of Government*. New York: Norton, 2006.

Garber, Marjorie. "Groucho Marx and 'Coercive Voluntarism' in Academe." *The Chronicle Review of the Chronicle of Higher Education* (January 10, 2003).

H20Playlist. The Berkman Center for Internet and Society, Harvard Law School, 2006, http://h2obeta.law.harvard.edu/home.do;jsessionid= C1FE5F9F3EBA119A676759CFE544A6FC.

Hajnal, Peter I., ed. *Civil Society in the Information Age*. Hampshire, UK: Ashgate, 2002.

Hick, Steven F., and John G. McNutt, eds. *Advocacy, Activism and the Internet: Community Organization and Social Policy*. Chicago: Lyceum, 2002.

Hunter, Dan. "Cyberspace as Place and the Tragedy of the Digital Anticommons." *California Law Review* 91 (2003): 439, 454–458, 472–497.

Kelty, Christopher M. *Two Bits: The Cultural Significance of Free Software*. Durham, NC: Duke University Press, 2008.

Keohane, Robert O. *International Institutions and State Power: Essays in International Relations Theory*. Boulder, CO: Westview Press, 1989.

Kim, Minjeong. "The Creative Commons and Copyright Protection in the Digital Era: Uses of Creative Commons Licenses." *Journal of Computer-Mediated Communication* 13, no. 1, article 10 (2007), http://jcmc .indiana.edu/vol13/issue1/kim.html.

Kirschenbaum, Matthew G. *Mechanisms: New Media and the Forensic Imagination*. Cambridge, MA: MIT Press, 2008.

Kling, Robert. *Computerization and Controversy: Value Conflicts and Social Choices*. San Diego, CA: Morgan Kaufmann, 1996.

Lastowka, F. Gregory, and Dan Hunter. "The Laws of the Virtual Worlds." *Legal Theory Research Paper Series, University of Pennsylvania Law School* 26 (2003).

Lessig, Lawrence. *Code and Other Laws of Cyberspace, Version 2.0*. New York: Basic, 2006.

————. *Free Culture: How Big Media Uses Technology and the Law to Lock Down Culture and Control Creativity*. New York: Penguin, 2004.

Reid, Elizabeth M. "Hierarchy and Power–Social Control in Cyberspace." *Communities in Cyberspace*, edited by Marc A. Smith and Peter Kolloc. London: Routledge, 1999.

————. "Text-Based Virtual Realities: Identity and the Cyborg Body." *High Noon on the Electric Frontier: Conceptual Issues in Cyberspace*, edited by Peter Ludlow. Cambridge, MA: MIT Press, 1996.

Rheingold, Howard. *Smart Mobs: The Next Social Revolution*. New York: Basic, 2003.

Sassen, Saskia. *Territory, Authority, Rights: From Medieval to Global Assemblages*. Princeton, NJ: Princeton University Press, 2006.

Strangelove, Michael. *The Empire of Mind: Digital Piracy and the Anticapitalist Movement*. Toronto: University of Toronto Press, 2005.

Von Hippel, Eric. *Democratizing Innovation*. Cambridge, MA: MIT Press, 2005.

Global Markets and Culture

Allison, Anne. *Millennial Monsters: Japanese Toys and the Global Imagination*. Berkeley: University of California Press, 2006.

Anderson, Chris. *The Long Tail: A Public Diary on Themes Around My Book.* Creative Commons, 2006, http://www.thelongtail.com.

———. *The Long Tail: Why the Future of Business is Selling Less of More.* New York: Hyperion, 2006.

Balsamo, Anne. *Designing Culture: The Technological Imagination at Work* (book in progress).

Brynjolfsson, Erik, Yu Jeffrey Hu, and Duncan Simester. "Goodbye Pareto Principle, Hello Long Tail: The Effect of Search Costs on the Concentration of Product Sales," 2007, http://ssrn.com/abstract=953587.

Brynjolfsson, Erik, Yu Jeffrey Hu, and Michael D. Smith. "From Niches to Riches: Anatomy of the Long Tail." *Sloan Management Review* 47, no. 4 (2006): 67–71.

Callon, Michel. "Some Elements of a Sociology of Translation: Domestication of the Scallops and the Fishermen of St Brieuc Bay." In *Power, Action and Belief: A New Sociology of Knowledge,* edited by John Law. London: Routledge & Kegan Paul, 1986.

Diamond, Jared. *Collapse: How Societies Choose to Fail or Succeed.* New York: Viking, 2005.

Elberse, Anita, and Felix Oberholzer-Gee. "Superstars and Underdogs: An Examination of the Long Tail Phenomenon in Video Sales." Working Paper No. 07-015, Harvard Business School, 2006.

Ghosh, Rishab Aiyer, ed. *CODE: Collaborative Ownership and the Digital Economy.* Cambridge, MA: MIT Press, 2005.

Granovetter, Mark. "The Strength of Weak Ties: A Network Theory Revisited." *Sociological Theory* 1 (1983), 201–233.

Grau, Oliver. *Virtual Art: From Illusion to Immersion.* Cambridge, MA: MIT Press, 2003.

Jenkins, Henry. *Textual Poachers: Television Fans & Participatory Culture.* New York: Routledge, 1992.

Johnson, Steven. *Emergence: The Connected Lives of Ants, Brains, Cities, and Software.* New York: Scribner, 2001.

————. *Everything Bad Is Good for You: How Today's Popular Culture Is Actually Making Us Smarter*. New York: Riverhead, 2005.

Kiesler, Sara, ed. *Culture and the Internet*. Mahwah, NJ: Lawrence Erlbaum Associates, 1997.

Leskovek, Jure Leskovek, Lada A. Adamic, and Bernardo A. Huberman. "The Dynamics of Viral Marketing." *arXiv.org*, Cornell University Library, 2006, http://arxiv.org/abs/physics/0509039

O'Hara-Devereaux, Mary, and Robert Johansen. *Global Work: Bridging Distance, Culture, and Time*. San Francisco: Jossey-Bass, 1994.

Peters, Michael A. *Building Knowledge Cultures: Education and Development in the Age of Knowledge Capitalism*. Lanham, Maryland: Rowman and Littlefield, 2006.

Rainie, Lee, and John Horrigan. *A Decade of Adoption: How the Internet has Woven Itself into American Life*. Washington D.C.: PEW Internet and Family Life, 2005.

Samuels, Robert. *Integrating Hypertextual Subjects*. New York: Hampton Press, 2006.

Saxenian, AnnaLee. *The New Argonauts: Regional Advantage in a Global Economy*. Cambridge, MA: Harvard University Press, 2006.

Shaffer, D.W. *Multisubculturalism: Computers and the End of Progressive Education*. WCER Working Paper No. 2005-5. Madison: University of Wisconsin-Madison, Wisconsin Center for Education Research, 2005.

Surowiecki, James. *The Wisdom of Crowds: Why the Many Are Smarter Than the Few and How Collective Wisdom Shapes Business, Economies, Societies and Nations*. New York: Anchor, 2005.

Youth Culture

Alvermann, D. E. *Adolescents and Literacies in a Digital World*. New York: Peter Lang Publishing, 2002.

Bennett, W. Lance, ed. *Civic Life Online: Learning How Digital Media Can Engage Youth*. The John D. and Catherine T. MacArthur Foundation

Series on Digital Media and Learning. Cambridge, MA: MIT Press, 2008.

Buckingham, David. *After the Death of Childhood: Growing up in the Age of Electronic Media.* Cambridge, MA: Polity Press, 2000.

Buckingham, David, ed. *Youth, Identity, and Digital Media.* The John D. and Catherine T. MacArthur Foundation Series on Digital Media and Learning. Cambridge, MA: MIT Press, 2008.

Bussière, Patrick, and Tomasz Gluszynski. "The Impact of Computer Use on Reading Achievement of 15-Year-Olds." Learning Policy Directorate, Strategic Policy and Planning Branch, Human Resources and Skills Development Canada, 2004, http://www.hrsdc.gc.ca/en/cs/sp/hrsdc/lp/publications/2004-002625/page00.shtml.

Grossberg, Lawrence. *Caught in the Crossfire: Kids, Politics, and America's Future.* Boulder, CO: Paradigm, 2005.

Ito, Mizuko, Sonja Baumer, Matteo Bittanti, danah boyd, Rachel Cody, Becky Herr-Stephenson, Heather A. Horst, Patricia G. Lange, Dilan Mahendran, Katynka Z. Martínez, C. J. Pascoe, Dan Perkel, Laura Robinson, Christo Sims, and Lisa Tripp. *Hanging Out, Messing Around, and Geeking Out: Kids Living and Learning with New Media.* The John D. and Catherine T. MacArthur Foundation Series on Digital Media and Learning. Cambridge, MA: MIT Press, 2010.

Latham, Rob. *Consuming Youth: Vampires, Cyborgs, and the Culture of Consumption.* Chicago: University of Chicago Press, 2002.

Lenhart, Amanda, and Mary Madden. *Teen Content Creators and Consumers.* Washington, D.C.: Pew Internet and American Life Project, 2005, http://www.pewinternet.org/PPF/r/166/report_display.asp.

Livingstone, Sonia. *Young People and New Media.* London: Sage Publications, 2002.

McPherson, Tara, ed. *Digital Youth, Innovation, and the Unexpected.* The John D. and Catherine T. MacArthur Foundation Series on Digital Media and Learning. Cambridge, MA: MIT Press, 2007.

Meier, Deborah, and George Wood, eds. *Many Children Left Behind: How the No Child Left Behind Act is Damaging Our Children and Our Schools.* Boston: Beacon Press, 2004.

Metzger, Miriam J., and Andrew J. Flanagin, eds. *Digital Media, Youth, and Credibility.* The John D. and Catherine T. MacArthur Foundation Series on Digital Media and Learning. Cambridge, MA: MIT Press, 2008.

Montgomery, Kathryn C. *Generation Digital: Politics, Commerce, and Childhood in the Age of the Internet.* Cambridge, MA: MIT Press, 2007.

Oblinger, Diana G., and James L. Oblinger, eds. *Educating the Net Generation.* Washington, D.C.: EDUCAUSE, 2005, http://www.educause.edu/educatingthenetgen.

Papert, S. *The Children's Machine: Rethinking School in the Age of the Computer.* New York: Basic Books, 1993.

———. *The Connected Family: Bridging the Digital Generation Gap.* Atlanta, GA: Longstreet Press, 1996.

Peterson, Paul E., and Martin R. West, eds. *No Child Left Behind? The Politics and Practice of School Accountability.* Washington, D.C.: Brookings Institution Press, 2003.

Rideout, Victoria, Donald F. Roberts, and Ulla G. Foehr. *Generation M: Media in the Lives of 8-18 Year-Olds.* Menlo Park, CA: The Henry J. Kaiser Family Foundation, 2005.

Rocheleau, B. "Computer Use by School-Age Children: Trends, Patterns, and Predictors." *Journal of Educational Computing Research* 12, no. 1 (1995): 1–17.

Tapscott, Dan. *Growing up Digital: The Rise of the Net Generation.* New York: McGraw Hill, 1998.

Race, Gender, and Ethnicity

Balsamo, Anne. *Technology of the Gendered Body: Reading Cyborg Women.* Durham, NC: Duke University Press, 1996.

Enders, Alexandra, and Steve Bridges. "Disability and the Digital Divide: Comparing Surveys with Disability Data." The Research and Training Center on Disability in Rural Communities, Missoula, MT: University of Montana Rural Institute, 2006.

Essed, Philomena, and David Theo Goldberg. "Cloning Cultures: The Social Injustices of Sameness." *Ethnic and Racial Studies* 6, no. 1: 2002 1066–1082.

Everett, Anna, ed. *Learning Race and Ethnicity: Youth and Digital Media.* The John D. and Catherine T. MacArthur Foundation Series on Digital Media and Learning. Cambridge, MA: MIT Press, 2007.

Kafai, Yasmin, Carrie Heeter, Jill Denner, and Jennifer Sun, eds., *Beyond Barbie to Mortal Kombat: New Perspectives on Gender and Computer Games.* Cambridge, MA: MIT Press, 2008.

Kolko, Beth E., Lisa Nakamura, and Gilbert B. Rodman, eds. *Race in Cyberspace.* New York: Routledge, 2000.

Nakamura, Lisa. *Cybertypes: Race, Ethnicity, and Identity on the Internet.* New York: Routledge, 2002.

———. "Race In/For Cyberspace: Identity Tourism on the Internet." *The Cybercultures Reader,* ed. David Bell. New York: Routledge, 2000.

History of Writing, Learning, and the Book

Albanese, Andrew Richard. "The Social Life of Books." *Library Journal* 131, no. 9 (2006).

Bolter, J. D. *Writing Space: The Computer, Hypertext, and the History of Writing.* Hillsdale, N.J.: L. Erlbaum Associates, 1991.

Davidson, Cathy N. *Revolution and the Word: The Rise of the Novel in America.* New York: Oxford University Press, 1986.

Davidson, Cathy N., ed. *Reading in America: Literature and Social History*. Baltimore: Johns Hopkins University Press, 1989.

Reports

ACLS Commission. *Our Cultural Commonwealth: The Final Report of the ACLS Commission on Cyberinfrastructure for the Humanities and Social Sciences*. 2006, http://www.acls.org/cyberinfrastructure/OurCulturalCom monwealth.pdf.

Council of Graduate Schools Advisory Committee on Graduate Education and American Competitiveness. *Graduate Education: The Backbone of American Competitiveness and Innovation*, http://www.cgsnet.org/por tals/0/pdf/GR_GradEdAmComp_0407.pdf.

Harley, Diane, and Shannon Lawrence. *Regulation of E-Learning: New National and International Policy Perspectives*. Berkeley, CA: Center for Studies in Higher Education, University of California, Berkeley, 2006, http:// cshe.berkeley.edu/publications/docs/ROP.Regulation_of_elearning.pdf.

NESTA Futurelab. *Looking At the Future of Learning*. Bristol, England: 2005, http://www.futurelab.org.uk/.

New Media Consortium (NMC). *The Horizon Report: 2007 Edition*. Austin, TX: NMC Emerging Technologies Initiative and EDUCAUSE Learning Initiative, 2007, http://www.nmc.org/horizon.

Novak, J. D., and A. J. Cañas. *The Theory Underlying Concept Maps and How to ConstructThem*. Technical Report IHMC CmapTools 2006-01. Florida Institute for Human and Machine Cognition, 2006, http://cmap.ihmc .us/Publications/ResearchPapers/TheoryUnderlyingConceptMaps.pdf.

Podesta, John D. Testimony before the House Committee on Health, Education, Labor, and Pensions. *NCLB Reauthorization: Modernizing Middle and High Schools for the 21st Century*, 2007.

RePAH Project Team. *Digital Resource Study: Understanding the Use of Digital Resources in Humanities and Social Science Undergraduate Education*. University of Sheffield, UK: Knowledge Media Design and The Humanities Research Institute, 2006, http://cshe.berkeley.edu/research/digital resourcestudy/report/digitalresourcestudy_final_report.pdf.

Shaffer, David Williamson, Kurt Squire, Richard Halverson, and James P. Gee. *Video Games and the Future of Learning.* University of Wisconsin-Madison and Academic Advanced Distributed Learning Co-Laboratory, 2005, http://www.academiccolab.org/resources/gappspaper1.pdf.

Squire, Kurt D. *Game-Based Learning: Present and Future State of the Field.* An x-Learn Perspective Paper Supported by a grant from the e-Learning CONSORTIUM. Madison, WI: Academic Advanced Distributed Learning Co-Laboratory, 2005.

Summit on Educational Games. *Harnessing the Power of Games for Learning.* Washington, DC: Federation of American Scientists, 2005, http://www.fas.org/gamesummit/reading/prepaper.pdf.

University of California Commission on General Education in the 21st Century. *General Education in the 21st Century.* Berkeley, CA: Center for Studies in Higher Education, 2007, http://cshe.berkeley.edu/research/gec.

Bibliography II: Resources and Models

K-12: Innovative Schools

Argyle Magnet School for Information Technology   Silver Spring, Maryland, http://www.mcps.k12.md.us/schools/argylems. At Argyle Middle School, all students must take a comprehensive technology course each year, earning them a national technology certification. However, students may choose to take a second strand of elective courses that focuses on either programming or digital media. The digital media program, in particular, encourages students to work in teams to develop, market, and create video games, digital music, and digital art. Students are taught to solve problems and explore new information with technological tools available in their Instructional Media Center.

Arthur F. Smith Middle Magnet School   Alexandria, Louisiana, http://www.rapides.k12.la.us/smithjr. At the Arthur F. Smith Middle Magnet School, students learn and gain professional training through a curriculum with an emphasis on communication arts. The program was the first in Louisiana to offer middle-school students the opportunity to learn animation and digital editing using current media industry standards. Students work throughout their time at Arthur F. Smith to build a digital and printed portfolio, acquiring cutting-edge technology skills in the process. The goal of this project is to allow students to experience the power of media communication and to give them an opportunity to develop their creative potential. Teachers at Arthur F. Smith are organized into cross-curricular teams, and they coordinate interdisciplinary and technology-enhanced lessons and projects in such a way that the students become active participants in the learning process.

Beacon School   New York, New York, http://www.beaconschool.org. The Beacon School was founded in 1993 by teachers from the Computer School (see below) who wanted to create a high school based on the same principles of technological knowledge and global awareness. The school is located in a converted warehouse that has been retrofitted to accommodate an impressive array of technologies. Beacon prides itself on its extensive use of the Internet: All teachers and students have their own email addresses, and many have created personal Web sites. However, this focus on electronic communication has not left students without avenues for personal contact and collaboration. For example, each year they must demonstrate their mastery of the curriculum by presenting independent research projects to a panel of teachers. In developing these projects, students are encouraged to make use of the school's many high-tech labs and resources. Another popular program is the annual film festival in which students share and critique each other's digital media projects.

Brooks Global Studies Extended Year Magnet School   Greensboro, North Carolina, http://schoolcenter.gcsnc.com/education/school/school.php ?sectionid=6952. At Brooks, they believe that rapid improvements in technology and communications have made it essential for today's young people to learn about the world and human cultures. Thus, the focus of the school is global literacy, with a commitment to collaborative learning and technology. The global studies program emphasizes the five major geography themes developed by the National Geographic Society: location (exactly where on the earth's surface places are found); place (the physical and human characteristics of specific places that set them apart from others); relationships within places (how humans interact with their environment); movement (how people, products, information, and ideas within and among countries change); and regions (how regions form and develop).

Center for Advanced Technologies, Lakewood High School   St. Petersburg, Florida, http://www.cat.pinellas.k12.fl.us/Default.aspx. The Center for Advanced Technologies is a public school magnet program housed within Lakewood High School. The program opened in 1990 and moved into its own building in 1991. Each year, students attending Lakewood must apply for one of the approximately 150 places in the selective CAT program. Aside from small class sizes and a team of highly trained teachers, the CAT program offers its students access to multimedia labs, computer workstations, and a fully equipped television studio where a daily live television show and weekly newsmagazine are produced for the local FOX network affiliate.

The Computer School New York, New York, http://www.thecomputer school.org/index.php. This middle school was founded in 1983 as a result of a grant from the developers of the Logo program at MIT. Although computer programming and technology have left Logo's green turtle far behind, the Computer School continues to focus on its original mission: to educate children to become technologically aware and to understand the power of the computer and related technology to access information and resources spread throughout the global community. In order to reach these goals, technology is integrated into all aspects of the curriculum and school life. The results are, ideally, well-rounded students who are able to express themselves clearly and coherently through a variety of technology and media.

Denali Borough School District Alaska, http://denali.ak.schoolweb pages.com/education/district/district.php?sectionid=1. Beginning in the fall of 2004, laptops were distributed to all sixth- to twelfth-grade students and teachers in the remote Denali Borough School District. Unlike many such programs, which often fail to see desired results due to the privileging of equipment over more fundamental change, the Denali Borough is committed to accompanying the laptops with a long-term revision of the curriculum and a new approach to learning. This program has created a classroom environment in which students take on greater responsibility for their own education and work together with their teachers to learn new skills and ways of approaching problems. The traditional classroom structure and environment has been replaced by a project-based curriculum in which students use networked programs to create digital research projects, electronic drop-boxes to turn in assignments, and school servers to store their work. In the years since the program was initiated, academic performance has increased, and discipline referrals have decreased. The borough's home-schooled students were also the only group in the state to meet the national AYP (Adequate Yearly Progress) standard. The mission of the project is as follows: The Denali Borough School District, with proactive student, parent, and community involvement, provides a nurturing, diverse, quality education that empowers students, promotes lifelong learning, and produces conscious locally involved citizens.

Francis Scott Key Technology Magnet School Baltimore, MD, http:// www.fsk.org/school/index.html. At Francis Scott Key, technology is integrated into instruction to create a curriculum that is able to adapt to a very diverse population, including developmentally delayed and ESOL students. For example, tools such as Smart-Boards and the Opass (an interpretive device) are used to enhance the learning environment for these students. Teachers and students also engage in learning activities in a Distance Learning Lab, in which the walls of the classroom are literally and figuratively broken down to encourage collaborative telecommunication activities with other students and teachers across the country.

Frost Lake Magnet School of Technology and Global Studies St. Paul, Minnesota, http://frost.spps.org. Frost Lake is a K-6 (including a full-day kindergarten program) school in which students use a variety of technology tools to explore the theme of global studies. It calls itself a school that is "technology infused, globally based, and literacy focused." What makes Frost Lake unique is its small class size (no more than 22 students in grades K-4) and an emphasis on collaborative instruction and the use of technology to enhance and support teaching and learning in every classroom.

Quest to Learn School New York, New York, http://www.instituteofplay .com/node/114. Slated to open in fall 2009, this gaming school is a joint venture between the Gamelab Institute of Play and the nonprofit organization New Visions for Public Schools. This innovative middle and high school redefines the learning paradigm and actively seeks to change the way institutions of learning are conceived of and built by blurring the traditional line between learning and play. It aims to prepare students for a digitally mediated future through a curriculum structured around the creation and execution of alternate reality games. The project will also act as a demonstration and research site for alternative trends in education funded, in part, by the MacArthur Foundation Digital Media and Learning Initiative.

Gary & Jerri-Ann Jacobs High Tech High School   San Diego (Point Loma), California, http://www.hightechhigh.org. Housed in a converted naval training warehouse, High Tech High School (HTHS) makes maximum use of an open floor plan, high ceilings, and low central walls to encourage students and teachers to interact more freely. Students learn in specialized labs equipped with computer workstations as opposed to traditional classrooms. This redefinition of conventional notions of face-to-face interactions within institutional learning spaces supports an integrated project-based curriculum in which digital portfolios and internships are part of the curriculum. The goal of this publicly funded charter high school is to provide its approximately 400 students (drawn from the ethnically diverse surrounding urban community) with the technical experience, academic excellence, and leadership skills that will allow them to succeed in today's high-tech industries. The school was originally conceived by a coalition of San Diego business leaders and educators who founded HTH Learning, a private nonprofit organization, to oversee the development and construction of the school. Since it was first authorized as a single-charter high school in 2000, HTHS has expanded significantly and is now part of a family of seven K-12 schools. The HTHS network does not believe in centralized management for its member schools but instead gives them the freedom to maneuver within the original set of design principles, thereby allowing them to continually adapt to local circumstances. The network has received significant funding from the Bill and Melinda Gates Foundation.

High School of Telecommunication Arts and Technology   Brooklyn, New York, http://www.hstat.org/main.asp. High School of Telecommunication Arts and Technology is dedicated to the integration of an interdisciplinary curriculum with the creation and modification of online content. It is the only high school in New York City to have its own Web server and to teach every student HTML. Among the school's high-tech offerings is a course specifically dedicated to creating and maintaining the school's Web site and a fully equipped television studio.

Johnson Street Global Studies K-8 Extended Year Magnet School   High
Point, North Carolina, http://schoolcenter.gcsnc.com/education/school/
school.php?sectionid=7019. Johnson Street Global Studies Magnet
School originated as an elementary school and expanded to include a
pre-kindergarten and middle-school program in July 2006. The Global
Studies theme provides an environment in which students learn about
global issues and the relationships and interdependence among peo-
ples and nations. Beginning in kindergarten, students study two different countries each year, and, by the end of eighth grade, they have
covered topics such as the economics, education, environmental conditions, cultures, and technologies of countries on each of the seven
continents.

Jonas Salk Middle School   Sacramento, California, http://www.jsms
.com. The Jonas Salk Middle School has achieved a complete turn-
around in student and teacher commitment to learning through the
implementation of a technology-infused curriculum. With the help of
funding and technology support from Apple Computers, the school now
organizes its days around the creation and execution of collaborative
assignments. One of the most popular of these programs is the daily
newscast, which is almost entirely student produced and stresses innovation through digital storytelling. The school has found, not surpris-
ingly, that when students were encouraged to share their work with their
peers via online networking the turn-in rate rose to nearly 100 percent.

Kellman Corporate Community School   Chicago, Illinois. Kellman Corporate Community School was founded in 1988 by Chicago business-
man Joseph Kellman. Kellman wanted to create a school in which
business concepts were integrated into the educational environment.
As in a well-run business, teachers and students are expected to meet
frequently, exchange ideas, and collaborate. Although the school is
public, the Kellman Family Foundation funds an extra hour of class
Monday through Thursday. These "banked" hours allow the students
to leave school at noon on Fridays, giving teachers the rest of the afternoon for professional development. Due to its location in one of Chicago's poorest African-American neighborhoods, the school's largest
obstacle was finding a way to give its students equal access to technology and media. Thus, Kellman seeks to level the playing field and

bridge the digital gap by giving each student in fourth through eighth grades a wireless laptop. As an added bonus, each graduating eighth-grader also receives the gift of a laptop to take to high school (the computers used during the previous years were leased).

New Technology High School   Napa, California, http://www.newtech high.org/Website2007/index.html.   New Technology High School (NTHS) advocates a union of technology and curriculum. Students are taught by teams of teachers who take a student-centered approach in the classroom, creating computer-based academic content through the development of problem-solving and experiential assignments. Classes are not organized around the traditional divisions of subject but are instead interdisciplinary and collaborative. For example, as a final project, students create an online portfolio of their NTHS career from tenth grade through twelfth grade that is then shared through digital networking. The school also offers a variety of other clubs and organizations, often technology oriented, that are student-created and student-driven. Although originally developed for the community of Napa, California, the NTHS network now includes 25 schools, with seven in Northern California, four in Southern California, six in North Carolina, two in Oregon and Louisiana, and one each in Alaska, Colorado, Illinois, and Texas.

NYC Museum School   New York, New York, http://schools.nyc.gov/ SchoolPortals/02/M414/default.htm.   The 400 high-school students at the NYC Museum School spend up to three days a week at a chosen museum (either the American Museum of Natural History, the Metropolitan Museum of Art, the Children's Museum of Manhattan, or the South Street Seaport Museum) studying with specialists and museum educators. Students work on different projects depending on which museum they choose (I.e., geometry and computer animation at the Children's Museum or navigation at the South Street Seaport Museum). At the end of their senior year, each student shares a thesislike project on a chosen theme. The NYC Museum School was founded in 1994 by a former Brooklyn Museum assistant director in partnership with a former teacher with the Lab School in New York. It has been featured in the Bill and Melinda Gates Foundation "High Schools for the New Millennium" Report.

Putnam Valley Middle School   Putnam Valley, NY, http://www.pvcsd .org/ms/index.php. Putnam Valley Middle School aims to create an environment where learning is a collaborative experience between teachers and students. The school is involved in Apple Computers' 1-to-1 learning program, which allows for every seventh and eighth grader to receive a personal laptop computer. Consultants from Apple were brought in to conduct workshops on how best to integrate the use of technology into the curriculum. Putnam, and other schools partici- pating in Apple's 1-to-1 learning program, hope that through consis- tent and extended access to technology, students will be better prepared for the job market of the future.

School of the Future   New York, New York, http://www.sofechalk.org/ home.aspx. The School of the Future in New York City is one of many schools successfully integrating the principles of the Coalition of Essential Schools (small class size, an emphasis on depth rather than coverage, teachers who function as coaches and guides, an interdisci- plinary curriculum, the creative use of technological resources, and collaboration between teachers, http://www.essentialschools.org). The curriculum at this sixth- to twelfth-grade institution is project-based and focuses on peer-to-peer evaluation. Eighth-grade students must present a portfolio (often, but not exclusively, digital) to a panel of sixth- and seventh-grade students at the end of the year. This portfolio is used to evaluate whether they are ready for high school. High school students, for their part, must complete four separate research projects (one per year) that are exhibited and presented to a panel of fellow stu- dents, parents, and teachers. These projects are designed and carried out entirely by the students, with guidance from a team of specialized teachers.

School of the Future   Philadelphia, Pennsylvania, http://www.micro soft.com/education/schoolofthefuture. The School of the Future in Philadelphia is unique in that it is the first urban high school to be built in a working partnership with a leading software company, Microsoft Corporation. The school opened in September 2006 and serves approximately 750 students in a state-of-the-art, high-tech, and "green" facility. The school is not a magnet school: It was built in a low- income, high-crime neighborhood in the belief that the "school of the future" must be accessible to all students, regardless of their economic status or existing skill sets. Thus, the school has set up a lottery system to ensure that every applicant has an equal chance to "cross the digital divide." Microsoft's Partners in Learning initiative played an integral part in the design and conceptualization of the school, not through a monetary donation (The School of the Future is funded by the School District of Philadelphia) but through the development of new technologies for both teaching and administrative purposes. Among the most innovative, and controversial, of these technologies is a smart card that allows access to digital lockers and that tracks calories consumed during school meals (breakfast and dinner are also served before and after school). Class schedules and locations change every day (the goal being to break down our culture's dependency on time and place), and all rooms are designed with flexible floor plans to foster teamwork and project-based learning. Instead of a library and textbooks, all students are given a laptop with wireless access to the Interactive Learning Center, the school's hub for interactive educational material. These laptops are linked to smartboards in every classroom and networked so that assignments and notes can be accessed even from home (eventually, through the "Wireless Philadelphia" initiative, Web access will be universal, but until then the School of the Future has decided to subsidize its students' home Internet access). The building itself is also unique in its holistic approach. Rainwater is caught and repurposed for use in toilets, the roof is covered with vegetation to shield it from ultraviolet rays, panels embedded within the windows capture light and transform it into energy, room settings auto-adjust based on natural lighting and atmospheric conditions, and sensors in all rooms turn lights on and off depending on whether the space is being used. The School of the Future is just the beginning for Philadelphia: It is part of a capital construction campaign that includes five new high schools, four elementary schools, and additions and improvements to existing schools. The goal of this program is to reconstruct the learning environment—an alternative to the more common approach of overlaying a traditional curriculum with high-tech tool. A rebroadcast of a segment on the school from The News Hour with Jim Lehrer is available at http://www .youtube.com/watch?v=2Mug66WnoSk.

Walt Disney Magnet School   Lansing, Michigan, http://www.disney.cps .k12.il.us. The Walt Disney Magnet School's approximately 1,500 lottery-selected students are drawn from a variety of ethnic and economic backgrounds. The school aims to meet the needs of its diverse students through an arts- and technology-focused curriculum that takes place in an open-space environment. Projects are arranged around themes such as art, music, dance, animation, and digital music. At least once a year, each student is able to carry out a two-week integrated art and technology project in the 30,000-square-foot Communication Arts Center, which includes, among other things, an animation lab and a digital music lab. The goal of the curriculum is to train students to be independent and creative thinkers who have the tools to problemsolve in today's technology-oriented landscape.

Webster High School   Tulsa, Oklahoma, http://www.tulsaschools.org/schools/Webster. Webster High School is a magnet school that includes three strands: the Digital Media and Broadcasting strand, the Information Technology strand, and the Journalism, Marketing, and Advertising strand. All paths aim to give students access to essential knowledge and skills to prepare them for careers in the visual and print media industries. The campus includes a state-of-the-art student-run television studio that encourages hands-on learning and collaborative thinking. The curriculum for Webster High School was developed in conjunction with leaders in professional associations, institutions of higher education and career technology.

K-12: Digital Learning Programs and Research

Consortium for School Networking (CoSN)   http://www.cosn.org. Consortium for School Networking (CoSN) is a consortium of K-12 education leaders who are committed improving the quality of teaching and learning through the strategic use of technology. One of its primary aims is to enable and empower K-12 leaders and policy-makers to increase their knowledge and to find innovative ways of incorporating emerging technologies into their curricula. Toward this end, CoSN works to develop programs and activities such as reports, analysis tools, and professional development resources. It also is deeply committed to supporting member advocacy efforts in order to ensure that law and policy changes serve the interests of students, not businesses or the government.

Digital Youth Research: Kids' Informal Learning with Digital Media   Berkeley, California, http://digitalyouth.ischool.berkeley.edu. Digital Youth Research is a research project administered by the Institute for the Study of Social Change at the University of California, Berkeley, with assistance from investigators at other schools in the University of California system. This project seeks to address the gap between young people's experiences with digital media (e.g., social networks and gaming) outside of schoolwork and their engagement with those same technologies in an in-school setting. Emergent modes of informal learning, such as communication and play, will be examined through a targeted set of ethnographic investigations in local neighborhoods in northern and Southern California and in virtual spaces, such as online games, blogs, messaging, and social networks. The objectives of the project are to describe a young person's role as an active innovator (rather than a passive consumer) in digital media, to think about implications of this for K-12 and higher education, and to advise software designers and educators about how to build better learning environments to take advantage of these new skill sets. This project is sponsored by The John D. and Catherine T. MacArthur Foundation.

FOCUS: Teen Voices on Digital Media and Society   http://www.focuson digitalmedia.org. Global Kids, a New York nonprofit, started an online focus group in April 2007 devoted to the topic of teens, digital media, and society. This short-term project (lasting only four weeks) was conceived as a way to make sure youth perspectives were being heard by policy-makers, teachers, and researchers. The discussion, in which 48 official participants took part, covered a range of topics that reflected the role that digital media plays in the lives of today's youth. Initial discussion topics were provided by Global Kids in conjunction with its partner institutions and grantees, the MacArthur Foundation's Digital Media and Learning Initiative and NewsHour EXTRA (the online youth forum for the NewsHour with Jim Lehrer), in the form of Digital Media NewzFlashes (articles paired with thought-provoking questions). Further content and discussion threads were created throughout the dialogue by the participants themselves. Although educators did not take part in the online dialogue, the FOCUS Web site provided information and suggestions for a digital media curriculum in the Teachers' Lounge forum.

From Lunch Boxes to Laptops State of Maine School System, http://
www.maine.gov/portal/education/k12.html. In the year 2000, the former governor of Maine, Angus King, persuaded his state to launch the
first large-scale distribution of laptop computers in the history of the
United States. That year, laptops were distributed to every seventh-
grade student in the state—42,000 computers in total. King believed
that only by reaching a student-to-laptop ratio of 1:1 would a technology program such as this have the power to make a true difference.
King hoped that the laptops would become the personal property of
each student, but this idea was met with skepticism. When the plan
was implemented, the computers remained the property of the school.
Furthermore, it was left up to each school to decide if the students
would be allowed to take the laptops home with them; about 50 percent of schools allowed this to happen. The program involved more
than just distributing the laptops; there was also a concerted effort
made to transform the classroom in order to take advantage of the possibilities offered by the new hardware. Teachers were organized into
teams and given comprehensive training on how to use the laptops
and also how transform their teaching styles to give their students
more independence and initiative. In other words, the teachers took on
the role of a coach and facilitator and worked with students toward the
common pursuit of knowledge. The program was largely a success; student engagement with course material was heightened and test scores
increased. The program is now being expanded into high schools, and
a private fund has been set up to help low-income families to apply for
Internet access at home.

Games and Professional Practice Simulations (GAPPS) Group   http://www
.academiccolab.org. The Games and Professional Practice Simulations
(GAPPS) Group is a digital learning and research initiative supported
by the Academic Advanced Distributed Learning (ADL) Co-Lab at the
University of Wisconsin, Madison, in partnership with a variety of
educational institutions and funded in part by the MacArthur Foundation. GAPPS studies the manner in which digital technology has been
(or has not been) incorporated into primary education and seeks to
find ways to improve this relationship. One of the primary interests of
the program is how video game technologies (both playing and creating games) can be used to effectively teach complex technical and

problem-solving skills. These skills can then be applied to any number of real-life situations, both in and out of the school environment. As a development program, the ultimate goal of GAPPS is to address the nation's poor performance in science and technology and to ensure the future success of the next generation in a global job market. GAPPS believes that the only way to do this is to give students the opportunity to become comfortable with the ever-changing field of technology and the creative application of media skills from an early age.

Georgia Institute of Technology College of Computing   http://www.cc .gatech.edu/gacomputes. In the summer of 2007, Georgia Institute of Technology College of Computing implemented a pilot program called "Introduction to Technology Design for Teenagers." The goal of the program was to facilitate active learning and skill acquisition through the creation of individually tailored projects that are both fun and instructive. These projects were designed by the students themselves and included activities such as redesigning a "Google interface for teens," writing a Facebook application, or prototyping a new multiplayer game. It is the hope of the program that courses like this will help prepare today's teenagers for future careers in high-tech industries.

Level Playing Field Institute   http://www.lpfi.org. The Level Playing Field Institute is a San Francisco-based nonprofit organization committed to promoting fairness in education, the workplace, and society at large. Founded in 2001 by Freada Kapor Klein, PhD, the Institute seeks to reveal and remove barriers that are threatening underrepresented groups in the realms of higher education and business. They believe that everyone should have equal access to all opportunities regardless of racial, cultural, or economic differences. This "leveling" would start in the early stages of education when all talented students would receive quality preparation for higher education and future careers. Educational projects such as the Summer Math and Science Honors Academy (SMASH) program for high-school students and the Initiative for Diversity in Education and Leadership (IDEAL) scholarship program for undergraduates are helping the Institute achieve its goal. Through these programs and others, the Level Playing Field Institute hopes to create an open dialogue about the sometimes subtle modes of discrimination at work in today's society and then work collaboratively to remove these hidden barriers.

New Media Literacies   http://www.projectnml.org. The New Media Literacies project (NML) is a new initiative headed by Dr. Henry Jenkins of MIT's Comparative Media Studies Program that intends to develop a theoretical framework and hands-on curriculum for K-12 students that integrates new media tools into broader educational, expressive, and cultural frameworks. NML believes that the most successful learning environments are student-driven, creative, and collaborative, all characteristics that can be enhanced by digital media and new network technologies. Through participation in this project, students will not only learn technical skills but will also develop a critical framework for thinking about the role of media in their lives. This project is funded by the John T. and Catherine D. MacArthur Foundation.

One Laptop Per Child   http://laptop.org/en/index.shtml. The One Laptop Per Child project was the brainchild of Nicholas Negroponte, the cofounder and director of the MIT Media Laboratory. In 2005, he launched a nonprofit organization whose goal was to provide $100 laptops to every child on earth. He reasoned that it was possible to stimulate children's innate capacity to learn, share, and create by providing them with the material means to explore their own potential. This, in turn, would result in a new generation of free thinkers and empowered youth. While the initiative has gone forward, it has also met with much criticism for a substandard product, insufficient testing, and poor marketing. However, despite these setbacks, the One Laptop Per Child initiative has been a revolutionary first step in lowering the cost and increasing access to technology throughout the world.

Open Education Resources (OER)   http://www.hewlett.org/oer. OER was founded by the William and Flora Hewlett Foundation as a way to make high-quality educational content and tools freely available to anyone with access to the Internet. This project is global in nature and aims to offer equal access to knowledge and educational opportunities regardless of geographical and cultural constraints (although the majority of the materials are in English). Resources offered on the Web site include entire course plans, modules, textbooks, videos, exams and evaluation materials, software, and much more. All materials reside in the public domain or have been released under an intellectual property license.

ThinkeringSpaces   http://www.thinkeringspace.org. ThinkeringSpaces is a research project that installs innovative and networked learning spaces in existing library environments. These spaces will draw on the collections and resources of each library and seek to encourage hands-on tinkering with materials, objects, messages, and images (both physical and virtual). Rather than imposing a particular structure onto a child's desire to learn, ThinkeringSpaces aims to tailor its environment to the way children actually perceive, interpret, and use learning opportunities, promoting open-ended and unfettered thinking. The goal of the program is to help facilitate the expansion of a wide range of interests and sets of skills and to allow children to move beyond conventionally defined projects. These learning environments take the shape of free-standing platforms that can be used individually or collaboratively. This project was designed by the Illinois Institute of Technology Institute of Design and funded by the MacArthur Foundation. The results of the research will be used to establish design principles, criteria, and specifications for the development of full-scale installations.

University of Chicago Urban Education Institute   http://uei.uchicago.edu. The Urban Education Institute at the University of Chicago has teamed together with Woodlawn High School and the North Kenwood/Oakland campuses of the University of Chicago Charter School to develop after-school media literacy programs for high-school students. The goal of this program, funded in part by a grant from the MacArthur Foundation, is to allow inner-city students access to digital media resources and instruction. Through an emphasis on creative design work, students learn skills used by media professionals and work collaboratively to produce video documentaries, podcasts, video games, and music videos.

Words Without Borders   http://www.wordswithoutborders.org. Words Without Borders is an online literary magazine where volunteers post free translations of short stories from around the globe. The organization also advocates literature in translation through the planning of events (often virtual) that connect non-English-speaking writers to students and academic institutions. The ultimate goal of Words Without Borders is to introduce international writers and writing to the general public and thus foster a global exchange of voices and ideas. Its Web site also contains units and lesson plans for high-school readers/teachers that are organized around the themes used in advanced placement classes (e.g., justice, exile, self-sacrifice). Words Without Borders is a partner of PEN American Center and the Center for Literary Translation at Columbia University. The Web site is hosted by Bard College.

Higher Education: Institutions, Research, and Projects

Humanities, Arts, Science, and Technology Advanced Collaboratory (HASTAC) http://www.hastac.org. HASTAC (pronounced "haystack") is a virtual consortium of humanists, artists, scientists, and engineers, researchers, and nonprofit research institutions who are committed to new forms of collaboration across communities and disciplines fostered by creative uses of technology. The HASTAC network consists of more than 80 institutions, including universities, supercomputing centers, grid and teragrid associations, humanities institutes, museums, libraries, and other civic institutions. HASTAC works to develop tools for multimedia archiving and social interaction, gaming environments for teaching, innovative educational programs in information science and information studies, virtual museums, and other digital projects. Its mission is two-fold: to ensure that humanistic and humane considerations are never far removed from technological advances and to push education and learning to the forefront of digital innovation. Similarly, HASTAC is dedicated to the idea that this complex and world-changing digital environment requires all the lessons of history, introspection, theory, and equity that the modern humanities (broadly defined) have to offer. The infrastructure of HASTAC is jointly supported by Duke University and the University of California Humanities Research Institute (UCHRI). Funding for HASTAC has come from grants from the National Science Foundation, the Digital Promise Initiative, and the John D. and Catherine T. MacArthur Foundation, as well as from its member institutions.

The John Hope Franklin Center for Interdisciplinary and International Studies Duke University, http://www.jhfc.duke.edu. The Franklin Center is a consortium of programs at Duke University that are committed to revitalizing notions of how knowledge is gained and exchanged. Inspired by the example of John Hope Franklin—Duke professor emeritus, historian, intellectual leader, and lifelong civil rights activist—the Center encourages participants from a broad range of disciplines, perspectives, and methodologies to come together and explore intellectual issues. The Franklin Center's mission is to bring together humanists and those involved in the social sciences in a setting that inspires vigorous scholarship and imaginative alliances. The Center is also committed to employing advanced technologies, such as multimedia and high-speed videoconferencing, not only as a means to an end, but as objects of critical inquiry themselves. In sum, the Franklin Center seeks to meld past knowledge and present questions, international perspectives, and technology with local concerns, timeless scholarship, and timely issues.

University of California Humanities Research Institute (UCHRI)   http://www.uchri.org. UCHRI is a multicampus research unit that serves all 10 campuses in the University of California system. Founded in 1987, UCHRI promotes collaborative work representing different fields and institutions both within and beyond the University of California. The Institute's research addresses topics traditional to the humanities such as literature, philosophy, classics, languages, and history, as well as the pressing human dimensions that arise in the social and natural sciences, technology, art, medicine, and other professions. UCHRI interacts with University of California campus humanities centers and with individual faculty to promote collaborative, interdisciplinary humanities research and pedagogy throughout the University of California system and the larger academic world. Stressing interdisciplinary research, UCHRI bridges gaps between disciplines across the humanities and human sciences and seeks to overcome the intellectual and institutional barriers that can separate the humanities from other fields.

HASTAC on Ning: A Synergistic Symposium for the Cybernetic Age   http://hastac.ning.com. HASTAC on Ning is a social network created by Mechelle De Craene. This network was started as a companion site to http://www.hastac.org and is a way for members of the HASTAC community to learn more about each other and share ideas and information. Members of this site can post videos, links, and participate in a group blog in order to promote new models for thinking, teaching, and research. Ning is a Palo Alto, California-based company that allows participants to create their own customizable social network about anything (http://www.ning.com/).

The Anthropology of the Contemporary Research Collaboratory (ARC) http://anthropos-lab.net. Anthropology of the Contemporary Research Collaboratory (ARC) is a collaboratory in the human sciences founded by Paul Rabinow (University of California at Berkeley), Stephen J. Collier (New School for Social Research, New York), and Andrew Lakoff (University of California at San Diego). The goal of this virtual institution is to explore the anthropology of the contemporary through the encouragement of collaboration, communication, and research inquiry across disciplines and academic institutions. ARC focuses on developing techniques and tools in fields such as synthetic anthropos, nanotechnology, vital systems security, biopolitics, and concept work. Through collaboration, ARC aims to create the conditions for successful creative inquiry and original research.

The Centre for Advanced Learning Technologies (CALT)   http://www.calt.insead.edu. CALT is a project launched by INSEAD, an international business graduate school with campuses in Singapore and France. CALT was officially founded in 1995 in order to promote the understanding and study of the effect of new media and technologies on management theory and practice. The CALT Research Agenda specifically studies the impact of new media and technologies on the virtual business environment (e.g., Internet-based business practices and the management of virtual communities) and on the way management skills are learned. CALT researchers produce materials in diverse formats, such as academic articles, technical papers, conference presentations, knowledge dissemination events and workshops, and online content.

Center for History and New Media at George Mason University   http://chnm.gmu.edu. Founded in 1994 by the historian Roy A. Rosenzweig, the Center for History and New Media (CHNM) researches and develops innovative ways to use digital media and computer technology to democratize history. By "democratizing history," the Center means working to incorporate forgotten voices and multiple viewpoints, reaching diverse audiences, and encouraging popular participation in presenting and preserving the past. In order to accomplish this goal, CHNM is currently working on more than two dozen digital history projects that include World History Matters, which helps teachers and their students locate, analyze, and learn from online primary sources; Echo: Exploring and Collecting History Online, which collects, organizes, and preserves digital materials in the history of science, technology, and industry; Interpreting the Declaration of Independence, which uses foreign translations to promote a richer understanding of the Declaration; History News Network, a Web-based magazine that places current events in historical perspective; and three Teaching American History projects in collaboration with Virginia public school districts. The Center also collaborates with the American Social History Project/Center for Media and Learning at the Graduate Center of The City University of New York on several digital archiving projects, most prominently the September 11 Digital Archive. CHNM also works to develop free tools and resources for historians. Many of these, such as Zotero, Web Scrapbook, Survey Builder, Scribe, Poll Builder, and Syllabus Finder, have had a significant impact on the way humanities research and education is being carried out.

Center for Information Technology Research in the Interest of Society at the University of California, Berkeley   http://ucberkeley.citris-uc.org. Center for Information Technology Research in the Interest of Society (CITRIS) brings together faculty and students from four University of California campuses (Berkeley, Davis, Merced, and Santa Cruz) with industrial researchers at over 60 corporations from the private sector in the common goal of creating information technology solutions for social, environmental, and healthcare issues. Founded in the late 1990s, CITRIS was one of the first organizations in the nation to create a public-private partnership specifically to explore the potential of technology. The Center is currently focusing on several fields of research, including the improvement of access to healthcare through the development of intelligent infrastructures and innovative technologies, finding sustainable and environmentally friendly energy solutions, and bringing technological knowledge to developing regions, both in the United States and throughout the world.

Center for Studies in Higher Education at the University of California, Berkeley   http://cshe.berkeley.edu. Center for Studies in Higher Education (CSHE) is currently implementing a number of projects that contribute to our understanding of how learning institutions are adapting to the digital age. The most relevant of these is the Higher Education in the Digital Age (HEDA) project directed by Dr. Diane Harley. The goal of the HEDA program is to research the policy implications for institutions of higher education trying to incorporate emerging technologies. Ongoing research takes place in one of two broad and interrelated areas of inquiry: the costs and benefits (economic, academic, and social) of digital technology in higher education, and patterns of institutional change during the process of integrating these technologies. Under the broad umbrella of the HEDA program are smaller, more focused projects such as the Digital Resource Study, which seeks to understand the use of digital resources in undergraduate education in the humanities and social sciences, the Future of Scholarly Communication, which researches the needs and desires of faculty for in-progress scholarly communication (i.e., forms of communication employed as research is being executed) as well as archival publication, and the Regulation of E-Learning, a project that explores current and ongoing debates in the regulation of technology-mediated higher education both domestically and internationally. HEDA is also tracking and analyzing all online distributed education projects that are taking place throughout the University of California system.

Connexions   http://cnx.org. Last year, Rice University started the first all-digital open-content university press, Connexions. Through Connexions, scholars are able to collaboratively develop, share, and publish academic content on the Web. For the most part, Connexions favors small modules of learning material (as opposed to complete books) that can be rapidly produced and easily incorporated into larger collections or courses. In this way, Connexions hopes to mimic the modular and nonlinear style of learning that is favored by today's younger generations. It also hopes to actively involve users in the development process by encouraging collaboration and additions, thereby allowing knowledge to be shared and lines of communication to be opened. Content is currently being developed for students and educators of all levels and is freely accessible under the Creative Commons "attribution" license.

Electronic Cultural Atlas Initiative at the University of California, Berkeley http://www.ecai.org. The Electronic Cultural Atlas Initiative (ECAI) is a consortium of scholars, archivists, and other members around the globe who share the vision of creating a distributed virtual library of cultural information with a time and place interface. Its goal is to create a global atlas of historical and cultural resources, using space and time to enhance understanding and preservation of human culture. They do this through TimeMap, a set of software tools developed by Ian Johnson and Artem Osmakov at the University of Sydney, Australia. The ECAI TimeMap is a customized version of these tools.

EDUCAUSE   http://www.educause.edu. EDUCAUSE is a nonprofit association made up of institutions of higher education and corporations serving the higher education technology market. Its mission is to advance education by promoting the intelligent use of information technology. In order to do this, it develops professional development activities, teaching and learning initiatives, provides online information services, and publishes relevant texts. Current major initiatives include the EDUCAUSE Learning Initiative (ELI), a community of institutions, organizations, and corporations committed to advancing learning through innovative technologies, and Net@EDU, which is working to promote advanced networking among institutions of higher education, governments, and business.

Electronic Learning Community Lab   http://www.static.cc.gatech.edu/ elc/index.shtm. Electronic Learning Community (ELC) is a research institute associated with the Georgia Institute of Technology College of Computing. It focuses on discovering how online communities are designed for learning and how this can be improved. ELC research is inspired by an educational theory called constructionism that posits that people learn best when they are making something that is personally meaningful to them. While constructivist learning traditionally focuses on individuals, the ELC Lab aims to incorporate this philosophy into the online environment. Current projects include Science Online, a science wiki that focuses on high-quality scientific information for students and educators, research into how large-scale collaboration occurs in online animation communities, and GameLog, a blogging environment where gamers can explore the features and design elements that make particular games successful.

EQUEL   http://www.equel.net. EQUEL (which stands for "e-quality in e-learning") is a virtual center that brings together researchers and practitioners from 14 European institutions of higher education in order to research innovations in and practices of e-learning. The organization is supported by the e-learning initiative of the European Commission. The primary goal of EQUEL is to foster increased knowledge and understanding of the effect of e-learning practice, theory, and philosophy through a network of researchers and practitioners. The center ultimately plans to offer a range of consulting and evaluation services, including e-learning courses, based on the tools and methods developed by its members and affiliates.

Euro Computer Supported Collaborative Learning   http://www.euro-cscl.org. Euro Computer Supported Collaborative Learning (CSCL) is a Web-based community that gives its members a forum where they can share and discover information about the field of CSCL. Membership is open to practitioners (teachers), researchers, and school administrators. The Web site is funded by The European Commission in the Information Society Technologies (IST) Framework, "School of Tomorrow."

Experiential Technologies Center at the University of California at Los Angeles   http://www.etc.ucla.edu. Originally founded in 1997 as the Cultural Virtual Reality Lab (CVRlab), the Experiential Technologies Center (ETC) explores the application of emerging digital technologies to cultural heritage projects. The CVRlab was originally established in order to facilitate a collaborative project to reconstruct Trajan's Forum in Rome, and the ETC has continued this work, bringing together the knowledge of experts in a variety of fields and creating a solid methodological approach that addresses all aspects of virtual environments: visualization, sound, temporalization, spatialization, and other experiential factors. Recently, the Center expanded its mission to include pedagogy (both for higher education and K-12 schools), performance, and the development of open-source tools for creating dynamic virtual environments.

Franklin W. Olin College of Engineering   Needham, Massachusetts, http://www.olin.edu. Olin College is a small, tuition-free college that is trying to reinvigorate the field of engineering by designing a new kind of engineer who will be able to easily bridge science, technology, enterprise, and society. The college opened in 2002 and was funded by the F.W. Olin Foundation, which literally put all its resources into the creation of the new school. Olin has not only redesigned the field of engineering but has redesigned traditional engineering curriculum: Instead of academic departments, there is a single, synthetic interdisciplinary program that focuses on entrepreneurship and humanities as well as technical skills.

The Game Pit at Northern Virginia Community College   http:// www .nvcc.edu. The Game Pit was originally dreamed up by the Dean of Business Technologies at Northern Virginia Community College, John Min, as a way to raise falling enrollments in the college's information technology classes. It is an open-access classroom equipped with consoles for Xbox and PlayStation and 15 high-end PCs devoted to playing games such as *World of Warcraft* and *Counter-Strike*. Administrators are also hoping that the availability of a gaming center on campus will give students a place to meet and socialize, creating an enhanced feeling of community and camaraderie in a largely commuter school. For video depicting the Game Pit and its most devoted users, see http:// chronicle.com/free/v54/i16/16a02601.htm.

Global Text Project   http://globaltext.terry.uga.edu. The Global Text Project was founded in January 2004 by Richard T. Watson of the University of Georgia and Donald J. McCubbrey of the University of Denver with the goal of delivering freely available open content electronic textbooks to developing nations (books will also eventually be available in hardcopy, CD, or DVD format). The project's first title, *Information Systems*, was released this past fall and is currently being used at Addis Ababa University in Ethiopia and Atma Jaya Yogyakarta University in Indonesia. A second book, *Business Fundamentals*, is slated for release early this year and nine others are in development. In order to produce these textbooks, the Global Text Project recruits professors and experienced professionals from around the world to write at least one chapter on a topic of their choice (all work is done pro bono). The chapters are reviewed and assembled into complete books by scholars and editors. At times, the chapters will be written using wikis, so that multiple participants can contribute to and edit the material during the writing process. The books will also constantly evolve to build on current events and to incorporate the expertise of those (both instructors and students) using the texts. The project aims to set itself apart from other open textbook efforts, such as Wikibooks, by making sure that scholars have editorial control over the finished project. Ultimately, the Global Text Project hopes to develop 1,000 titles in a variety of languages, an endeavor that will require approximately 20,000 volunteers.

Human Sciences and Technologies Advanced Research Institute at Stanford University   http://www.stanford.edu/dept/h-star/cgi-bin/hstar.php. Human Sciences and Technologies Advanced Research Institute (H-STAR) is an interdisciplinary research center initiated by Stanford University with the goal of furthering our understanding of how we are affected by technology. Some key questions asked by the center are: How do people use technology, how can we improve technology to make it more user-friendly (and competitive in the marketplace), how does technology affect our everyday lives, and how is technology used to create innovation in learning, business, and entertainment? H-STAR researchers use these questions to develop projects that aim to reduce the complexity of technologies, close the digital divide, create technologies that respond to specific human needs, and address issues of trust and security in widespread use of technology. Within H-STAR are two smaller interdisciplinary centers that focus on particular projects, the Center for the Study of Language and Information and the Stanford Center for Innovations in Learning (see below), as well as an industry partners program, Media X.

HUMlab at the University of Umea in Sweden   http://www.humlab.umu .se/about. HUMlab is both a virtual and real-life organization where the humanities, cultural studies, and modern information and media technology can work together. It aims to combine ideas from different times, cultures, environments, and fields of study. The virtual environment is funded by the Kempe Foundation and the Bank of Sweden Tercentenary Foundation, while the organization of HUMlab is centered under the Faculty of Arts at Umea University.

Institute for Advanced Technology in the Humanities at the University of Virginia http://www.iath.virginia.edu. The goal of Institute for Advanced Technology in the Humanities (IATH) is to explore and develop innovative ways of incorporating information technology into scholarly humanities research. At the Institute, humanities and computer science research faculty, computer professionals, student assistants and project managers, and library faculty and staff come together in a collaborative effort to document and interpret the record of human achievement in digital form. IATH was founded in 1992 with a major grant from IBM as a way to enable use of sophisticated technical tools in the arts and humanities. Its mission has since evolved to specifically address the problem of making sure that humanities research is able to persist through time and across media in a constantly changing digital world.

The Illinois Center for Computing in the Humanities, Arts, and Social Science at the University of Illinois, Urbana-Champaign   http://www.chass .uiuc.edu/index.html. The Illinois Center for Computing in the Humanities, Arts, and Social Science (I-CHASS) is a recently formed collaboration venture between the humanities (e.g., humanists, artists, and social scientists), computer sciences, and engineering. The Center seeks to foster innovation by bringing these fields together in order to identify, create, and adapt computational tools that can be used in humanities education and research. I-CHASS's mission is to bring together the expertise and experience of humanists and information technology specialists in a way that is mutually beneficial to the future development of both fields, as well as other fields in the sciences and technology. I-CHASS is also making a concerted effort toward the democratic redistribution of technological knowledge through participation in programs such as the National Science Foundation's Engaging People in Cyberinfrastructure (EPIC). The Center believes that because technology is evolving at such a fast pace it is increasingly important that a concerted effort be made to close (or at least shrink) the information gap before it spins out of control.

Immersive Education   http://immersiveeducation.org. Immersive Education is a nonprofit initiative that encourages international collaboration in the development of virtual-reality software for educational purposes. The currently available software package, which uses interactive three-dimensional graphics, Web cameras, Internet-based telephony, and other digital media, is designed to work within already existing open-code virtual worlds, such as Second Life. The endeavor was founded by Aaron Walsh, an instructor at Boston College, in the hopes of creating three-dimensional, interactive learning environments that would have the same attraction to students as popular massive multiplayer games. These games encourage self-directed learning and collaborative action in ways that many scholars would like to see transferred to the classroom. Originally only available to university students, the next generation of Immersive Education software is broadening its scope to include K-12 education and nonacademic users (e.g., corporate training programs).

Institute for Digital Research and Education at the University of California at Los Angeles   http://www.idre.ucla.edu. Institute for Digital Research and Education (IDRE) is a newly organized institution committed to researching and supporting innovative scholarship that takes advantage of new technologies. The Institute encourages collaboration between faculty from different departments and disciplines at UCLA, the opening of new research questions, and the enrichment of the learning environment. IDRE is meant to be a convergence point for interdisciplinary expertise, perspectives, and methodologies through the implementation of networked local, national, and international digital environments.

Institute for Multimedia Literacy at the University of Southern California http://iml.usc.edu. The Institute for Multimedia Literacy (IML) was founded in 1998 by the University of Southern California's Dean of Cinematic Arts, Elizabeth Daley. Daley was inspired by a conversation with filmmaker George Lucas about the lack of educational programs dedicated to researching and addressing the changing nature of literacy in a networked culture. In order to remedy this situation, the IML began developing educational programs that promoted effective and expressive communication through the use of multimedia applications and tools. Originally a program embedded within the Annenberg Center for Communication, the IML has since broadened its scope to include faculty and students from many different departments and backgrounds. The Institute works closely with faculty and researchers to integrate multimedia literacy skills and analysis into a wide range of classes. It also supports an honors program in Multimedia Scholarship and has recently instituted a core curriculum aimed at teaching students across fields how to use and develop new multimedia technologies.

The Knowledge Media Laboratory   http://www.carnegiefoundation.org/programs/index.asp?key=38. The goal of the Knowledge Media Lab (KML) is to create a future in which communities of teachers, faculty, programs, and institutions collectively advance teaching and learning by exchanging educational knowledge, experiences, ideas, and reflections. KML is currently working to develop digital tools and resources (e.g., the KEEP Toolkit) for educators as a way to facilitate the sharing and creation of effective teaching practices. They are also researching how best to combine various technologies to create learning environments that entirely re-think traditional methods of teaching and learning. This initiative is funded by the Carnegie Foundation for the Advancement of Teaching.

MATRIX: The Center for Humane Arts, Letters, and Social Sciences Online at Michigan State University http://matrix.msu.edu. MATRIX was originally established to host the computing activities of H-NET: Humanities and Social Sciences Online, an independent scholarly initiative by humanists and social scientists to find more innovative ways to use the Internet. However, MATRIX's mission was soon extended far beyond this, and it became a full-fledged interdisciplinary center involved in research, educational practice, networking, publications, and outreach. As the best-funded humanities technology center in the country, MATRIX is deeply committed to not only advancing critical understanding of human nature and access to knowledge within academia but also to expanding its influence into developing nations. For example, the Center is currently working to build open-source inexpensive hardware and software that will be freely available worldwide. Through this project and others, MATRIX hopes to become a true "matrix" of interdisciplinary and international research.

MIT OpenCourseWare http://ocw.mit.edu/OcwWeb/web/home/home/index.htm. MIT's OpenCourseWare (OCW) is a revolutionary Internet site that allows open access to course materials used in MIT's general curriculum. It was proposed by a faculty committee in the year 2000 as a way to advance lifelong education around the world and was officially launched in 2003. Since that time, OCW has grown to include syllabi, lecture notes, readings, videos, and other course materials for over 1,800 courses. Over 90 percent of faculty members at MIT have participated in this venture, voluntarily contributing their teaching materials to the Web site. All materials are published under an open license that encourages reuse, redistribution, and modification for educational purposes. In 2004, OCW began to create mirror sites at university campuses all over the world in order to facilitate access and to make translations available. OCW's most recent venture has been to launch a new Web site, Highlights for High School, that reorganizes already existing course materials into a format that matches Advanced Placement curricula and thus makes the tool more accessible for high school students and teachers. MIT's OpenCourseWare has inspired a global movement that has resulted in universities from around the world creating their own open courseware sites.

Maryland Institute for Technology in the Humanities at the University of Maryland http://www.mith2.umd.edu. Maryland Institute for Technology in the Humanities at the University of Maryland (MITH) was founded in 1999 as a collaboration between the University of Maryland's College of Arts and Humanities, its libraries, and the Office of Information Technology. The Institute functions as a think tank for research into digital tools, text mining and visualization, and the creation and preservation of digital information. Among its many current projects are the Electronic Literature Organization, an internationally recognized group devoted to the writing and publishing of electronic literature; the Preserving Virtual Worlds project, which develops methods to preserve the notoriously ephemeral world of virtual environments; and the production of Web-based tools for archives and networking.

Multimedia Research Center at the University of California, Berkeley http:// bmrc.berkeley.edu. Founded in 1995, the Multimedia Research Center at the University of California, Berkeley (BMRC) is an interdisciplinary group of artists, educators, professionals, and scientists who are committed to building partnerships between academia and the media industry. All participants are joined by a common interest in experimenting with interactive multimedia technology and finding new ways to incorporate this into professional practice and education. The group focuses on four areas: multimedia authoring (including the development of advanced learning environments), teaching and learning (distance learning as well as interactive and collaborative course materials such as the Open Mash Toolkit), infrastructure (e.g., a system to support the networking of all multimedia content at the University of California, Berkeley), and public programs (lectures, seminars, and symposia).

New Media Consortium (NMC) http://www.nmc.org. The New Media Consortium (NMC) is an international nonprofit consortium of nearly 250 educational organizations dedicated to the exploration and use of new media and new technologies. Member institutions include colleges, universities, museums, research centers, and private companies across the United States, Canada, Europe, Asia, and Australia. The Consortium has identified three core areas of long-term research and activity: These are the Dynamic Knowledge Initiative, which explores how developing technologies are driving the formation of new knowledge; the Emerging Technology Initiative, which seeks to identify and make public emerging technologies that have educational relevance; and the New Collaborations Initiative, which encourages interdisciplinary and cross-sector idea sharing. Through collaborative research and development programs in each of these core areas, the NMC aims to promote the use of new technologies to support learning and creative expression.

MIT Media Lab   http://www.media.mit.edu. The Media Lab opened its doors in 1985 with the mission of "inventing and creatively exploiting new media for human well-being without regard for present-day constraints." This statement set the tone for the Lab's ongoing reputation as a cutting-edge innovator in radical technology. The Lab was originally conceived in 1980 by Nicholas Negroponte (who would go on to found One Laptop Per Child) and former MIT President Jerome Wiesner. It was, and still is, housed within MIT's School of Architecture and Planning—a location that is indicative of its commitment to interdisciplinary collaboration between the arts and sciences. The Lab is not solely interested in information technology innovations but in inventing and reinventing how human beings experience technology and, by extension, how technology is changing the way we experience the world. All its myriad projects and inventions have been bound by a common goal: designing the technology to allow people to create a better future. Currently the Lab is in the process of a major expansion. When finished, the new complex will house the Okawa Center, which focuses on exploring how children live, learn, and play in the digital age; the List Visual Arts Center; the Center for Advanced Visual Studies; and other pedagogical and lab-based programs.

PERSEUS at Tufts University   http://www.perseus.tufts.edu. Perseus is an evolving digital library, edited by Gregory Crane, promoting interactions through time, space, and language. Its primary goal is to bring a wide range of source materials to as large an audience as possible in anticipation that this greater accessibility to the sources for the study of the humanities will strengthen the quality of questions, lead to new avenues of research, and connect more people through the intersection of ideas. PERSEUS is a nonprofit enterprise, located in the Department of the Classics at Tufts University. The project is also funded by the Digital Libraries Initiative Phase 2, the National Endowment for the Humanities, the National Science Foundation, and the Institute of Museum and Library Services.

The Pittsburgh Science of Learning Center at the University of Pittsburgh and the Carnegie Mellon University   http://www.learnlab.org. The Pittsburgh Science of Learning Center is creating a research facility known as LearnLab, designed to dramatically increase the ease and speed with which learning researchers can create theory-based experiments that pave the way to an understanding of how people learn. LearnLab makes use of advanced technologies to facilitate the design of experiments that combine the realism of classroom field studies and the rigor of controlled laboratory studies. LearnLab's activities include authoring tools for online courses, experiments, and integrated computational learner models as well as running in vivo learning experiments

Stanford Center for Innovations in Learning   http://scil.stanford.edu/index.html. Stanford Center for Innovations in Learning (SCIL) was established in 2002 as an independent center within the Human Sciences and Technologies Advanced Research Institute (H-STAR; see above) program. It is devoted to advancing scholarly research in the science, technology, and practice of learning and teaching. The center is housed in Stanford's new Wallenberg Hall, an experimental facility where educators and administrators can explore new ways of integrating technology into the classroom environment. SCIL is dedicated to cross-cultural collaboration: The center's goal is to bring together teachers, researchers, and students from across the world to develop improvements in formal and informal learning environments of all types. The center is codirected by Roy Pea, professor in learning sciences and technologies, and Stig Hagstrom, professor in materials science and former chancellor of the Swedish university system.

UCLA Center for Digital Humanities http://www.cdh.ucla.edu. The Center for Digital Humanities seeks to be an international leader in the development, application, and interpretation of digital technologies for use in the humanities. Its primary function entails enabling the faculty, students, and staff of the Division of Humanities at UCLA to explore innovative uses of technology. The Center also hopes to foster an understanding of how these technologies affect the humanities through ongoing research projects that have implications reaching far beyond the UCLA campus.

Virtual Knowledge Studio http://www.virtualknowledgestudio.nl/index .php. Launched in the fall of 2006, the Virtual Knowledge Studio (VKS) for the Humanities and Social Sciences is an international research and teaching institute hosted by the International Institute of Social History in Amsterdam and the Royal Netherlands Academy of Arts and Sciences. The VKS supports e-research in the creation of new scholarly practices in the humanities and social sciences and encourages the incorporation of this research into the learning environment. Social scientists, humanities researchers, information technology experts, and information scientists work together to integrate elements of design, analysis, and knowledge across academic and geographic boundaries. In June 2007, VKS partnered with the Erasmus University in Rotterdam to open the Erasmus Virtual Knowledge Studio, the institute's first physical campus, as a point of contact for visiting fellows, collaborators, and students.

Voice of the Shuttle http://vos.ucsb.edu. Voice of the Shuttle is one of the oldest humanities resources on the Web. While it was initially conceived as an introduction to the Internet for humanities scholars within the University of California, it became a public resource in early 1995. Voice of the Shuttle provides links to online humanities and humanities-related resources. Links can be submitted by anybody, but all suggested links are checked and, where necessary, edited to ensure quality and reliability.

Continuing and Distance Education

Academic Advanced Distributed Learning Co-Lab http://www.aca demiccolab.org. The Academic Advanced Distributed Learning (ADL) Co-Lab was established to enable global access to high-quality, reusable content for distributed learning. Supported by the Department of Defense and the University of Wisconsin at Madison, the Co-Lab serves as a focal point for academic research and evaluation of the ADL tools and content that have been developed by the federal government, academia, and industry. By creating a set of guidelines and standards to identify, assess, develop, and disseminate distributed learning tools and strategies, the Co-Lab hopes to provide the education community with open access to innovative, effective educational material. Topics currently being explored by the Co-Lab are mobile learning, games and simulations for learning, and the construction of digital repositories for ADL content.

Center for the Advancement of Distance Education   http://www.uic.edu/sph/cade. Center for the Advancement of Distance Education (CADE) is an organization supported by the University of Illinois at Chicago School of Public Health. It provides integrated online services to support projects in the health sciences, developing customized Web-based learning, data management, and webcasting solutions to enhance communication and improve information delivery. Currently, CADE is working on a project called Virtual Worlds, which aims to enhance the technologies used by public health and business, including emergency response training, business continuity planning and execution, and human resource counseling. It has created a virtual human resources department where employees can go for information and support. They have also designed a virtual situation room, which bypasses the need for a physical meeting space. In this virtual environment, company leaders can meet, get up-to-date information, or strategize in the wake of a disaster.

COOLSchool   http://www.coolschool.k12.or.us. COOLSchool advertises itself as an "electronic alternative for K-12 education." It is a virtual learning institution that provides electronic learning opportunities to Oregon school districts by working with local teachers to develop and offer online courses, training and mentoring teachers, and providing technical support for school districts wanting to establish an online course selection. What sets it apart from other distance-learning organizations is that it does not offer diplomas and does not believe in replacing face-to-face education. Instead, it aims to supplement the local school system and make advanced learning opportunities available to motivated students who can then adapt the course materials to fit their individual needs.

EDEN: European Distance and E-Learning Network http://www.eden -online.org/eden.php. EDEN was established in 1991 to function as an international educational association open to all institutions and individuals whose work involved e-learning, open, and distance education. The network's primary goal is to facilitate the sharing of knowledge and the creation of open avenues of communication across Europe and beyond. They are a meeting place and information locus for new technologies and current research, and they also work to bridge cultural and educational gaps that exist between members. EDEN represents all areas of education and training, formal and non-formal alike, and currently lists members from over 50 countries. Although EDEN is registered as a nonprofit under English law, the current home of its secretariat is the Budapest University of Technology and Economics.

Florida Virtual School http://www.flvs.net. Florida Virtual School was founded in 1997 as the country's first state-wide Internet-based public high school. The school aims to deliver a high-quality, technology-based education to students who have not excelled in the traditional school system. Students are given the flexibility to work at their own pace, select their own classes, and to choose their own environments. However, despite the lack of a physical community of students and teachers, FVS makes sure to give students individual guidance, personal feedback, and opportunities for collaboration through a variety of means, including via phone, email, chatrooms, instant messaging, and discussion forums.

Hispanic Educational Telecommunications Systems http://www.hets .org. Originally founded in 1993 by a group of higher education institutions interested in sharing access to distance education, the Hispanic Educational Telecommunications Systems (HETS) consortium has since expanded its vision to include not only the use of telecommunications in education but all types and levels of asynchronous learning. They are particularly interested in using technology to promote greater collaboration within and among educational institutions. As a Hispanic organization, it works with individuals and institutions in Spanish-speaking cultures to increase their competitiveness on a global scale and to foster open communication with distance education users throughout the world.

Michigan Virtual University http://www.mivu.org. Michigan Virtual University is a private, not-for-profit Michigan corporation established in 1998 to deliver online education and training opportunities to the citizens of Michigan. It is the parent organization of the Michigan Virtual School (K-12) and the Michigan LearnPort professional development portal for teachers, administrators, and school personnel. MVU and its offshoots seek to offer high-quality course offerings and educational materials to those students for whom traditional education is not feasible. MVU is unique in the distance education world in that it is a learner-centered, solution-based organization that has strong ties to the physical classroom.

OpenLearn LearningSpace: The Open University http://openlearn.open.ac.uk. The Open University is the only university in the United Kingdom dedicated to distance education. It offers a variety of courses and materials to students of all ages (although one has to be at least 18 to enroll) and nationalities. The OpenLearn LearningSpace Web site gives free access to learners anywhere in the world to course materials and discussion forums based on classes offered by the Open University's more traditional learning programs.

Research in Presentation Production for Learning Electronically http://manic.cs.umass.edu. The Research in Presentation Production for Learning Electronically (RIPPLES) project at the University of Massachusetts, Amherst, investigates, develops, and deploys multimedia learning technologies and explores how to most effectively use them both inside and outside of the classroom. It focuses on developing asynchronous learning environments for distance learning, in which students proceed at their own pace and can access course materials at any time and from any location. RIPPLES delivers lectures in digital audio or video formats and synchronizes them with slides, overheads, or other materials. All course material on its growing Web site can be accessed freely. This project was made possible by a grant from the National Science Foundation.

United States Distance Learning Association http://www.usdla.org. Founded in 1987, the United States Distance Learning Association (USDLA) is an alliance of educational institutions, businesses, healthcare facilities, and government organizations dedicated to advocating and promoting the use of distance learning. The association works with learning communities of all types, including K-12, higher education, continuing education, corporate training, military and government training, home schooling, and telemedicine. The USDLA was the first nonprofit distance-learning association in the United States to support research and development across all fields of education, training, and communication. It has taken a leadership role in fostering dialogue and providing advocacy, information, and networking opportunities for its member institutions. The USDLA has established chapters in all 50 states, and each chapter works closely with local distance learners and educators to help them reach their potential.

Wikiversity http://en.wikiversity.org/wiki/Wikiversity:Main_Page. An offshoot of the Wikibooks project, Wikiversity was founded in 2006 as a community for the creation and use of free learning materials and activities. Wikiversity is not a formal institution but is a multidimensional social organization dedicated to learning, teaching, research, and service. Its primary goals are to create and host free content, multimedia learning materials, resources, and curricula for all age groups in all languages (although currently French is the only language besides English offered) and to develop collaborative learning projects and communities around these materials. Learners and teachers of all kinds are invited to join the Wikiversity community as editors of the Web site and contributors of content.

Journals and Online Resources

Association for Learning Technology Journal http://www.alt.ac.uk/alt_j .html. This is an international, triannual, peer-reviewed journal produced by the Association for Learning Technology (ALT-J). It is devoted to researching and exploring practical applications of learning technologies in higher education. The ultimate goal of this research is to facilitate collaboration between practitioners, researchers, and policy-makers in education. ALT-J was originally published by The University of Wales Press and is now published by the Routledge Taylor & Francis Group.

The American Journal of Distance Education http://www.ajde.com/index .htm. The American Journal of Distance Education (AJDE) is an internally distributed and peer-reviewed journal of research and scholarship in the field of American distance education. Articles address digital teaching techniques such as audio and video broadcasts, teleconferences and recordings, and multimedia systems. The principal focus of current research is the World Wide Web, and its related fields of online learning, e-learning, distributed learning, asynchronous learning, and blended learning. AJDE aims to provide a solid foundation of valuable research-based knowledge about all aspects of pedagogy and resources in distance education.

First Monday http://www.uic.edu/htbin/cgiwrap/bin/ojs/index.php/fm. First Monday (which is issued on the first Monday of every month) is one of the first openly accessible, peer-reviewed journals on the Internet. It was founded in May 1996 as a forum for discussion on the emerging technologies associated with the World Wide Web. The journal published on a range of topics, stipulating only that they be original research papers addressing the Internet and related technologies.

Game Studies http://www.gamestudies.org. *Game Studies* is a peer-reviewed journal whose primary focus is on the aesthetic, cultural, and communicative aspects of computer games. It publishes articles on topics ranging from the nature of narrative in games to virtual economies and forms of interaction and communication in multiplayer games. It is a cross-disciplinary journal dedicated to exploring the cultural implications of gaming and to providing an academic channel for the ongoing discussions on games and gaming.

innovate: journal of online education http://www.innovateonline.info. *innovate* is an open access, bimonthly, peer-reviewed online periodical published by the Fischler School of Education and Human Services at Nova Southeastern University. The journal focuses on the creative use of digital technology to enhance learning processes in academic, commercial, and governmental settings. Its goal is to foster communication about innovative uses of technology across sectors and to encourage the sharing of ideas and resources.

International Journal of Computer-Supported Collaborative Learning (ijCSCL) http://ijcscl.org. ijCSCL is a new journal founded by the International Society of the Learning Sciences (ISLS). It is a peer-reviewed academic journal whose primary aim is to promote a deeper understanding of the nature, theory, and practice of the uses of computer-supported collaborative learning. The goal of the journal is to facilitate an understanding of how people learn in the context of collaborative activity and how to design the technological settings for collaboration.

International Journal of Emerging Technologies in Learning (iJET) http://www.online-journals.org/index.php/i-jet. The *iJET* publication is an international journal published out of Germany that promotes the exchange of trends and research in technology enhanced learning. It aims to bridge the gap between pure academic research journals and more practical publications meant for a general public. Thus, it publishes interdisciplinary articles not only on research but also application development, experience reports, and product descriptions.

Journal of Computer-Mediated Communication (JCMC) http://jcmc.indiana.edu/index.html. JCMC is one of the oldest Web-based Internet studies journals and has been published continuously (with one issue appearing every three months) since June 1995. It is a Web-based, peer-reviewed scholarly journal focused on social science research on computer-mediated communication via the Internet and wireless technologies. The journal was founded as an interdisciplinary platform for discussions on these subjects and publishes work by scholars in communication, business, education, political science, sociology, media studies, information science, and other disciplines. In 2004, JCMC became an official journal of the International Communication Association.

The Journal of Technology, Learning, and Assessment (JTLA) http://eschol arship.bc.edu/jtla. JTLA is a peer-reviewed, scholarly online journal housed jointly in the Technology and Assessment Study Collaborative (inTASC) and the Center for the Study of Testing, Evaluation, and Educational Policy (CSTEEP) at Boston College. The journal's goal is to address the intersection of computer-based technology, learning, and assessment. It publishes articles that examine how teaching and learning are altered by new technologies and seeks to measure the impact that this has through nontraditional assessment methods. The journal is currently supported by the William and Flora Hewlett Foundation and the Bill and Melinda Gates Foundation.

Language Learning and Technology   http://llt.msu.edu. *Language Learning and Technology* is a refereed journal that was founded in July 1997 in order to disseminate research and pedagogical information to foreign and second language educators around the world. Articles specifically focus on the intersections between language education and the use of new technology. The focus of the publication is not technology in and of itself, but rather how technology is used to enhance and change language learning and language teaching. *Language Learning and Technology* is sponsored and funded by the University of Hawai'i National Foreign Language Resource Center (NFLRC), the Michigan State University Center for Language Education And Research (CLEAR), and the Center for Applied Linguistics (CAL).

Learning Inquiry   http://www.springerlink.com/content/1558-2973. *Learning Inquiry* is a new, refereed scholarly journal devoted to the exploration of "learning" as a focus for interdisciplinary study. The journal's goal is to be a forum for a dialogue on all types and manifestations of learning, including informal as well as formal environments. Contributions will come from business professionals, government organizations, institutions of education at any level, and lifelong informal learners. The journal is intended to be of interest to the general public, or more specifically to anyone invested in learning, understanding its contexts, and anticipating its future. *Learning Inquiry* strives to strike a balance between presenting innovative research and documenting current knowledge to foster scholarly and informal dialogue on learning independent of domain and methodological restrictions.

Vectors: Journal of Culture and Technology in a Dynamic Vernacular   http://www.vectorsjournal.org. *Vectors* is a peer-reviewed online multimedia journal that highlights the social, political, and cultural stakes of our increasingly technologically-mediated existence. The journal focuses on the way in which technology shapes, transforms, reconfigures, and/or impedes our social relations, both in the past and in the present. As such, the journal is inherently cross-disciplinary and accepts submissions from scholars and experts in any field. *Vectors* is also unique in that it is published as a multimedia production: Its "articles" are made up of moving and still images, sound, computational structures, software, and text. The goal of the journal is to fuse the old and new in terms of media, subject matter, and style.

Blogs

boyd, danah. "apophenia: making connections where none previously existed." http://www.zephoria.org/thoughts

Chronicle of Higher Education. "Wired Campus Blog." http://chronicle.com/wiredcampus

Davidson, Cathy. "Cat in the Stack: Cathy Davidson's HASTAC Blog on the Interface of Anything." http://www.hastac.org/blog/79

De Craene, Mechelle. "HASTAC on Ning: A Synergistic Symposium for the Cybernetic Age." http://hastac.ning.com

Digital Youth Research. "Kids' Informal Learning with Digital Media." http://digitalyouth.ischool.berkeley.edu

Epistemic Games. "epistemic games: Building the Future of Education." http://epistemicgames.org/eg/?cat=63

Eyebeam Art and Technology Center. "Eyebeam reBlog: Distilling Art and Technology." http://www.eyebeam.org/reblog

Games for Change. "Games for Change (G4C)." http://www.gamesforchange.org

Global Kids' Digital Media Initiative. "Blog." http://holymeatballs.org

Hargittai, Eszter. "Eszter's Blog." http://www.esztersblog.com

The Institute for the Future of the Book. "if:book." http://www.futureofthebook.org/blog

Ito, Mimo. "Mimo Ito—Weblog." http://www.itofisher.com/mito/weblog

Jenkins, Henry. "Confessions of an Aca/Fan: The Official Weblog of Henry Jenkins." http://www.henryjenkins.org

———. "henry3@mit.edu." http://web.mit.edu/cms/People/henry3

Jussel, Amy. "Shaping Youth." http://www.shapingyouth.org/blog

Levine, Peter. "Blog." http://www.peterlevine.ws/mt

Lopez, Antonio. "Mediacology: Composting the Western Mind." http://mediacology.com

Losh, Liz. "Virtualpolitik." http://virtualpolitik.blogspot.com

The MacArthur Foundation. "Spotlight: Blogging the Field of Digital Media and Learning." http://spotlight.macfound.org

MIT and Stanford University. "Tomorrow's Professor List Serve." http://amps-tools.mit.edu/tomprofblog

New Media Consortium. "NMC Campus Observer." http://sl.nmc.org

Pacifici, Sabrina. "beSpacific: Accurate, Focused Law and Technology News." http://www.bespacific.com/index.html

Raynes-Goldie, Kate. "Everything is Relative." http://oceanpark.live journal.com/tag/academic

Rheingold, Howard. "DIY Media Weblog." http://www.video24-7.org.

Salen, Katie. "Missives from the Mob." http://www.gamersmob.com/weblog

Schussman, Alan. "schussman.com." http://www.schussman.com

Stutzman, Fred. "Unit Structures: Thoughts about Information, Social Networks, Identity and Technology." http://chimprawk.blogspot.com

Terra Nova. "Terra Nova." http://terranova.blogs.com

Vaidhyanathan, Siva. "Sivacracy.net." http://www.sivacracy.net

Water Cooler Games. "Videogames with an Agenda." http://www.water coolergames.org

Works by the Principal Investigators

Cathy N. Davidson's work for the last decade has focused on the role of technology in the twenty-first century. In 1999, she helped create the program in Information Science+Information Studies (ISIS) at Duke and, in 2002, cofounded the Humanities, Arts, Science, and Technology Advanced Collaboratory (HASTAC) with David Theo Goldberg. Davidson blogs regularly as Cat in the Stack at http://www.hastac.org.

Davidson is the author or editor of 18 books on wide-ranging topics including technology, the history of reading and writing, literary studies, travel, Japan, and women's and Native American writing. Her *Revolution and the Word: The Rise of the Novel in America* (Oxford University Press, 1986) is a study of mass literacy and the rise of American democracy. With documentary photographer Bill Bamberger, she wrote the prize-winning *Closing: The Life and Death of an American Factory* (Norton, 1998). Davidson has served as the editor of *American Literature* (1989–1999) and President of the American Studies Association. From 1998 until 2006, she was Vice-Provost for Interdisciplinary Studies at Duke and, in this role, oversaw more than 60 interdisciplinary programs and institutes, including the Center for Cognitive Neuroscience. The changes in this rapidly growing and by no means unitary field, along with Davidson's ongoing work with the MacArthur Foundation Digital Media and Learning Initiative and with HASTAC, are the background and motivation for *The Rewired Brain: The Deep Structure of Thinking in the Information Age* (forthcoming, Viking Press).

She is currently the Ruth F. DeVarney Professor of English and the John Hope Franklin Humanities Institute Professor of Interdisciplinary Studies at Duke University.

David Theo Goldberg directs the systemwide University of California Humanities Research Institute. He is also Professor of Comparative Literature and Criminology, Law, and Society, as well as a Fellow of the Critical Theory Institute at the University of California, Irvine. He has authored several books, including *The Racial State* (Basil Blackwell, 2002) and *Racist Culture: Philosophy and the Politics of Meaning* (Basil Blackwell, 1993). He has also edited or coedited many books, including *Anatomy of Racism* (University of Minnesota Press, 1990), *Multiculturalism: A Critical Reader* (Basil Blackwell, 1995), *Between Law and Culture*

(University of Minnesota Press, 2001), *Relocating Postcolonialism* (Basil Blackwell, 2002), and *The Companion to Gender Studies* (Basil Blackwell, 2004). His most recent book is *The Threat of Race: Reflections on Racial Neoliberalism* (Oxford, UK: Wiley-Blackwell, 2009). He is a co-founder of HASTAC: Humanities, Arts, Science, Technology Advanced Collaboratory, the international consortium for humanities and digital technologies, networking centers, institutes, and programs at more than 75 institutions of higher learning. He has been active in advancing digital technologies for pedagogy and research across the University of California, serving on various University of California-wide committees overseeing the future of research information and its stewardship for the University of California system.